HERE'S WHAT PEOPLE ARE SAYING ABOUT THIS BOOK...

"THE HOTTEST SOURCE IN TOWN"
Julian McRoberts, HOLLYWOOD CASTING DIRECTOR

"BUY THIS BOOK! If you want the fastest way into the movies! I used Cullen's method and made over $2,000.00 my first month! And in only three months I have a solid position in the movie industry making over $25,000.00 per year."
La Mar K. Pugh, Actor

"Cullen's tips, tidbits & tricks saved me months of leg work and phone calls. With the advice I received I was able to find good assignments as an Extra. In fact I made over $1,300.00 a day on one film and almost $10,000.00 in four weeks.!!"
Victor Lucas, Actor

"A lot of compilation of info... many will find it useful and informative... Outstanding... looks GREAT!!"
Kelley Palmer, Kelley Kalls

"... No one should start out in this business without this book... or even after you have been in it for years... GREAT... BACK TO ONE is the beginning Actor and Extra's BIBLE!!"
Gary Clement, Actor

"BACK TO ONE captures audiences attention in the business of acting... Applause... for the time, energy, research and hands-on experiences you shared... BRAVO!"
Paula Boger, Actress

"... Enjoyed your book and have started seeing it pop up everywhere, perhaps it is it's own testimonial."
David Calhoun, Actor

"I recommend Cullen's book to everyone desiring to be well informed and proficient... using the information from BACK TO ONE, I was able to land GOOD jobs and travel to exotic locations.!"
Kenneth R. Taylor, Actor,

"I recommend that all my beginning students read Cullen Chambers' book BACK TO ONE... It is a real treasure; you get all the education you need to become an extra for... A BARGAIN!"
Judy Kerr, Hollywood director and coach

...FEATURES & STORIES by

BACK STAGE WEST entertainment news
SPOTLIGHT CASTING
DRAMA-LOGUE Entertainment News
HOLLYWOOD REPORTER
VARIETY
1996 PEOPLE MAGAZINE Entertainment Almanac
THE LOS ANGELES TIMES
THE HOLLYWOOD INDEPENDENT
THE LIMA NEWS
CNN
NBC DATELINE
THE LOS ANGELES DAILY NEWS
E! ENTERTAINMENT TV
ARSENIO HALL SHOW
JUDY KERR SHOW
THE ANITA DeFRANCESCO SHOW
THE RIC BRATTON SHOW, WLIO-TV
GOOD MORNING L.A.
KTLA - KCBS - KABC - KJLH - KKGO - KPWR -
WLIO - WOSU - KIEV - KCLA - KKLA - KBET - KGFJ
- KMPC -KACE-
1996 YEARBOOK OF EXPERT,
AUTHORITIES & SPOKESPERSON

R. H. STAHCHILD

BACK TO ONE

The MOVIE Extras Guidebook

*How to Make GOOD Money as a Background
Actor in Film and TV*

by

Cullen Chambers

Completely Revised and Expanded

ISBN 0-9624577-0-1

BACK TO ONE Publications
HOLLYWOOD CALIFORNIA U.S.A.
backtoone@earthlink.net

"BACK TO ONE"

The MOVIE Extras Guidebook

By Cullen Chambers

Published by:

Back To One Publications
P.O. Box 753-1
Hollywood, California 90078 U.S.A
(213) 969-4897 FAX (818) 907-0908

Copyright © 1987, 1989, 1990,1991, 1992, 1993, 1994, 1995, 1996
by Back To One Publication/Cullen Chambers
First Edition 1987
Second Edition 1989
Third Edition 1990 - 1st printing, 2nd printing
Fourth Edition 1991 - 1st printing, 2nd printing
Fifth Edition 1992 - 1st printing, 2nd printing
Sixth Edition 1993 - 1st printing, 2nd printing, 3rd printing
Seventh Edition 1994 - 1st printing, 2nd printing
Eighth Edition 1995 - 1st printing, 2nd printing, 3rd printing
Ninth Edition 1995 - 1st printing
Tenth Edition 1996 - 1st printing

Library of Congress Cataloging in Publication Data
Chambers, Cullen G.
Back To One, The MOVIE Extras Guidebook:
How To Make Good Money As A HOLLYWOOD EXTRA
Bibliography:c
Includes index, appendix, glossary, photos, charts, and illustrations.
1. Acting-Guidebooks, handbooks, manuals, etc.
2. Movie Extras-Guidebooks, handbooks, manuals, etc.
3. Career-Guidebook, handbook, manuals, etc..
CIP 89-92435
ISBN 0-9624577-0-1: $19.95 Softcover
ISSN 1047-3629
10 9 8 7 6 5 4
Printed and bound in the United States of America

Dedicated to

Poppa Brown Chambers, my sisters Carol
Florence, Jamesy Renfro, Jollon Duncan and
Mary Monford

and my friends
Tracey Poree' and Jules Koenigsberg
for their loving support,

Mike Lackey , The Lima News &
Ric Bratton,The Ric Bratton Show, WLIO-TV, Lima OH,
for making it great to come "HOME"!

IN MEMORY OF

Emma Dickey
1946 - 1995
Loving Sister & Co-Founder of Back To One Publications,
A Chambers & Chambers Entertainment Group

Bernard Weisman
HOLLYWOOD WORLD BOOK & NEWS

With much love, Cullen

EXTRA SPECIAL THANKS

Almighty God, Lord and Savior Jesus Christ.

Doc Christopher For His Inspiration, Poppa Brown, Momma Inez, LaMar K. Pugh, Emma Dickey, Joe Wilson, Arthur Chambers, Norman Chambers, Cheryl Allen, Mary Monford, Carol Florence, Jamesy Renfro, David Chambers, Jollon Duncan, Greg Chambers, "FISH" Adkins for the faith, Adele Simmons, Marvin Rush, Arlene Fukai & "LACEY".

Keenan Ivory Wayans for both my S.A.G. & A.F.T.R.A. union cards. Retha Grey, Carl Joy, Rodney Epps & Mary Ann Lee of Cenex Casting, Jeff Olan & Terry & Jerry of Rainbow Casting for keeping their word. Gwen Feldman, Juanita Arneaud , Tracey Poreé & Jules Koenigsberg for their faith.

Bishop Charles E. Blake, Les Brown, Dr. Nathan & Shirley Miller, Vann Johnson, W. George Hubbard, Nannette Tancheron, Dr. Manisfield Dean, Bobbie Jean Skipworth, Andre Johnson, Stacey Harris, Al Foster, Arlema Callahan, Mike Lackey -The Lima News, Ric Bratton -The RIC BRATTON Show, Sheryl Kay-Jordan, Daniel Goldsmith, Carolyn Rivers, Maureen Mottley, Cheryl Felton & the "Elisha *of* Choice".

Jean & Kasey Kasem, Lorraine Montgomery, George Asturias - Debbie - Anna - Dinah - Sylvia - Kevin - Willie - Mary & Mary - Linda - Godoy - Azeb of First Interstate Bank - Hollywood, Gordon Lowe - L.A. Times, Diane Nelson, Shelia Manning of Shelia Manning Casting, Robert Townsend, Ima Rosario, Phoenix Nugent.

Samuel L. Jackson, John Travolta, Quentin Tarantino, Larwence Bender, Frank Mahoney, Kelley Kiernan, Scott, Careron, Rory of Brown 25's "Pulp Fiction", Maya Wallach, Forest Whittaker, Jeff Goldblum, Jana Sue Memel & Jonathan Sanger of Chanticlier Films' "Lush Life", Hal Davis - Rize Prods., H. B. Barnum, Jeanie Long, Dr. Cliff Brown, Cristal Mitchell, Jack McClain, Brenda Strange, Dewayne Hargray, Hans Tresvan, Lorenzo York - Clarence, Dawn Emerick, Randy Ordonez & Staff - Nextmedia, Rick Gunderson - ETC Casting, Nancy Mott, Michael Moorehead, Marianne Donahoe, Lady Aisha Johnson.

Uriah Carter, Raquel Rebollero, "Laura Lee Kasten", Victor Davis of Victor Davis Casting, Gil Arnold & Debbie Rock of Debbie Rock Group, Lynn Brown, Dolia Gomez, Lisa Gordon, Jim Kelly Durgin, Kathy Fritzgerald, Leann of Central Casting, Tony Cruz, Samara Lynn and Candice Clark.

Michael McCarthy, James Foxx and Jack Rowe of Samuel French Bookstore, Bess - Amy - Ric former Cast & Crew, Anthony of AV Prods., Steve Spiker - Mark - Ajay - Rich - Rodney & Gary formerly of D.I.S.C. now with Central, Rosemary Houston, Kymeee Solano & Kat Nelson, Fred

Green, agent Gary Aggas and personal manager "Betty Mccormick Aggas & Pierre Robin of Actors & Directors Studio", William & Jimmy Allard, David Calhoun, Liz Willow, Gary Johnson of F.F.M.P.C, Sherri Maddox, Ray Victor, Maurice & Joyce Lewis, Venai "Leck"Dhanasunthon
Richard Turner, Lisa Kishi, Cheryl McDowell, Edward James Olmos, Sally Perle, Cari formerly of Sally Perle Casting, Jim & John, The Learning Annex, Gary Clement, Kevin Jordan, Randy and Cyndie of Theta Data, Gregory Levi aka Stevie Wonder, Robert Wegner, The Hollywood Extra Casting Directory, Haskell Hooks, Dametta Poindexter, Rick - Dan - Dixie - The Casting Group, Harriett Walker. "Pretty Eyes Joan" - In Living Color.
Audrianne Norwood, Richard Icamen, John Lafreniere, Josef Hill, P.M. Productions, Sara Chambers, Barbara Blosvern-Suzanne Anaya-T.B.S. Casting, Jim Gribble, Mark Lucas, James Bratton, "Tit For Tat", Lisa & Paul-S.K.L., Michael Lofgren Aixia Maldonaldo, Franz Pierre Gatlin, Marvin Lewis.
Louise Pask, Jim Brown - R.O.W. Goals, Hal Levi - Hollywood Reporter, Terrence Harris, Reuven Harris, Ron O'Neal, K-Dean, Romy Walthall, Sidney Poitier, Washington Carter, Paula Boger, Samara - Mary Anne -of Cenex Casting, Julian McRoberts, Roxanne McBride, Jerry Belson, Anna Mary Johnson, Joe Romano, John Ponomarev of Newsways, "Rock" Riddle, Joel Colman, Willie Brown, Janet Cunningham and Michael Young.
Mark Kostopoulos, Bert Beecham, Sarah Kane - "Hot-Head", George Hill, Geri Grey, John Ronge, Mary Douglas, Harry Stanback - Dewayne of Location Security, Alan Ames - TBM, Tanya York, Pearl Brody - Dramalogue.
Woody Bryant, Claude Oates, Burt - Wilshire News, Carolyn Copeland, Jack Cloud, Agnew - Rudy - Universal News, Rich Hogan, Sylvia Anderson, Paulette & Ed Vandell, Tom Cannan - S.A.G., Prince Zaire - Phonet, D.E. Buford, Colleen Barber, Kandahsi, Ben Nash, J.J. Jones, Randy & Rocky, Barry Thomas-1st A.D., Christopher Gray Casting and Dwight Dwyer.
Carl Joy - Frank - Andy - Helen - Dan - Jim - Arnie - Pamela - Chuck & J.J. of Central Casting, Brenda Glynn aka Brenda Starr, Don Mitchell, Anastashi, Robert Hooks, Paulette Smith, Lisa Dunn, Belle McBeth, Valerie Harper - Tyra Ferrell - Howard Storm - Liz Torres - Todd Susman - Joan - Carol Vitkay - Woody - Audrey - Cynthia - Jeff and the entire C & C of "City".
Kelley Palmer of Kelley Kalls, Craig Turkel, Charles T. Hudson - Copymatic, Veda Best, Curtis Milan, Charles Ross, Jerry - Donna - Peter of V.M.I., Kathy Gallagher, Karla Edwards, Jack Hall, James Flannigan, Bob Tietelbaum & Marty of L.A. Casting Express, Merry Williams, Peter of Prime Casting, Steve Snyder, Mark Avis, Margaret Blanchard and Ms Gail.
Lisa-Krisha-Laura-Jennifer-Eden of Extra Phone, Anthony Degeure, Gwen Durham, Malcom, Clinton Carroll, Arlema Callahan, Judi Keppler,Tony Burton, Anthony Angulo, Lydia Laurans, Harry Medved-Robert Todd-Antoinette Mosley-Toloria Milner (world greatest receptionist) of the Hollywood SCREEN ACTORS GUILD and the beautiful Lauren Bailey - AFTRA rep.

And To All of Those Who Helped By Inspiration, Motivation, Dedication, Encouragement & Support, & Especially To "Hollywood Extras" everywhere.

ACKNOWLEDGMENTS

Cheryl Felton- Executive Editorial Assistant
Lamar K. Pugh & Computerization Manipulation
Rich Hogan - photographer
Joe & Cher Wilson- Computer Consultants
Paula Boger – That Special Touch
Reuven "Rudy" Harris - illustrator
Marion Mickens- Computer Technician
Jules Koenigsberg - associate editor
Les Pollack - senior research associate
Monty & Sam: Input/Output Center -West Hollywood
Lynn McLaughlin - Digital Composition Assistant
Maurice Lewis - production associate
Drew Barten - production associate
Kathleen Sandoval - Kay Shoemaker
Marianne Donahoe - editor
Pete Bateman-publicity stills research-
Larry Edmunds Books
Hyundai Electronics Co., Ltd And Kenneth R.Taylor
State Of California Labor Commissioner
Emma Dickey
V.M.I. Answer Service
Richard Rodriguiez Holiday- Exec. Prod. "ME" Awards
(Co-Contributor OVERNITE SENSATIONS , ACTOR WHO WERE EXTRAS?)
Samuel Clauder II, Sgt. Booker, Neil Eisman, Mick Lehr,
Kiyoko Ono Yamaguchi

Cover Concept: Cullen Chambers
Original Cover Design: Randy Ordonez - Next Media
Cover Recreation: by Randy Tobin & Joe Wilson
Back Cover Design: Cullen Chambers
Photographs: Rich Hogan Photography, Hollywood, CA
Cullen & DocChristopher Chambers
R.H. Stahchild Creator: REUVEN

TABLE OF CONTENTS

HOW TO MAKE GOOD $$$$$
AS A HOLLYWOOD EXTRA

-Chapter Four-

FOREWORD

ADELE SIMMONS

FIRST ASSISTANT DIRECTOR,
STAR TREK:
THE NEXT GENERATION

Welcome to the wonderful
world of motion picture
and TV production. The
opportunity to be a part of
the entertainment industry

is a dream shared by millions the world over. You have in your hands
the information that can begin, or further your acting career. The
"business" as it is called is truly unique. It can be fun and exciting.

I am a tremendous admirer of actors. I respect them. I feel that
I work well with them. Film and television production is a team
effort, from the director, the producer, the crew, the principal actors
and background actors or extras.

Back To One is the first book to bring together all the vital
information and tools beginning and experienced principal and
background actors need to work and gain valuable insight into the
film and television making process.

The book reveals to the reader the practical things that are
essential to building a successful acting career and surviving
until their big break comes. And come it shall if you plan your
career with knowledge you discover from talking to other professionals and reading. Both the experienced and beginner will find
a greater understanding and appreciation of the acting business.
But more so from following the steps and applying the indispensable information found in the pages of this book to their own
acting career building plan. In the beginning of an acting career
the hardest thing to come by is inside knowledge; the tips, tricks
and tidbits of making it happen for you. If you are just starting
out, it is vital to have an overview of just what is expected of you
so that you can decide if a career in show business is for you.

Beginning as a background actor is the perfect way to find out. It is a major stumbling block for most actors starting out to break into the business, especially those without family, friends or contacts or those with limited knowledge of how to go about getting **IN** show business. The problem is that you have to get in before you can find out how; sort of a Catch 22 situation. As in any business, contacts are important to success, especially in show business. The competition is fierce, but success is possible.

Cullen Chambers using his many contacts and invaluable resources provides you with direction as to where and how to go about looking for work.

Being a background actor or extra may look easy. Obtaining jobs as a professional background actor is anything but easy. This book will help show you how.

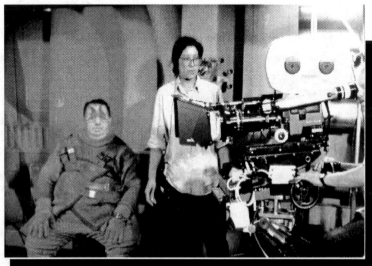

Adele Simmons and "Alien" on the set of 'STAR TREK: T.N.G.'

Author's Note

I felt this book was needed to answer the questions of thousands of people who have approached me while I was working on various HOLLYWOOD movie and commercial sets. Asking how to get started, is the work fun, how much money I made and etc., etc.?

My goal in presenting this informative guide book to you is to give sound, practical STEP-BY-STEP information and advice to the people who have thought it would be fun and exciting to be in the movies, while making good $$$$. Believe me it is, as well as valuable insight to the people who are considering professional acting as a career.

Cullen Chambers

For those of you who are talented, dedicated, willing and able to make the commitment to being an actor or actress, I have collected some valuable information and suggestions to help you make decisions about your career. Ways to make good money as a "HOLLYWOOD EXTRA" and as a stepping stone so that you will live comfortably until your big break comes. The first question you need to ask yourself is:

"Do I really want to work in film and television, or is it the glamour and the bright lights I'm attracted to?" If it is the latter, you are bound for a letdown. Eventually the glamour wears off and the lights go dim and what you are left with is work; although fun and excitement as well as financial rewards can be yours, it is work! (Twelve to 18-hour days, six and sometimes seven day work week, 5:00 a.m. wake-up, all night shooting, hot and dusty locations, some rude and egomaniacal crew people and sometimes cold coffee.)

If you still have stars and dollar signs in your eyes, you're ready. Let's move on to the TOOLS of... "HOW TO MAKE GOOD $$$$$ AS A HOLLYWOOD EXTRA."

OVER-NITE

ACTORS WHO

LUCILLE BALL	WALTER BRENNAN
TOM SELLECK	ROBERT DUVALL
BURT REYNOLDS	DUSTIN HOFFMAN
WHOOPI GOLDBERG	ROBERT DENIRO
SYLVESTER STALLONE	BILL COSBY
KEVIN COSTNER	JACK NICHOLSON
KEVIN DOBSON	CLINT EASTWOOD
SUZANNE SOMMERS	JOHN TRAVOLTA
MICHAEL LANDON	ROBERT REDFORD
ROBERT TOWNSEND	JULIA ROBERTS
MARILYN MONROE	DON STROUD
DONALD PLEASENCE	LAURENCE FISHBURNE
JOHN WAYNE	BRUCE WILLIS
BOB HOPE	HENRY WINKLER
CLARK GABLE	LEONARD NIMOY
GARY COOPER	ANGELICA HUSTON
SOPHIA LOREN	ISMAEL CARLO
JOAN CRAWFORD	WILFORD BRIMLEY
WALT WILLEY	CASEY KASEM
ALAN LADD	CARL LUMBLEY
MARY TYLER MOORE	BRAD PITT
TERRI GARR	JAMES GARDNER
TOM CRUISE	LEON ROBINSON

SENSATIONS?

WERE EXTRAS ?

BRAD PITT
DAVID NIVEN
JEAN HARLOW
GERI GRAY
MARK HARMON
DANA PLATO
VALERIE HARPER
DONALD SUTHERLAND
MICHAEL MOOREHEAD
PAT NIXON
ROMY WALTHALL
SAL LOPEZ
AARON SPELLING
KEN WAHL
JOE PESCI
TESS HARPER
JANET GAYNOR
GERI GRAY
PRESIDENT RONALD
REAGAN

P.S. IF YOU HEAR ANY GOOD RUMORS ABOUT OTHERS, PLEASE CALL ME:

CULLEN CHAMBERS
(213) 969-4897

OR SIMPLY DROP ME A NOTE AT;

BACK TO ONE
P.O. BOX 753,
HOLLYWOOD, CA
90078-0753

IT WOULD BE GOOD TO HEAR FROM YOU.
THANK YOU !

PRESENTED BY
Richard Rodriguez Holiday
on **Wednesday, March 25, 1992** at **8:00 P.M.**, from **Carlos 'N Charlie's** at **8240 Sunset Boulevard** in **Hollywood, California**
That night tribute was paid to the hitherto unrecognized stars of the "atmosphere". This was the Doo-Dah Parade of award shows. The trophies were recycled garage sales - tributes to former bowlers, tennis & baseball players... all purchased in the Hollywood area, to keep the karma intact. Recipients were self-nominated, because they had good stories to tell. Trophies were awarded to the most deserving by all who were there. Without the Extras, (*those paid professional actors in non-principal roles*) movies would look like they were shot in a ghost town. Without their tireless efforts, take after take, to provide consistent performances, the lives of editors would be a nightmare. Extras show up in all weather, at all hours, toting their three changes of clothes, patiently waiting to be called for the next take. Eat with the cast & crew ? You must be kidding! These people deserved to be recognized and this was their night long overdue and a wonderful time was had by all. See you there next time!

Richard Rodriguez Holiday

Executive Producer, of Richard Rodriguez Productions, an independent production company of major television events, including the awards ceremony for the Los Angeles Olympic Organizing Committee, the 16th Annual Golden Eagle Awards and currently the Annual Movie and TV Extra Awards Show, the "ME" Awards, for which he is creator, executive producer and co-writer. He has been involved in numerous production in varying capacities as executive producer, director, writer, casting director, actor and production consultant.

GUARANTEE

I would like to personally thank you for purchasing this book.

The research and development took thousands of hours. It was worth the effort! You see, after all my research, I know for a fact that if you read this manual and follow the instructions, you will be successful. It is based on proven methods of the most successful people already in the "Hollywood Extra" business.

This book is sold with a highly unusual money back guarantee. The guarantee is simple, here is how it works. If you actually follow the step-by-step instructions contained in this book for a trial period of six months and you fail to get work, you may return the book for an immediate refund of your entire purchase price.

All that is required is that you use the information in the book and give it an honest chance to work for you. If you try and fail, simply drop me a note telling where you feel the book went wrong and your availability for work along with proof you have registered with 10 rated Extra Casting Agents. When I receive this information along with the book, I'll give you as promised, an immediate refund of your entire purchase price. That's all there is to it.

It's like buying body-building equipment to build your body. If you use the equipment regularly and do the exercises, you will be rewarded with a better body. But it won't happen just because you bought the equipment. You have to follow through.

So thanks again, and might I suggest you... GET BUSY!! There's a lot of good money and big opportunities out there waiting for you, go get it.

Break a leg and I'll see you in the movies!!!

EXTRA NOTES

Chapter One

TOOLS OF THE TRADE

Getting off to a good start is a sure fire way to get ahead. It requires 10 (ten) specific TOOLS OF THE TRADE in order for you to make GOOD money as a "HOLLYWOOD EXTRA". Study each one carefully and check off the box when completed. These tools are vital to your success. GET BUSY!!!

☑   1. "BACK TO ONE" The MOVIE Extras Guidebook.

❑   2. Telephone/Answering Service/Pager.

❑   3. Photos.

❑   4. Resumé.

❑   5. Colleagues.

❑   6. Up-To-Date Information.

❑   7. Extra Casting Agencies.

❑   8. Extra Calling In Services.

❑   9. Thomas Brothers Guide Mapbook.

❑   10. Dependable Transportation.

1. "BACK TO ONE" The MOVIE Extras Guidebook

B ACK TO ONE' contains the vital information, advice, contacts and sources that will put you in the know of how to make good money as a Background Actor. Although this book is geared to the "Hollywood Movie & TV Production Scene", the methods and tidbits are applicable to film production everywhere in the world.

The Hollywood casting agents and the Association of Film Commissioners from around the globe, names, addresses, telephone numbers and the Hollywood map locations, "HOT LINES", fees, types of actors needed, kinds of productions that are casting, unions, wardrobe, working rights, "extra etiquette", studios, record keeping, pay rates and schedule, "**Acting For The Background**" plus other practical and pertinent information you will find invaluable. Everything you will need and want to know about becoming a working actor.

Read it again & again. Write in it. Highlight special sections that interest you. Make it your personal manual, handbook and/or reference guide to the "HOLLYWOOD WORLD" movie business and your professional acting career. Fill in completely the various forms and notes sections. Use them daily. You'll be quickly convinced how much the forms and notes will assist you in planning your dazzling career in show business. Also keep in mind that it's called "Show *Business*". The business side is more than half of the phrase. You'll find that strategy and planning will pay off more handsomely than talent and good looks.

Your questions and comments are welcomed and very much appreciated. The thousands of cards and letters I have received have been extremely vital in making "BACK TO ONE" Bigger and Better! The most comprehensive! The most accurate! The most exact! The most complete! The most widely read book of it's kind in entertainment history!!

Please keep the cards and letters coming. Information you make known to me that appears in future editions of "BACK TO ONE" will be greatly appreciated. A $5.00 finders fee will be given for each reputable new casting agency that I am apprised of that appears in future editions of BACK TO ONE.

2. Telephone/Answering Service/Pager

Next to BACK TO ONE, a telephone, an answering service and/or pager are the essential "TOOLS OF THE TRADE." You must be reachable! Forget the U.S. Mail. It just isn't used. Some background actors I know do not have a home telephone or an answering machine. They employ an outside telephone answering service. This service eliminates the necessity of waiting around for the telephone to ring.

The new computerized voice mail-box systems that high-tech answering service companies now use, allows all of your messages to be answered in your voice and kept confidential until retrieved with your own secret passcode. With an optional pager you will be beeped every time a message is received. Simply call your service and enter your secret code to retrieve your messages.

It has become essential for an actor to carry a pager for those all important "Rush Calls," (a casting call sent out for an actor or actress, needed for a specific assignment on the set immediately).

Most background actors and actresses have the new vibrating digital display pager that an agent can dial direct and leave a telephone number for you to call back at your earliest convenience. The vibrating mode is great because during a very quiet intense scene it is very embarrassing, not to mention extremely unprofessional to have your pager sounding off, the true sign of an inexperienced background actor.

The answer/pager service I recommend and personally use in Hollywood is: **V.M.I., 1335 N LaBrea Ave. Store #2 Hollywood, CA 90028., (213) 850-1414 or (818) 766-5090,** in New York City, **V.M.I., 853 Broadway, # 1516, New York City, 10003, (212) 428-8200**

V.M.I. even has mail box for rent for persons who need a place to receive their checks and other mail. Give them a call. Ask Jerry or Donna about the details. You can get set-up over the telephone. You don't have to visit their office.

Please tell them Cullen sent you and receive a certificate good for 50% off an EXTRA CALLSHEET record-keeping book, regularly $4.00, (*also available by mail see ORDER FORM*).

For those who desire to be serious players...

Cellular phones, the wave of the future are here now at incredibly affordable prices. Now you do not have to miss that all important casting call again. This could be the second best investment that you could make toward your career!

3. Photos

Your photographs are your calling cards. You are the product you are selling. You are the business. You perform a service for which you will be paid. No one knows that you exist unless they see your photographs. Some agencies will accept amateur photographs but without professional photographs it is almost impossible to get work. You can not do without them. There are two basic types:

A. Photographs for distribution, which are duplicated in mass quantities and sent along with your resumé.

B. Photographs in your portfolio, that you carry with you to interviews, auditions, registrations and visitations to casting agencies.

When selecting your photographs, select one or two to duplicate, one for theatrical (film, television & video) and one for a commercial look, and others to go into your portfolio. Take them to a professional quantity photo reproduction house. In Hollywood go to:

CHOICE PHOTO LAB 1550 Cahuenga Blvd., Hollywood, 90028,**(213) 463-5381**

SUNSET PLAZA One Hour Photo, 8539 Sunset Blvd., West Hollywood, 90069,(213) 854-7740

For the best prices on B&W
HOUR IMAGE,
6399 Wilshire Blvd.
Suite 102, Los Angeles, CA 90048
(213) 653-0130

For the best prices on
Litho Reproductions
BIGSHOTS
4942-B Vineland Ave.
North Hollywood, CA 91601
(818) 763-2202

PRINTS CHARM'N   (3 locations)
9054 Santa Monica Bl., W. Hollywood, 90069
(310) 288-1786
11020 Ventura Blvd., Studio City, 91604 (818) 753-9055
1657 Sawtelle Blvd., West Los Angeles, 90025
(310) 312-0904
DUPLICATE PHOTOS
1522 Highland Ave., Hollywood, 90028
(213) 466-7544
PAPER CHASE
7176 W. Sunset Blvd., Hollywood, 90046
(213) 874-2300
GRAPHIC REPRODUCTIONS
1423 N. LaBrea Ave., Hollywood, 90046
(213) 874-4335

   Sunset Plaza will even give you 20% off all 5 x 7 or 8 x 10 prints.
   Check the local yellow pages for others.
   Photos you take and/or send to EXTRA CASTING AGENTS should be color 3 ½ x 5, shot from the waist up. Photographs that will go into the Extra Casting Agency Commercial Photo Books should be taken outdoors. Your portfolio should contain 8 x 10 B/W (black and white) and/or color glossy prints. You will want to change them from time to time until you have a very diversified collection. Include some single headshots (from neck up photos), composite head shots (a variety of from neck up photos), composite head and the new 3/4 body shots (a variety from neck up and a variety from waist up, from knees up and full body (head to toe photos). They should be the best shots you can get. My thought is that if I can get two or three good shots out of a roll to add to my portfolio I'm satisfied.

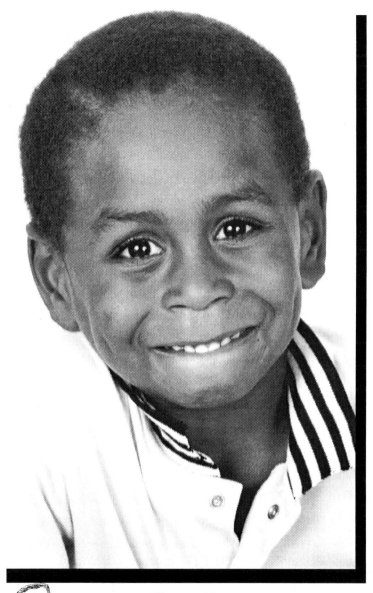

DOC

DocChristopher Gary Chambers
SAG   AFTRA

DOC
DocChristopher
Gary Chambers

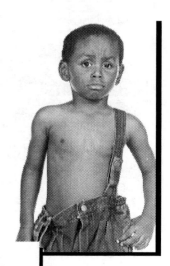

DOB: 12-1-85
SS# 000-00-000
(213) 969-4897
(213) 969-4889
(213) 871-7567

REPRESENTED BY:
JeanPage
MGMT.

TAMARA LUNT
COMMERCIAL HEADSHOT

STAN FLEISHMAN
THEATRICAL HEADSHOT

JULIE HOWELL
FULL BODY SHOT

Cheryl Felton
Commercial Headshot

R.C. BATES
CHARACTER SHOT

ALICIA SASSANO
3x5 color w/ white background

Phoenix Nugent
Theatrical Half-body

CLOYDE HOWARD
Commercial-extra (outdoor)

JOSEF HILL
OUTDOOR COMMERCIAL

AISHA JOHNSON
COMMERCIAL HALF-BODY

Following is a list of reputable professional photographers. The buzz on the boulevard is that these professional photographers will provide you with some of the finest photographs in Hollywood.

RICH HOGAN PHOTOGRAPHY

(213) 467-2628 (Hollywood)

Rich is considered by most of the biggest & best casting agencies to be one of "THE" photographer in Los Angeles. He has photographed over 10,000 actors & actresses as well as top celebrities and models. He shoots for most of the major casting companies & knows exactly what they want. He is offering two "Back To One" specials. A color starter package includes 8 exposures, 2 outfits, 8 3x5 prints and all the negatives for only $49.00. Package B includes the "Back To One" special and Sunset Casting and Hagerman & Associates registration for $89.00

New to his studio is a Special Services Department. Rich can provide **resumés** and other tools to help you <u>make it</u>.

CAVALIER PHOTOGRAPHY

(818) 840-9148 (818) 566-8291 Burbank

Cavalier Photography has a "BACK TO ONE" Special as well. You'll receive 36 4 x 6 or 3½ x 5 color prints for $135.00. It includes 36 poses/six outfits, processing and negatives. Cavalier will shoot an additional 36 B/W - $75.00.

CHARLES FRETZIN PHOTOGRAPHY

(818) 876-1783 Los Angeles

Mango Photography has a "BACK TO ONE" Special as well. You'll receive 36 3½ x 5 color prints for $135.00. It includes 36 poses/six outfits, processing and negatives. Mango will shoot an additional 36 B/W prints for $75.00.

Hogan, Cavalier & Fretzin all specialize in great theatrical and commercial headshot photographs! Choose carefully when selecting other photographers. Fees can vary enormously, ranging from $10.00 to <u>$1,500.00</u>. So check around!

4. Resumé

A resumé is a summary of your personal characteristics and experiences, a listing of characters and roles you have played and where. Include basic information such as name, height, weight, hair color, eye color, age range (*5 to 15 years maximum*) and telephone numbers. It should also contain any pertinent information that might be helpful to a casting agent, in evaluating and determining your qualifications for a special bit part or other additional acting assignments. Duplicate and attach the resumé to your photo.

Information you should list, such as your physical characteristics should be realistic. Specify a narrow age range or simply give your current age.

Your credits should include your professional experiences only, however, amateur experiences may be included when you are first starting out. Experience is not necessary but a strong desire to do whatever you do well is! If you choose to be affiliated with a union, this goes on the resumé next to your name. If you have acted with a union company, that should be at the top of the list. If you have been a stand-in on a movie or an extra on a T.V. Pilot, that takes priority over any leading role you may have had in a community play or a local cable television show. Whenever you have acted with known stars, known directors or known actors or actresses be sure this information takes precedence over any other information on your resumé.

Things to also include are your hobbies and special skills/abilities... singing, dancing, swimming, skating, diving, horseback riding, sports, biking, etc. (*see sample list at the bottom of EXTRA PERSONAL DATA SHEET on page 283*). Your training along with your instructors name. Languages you speak fluently are also important. A resumé should show your experiences at a glance.

TRACEY POREÉ

AFTRA   **SAG**

MOTION PICTURE

LET IT RIDE	*SPECTATOR*	ALLEGED PRODUCTION
HE'S MY GIRL	*FEATURED DANCER*	SCOTTI BROS.
PENITENTIARY III	*SPECTATOR #3*	CANNON GROUP
FIVE HEART BEATS	*GROUPIE LADY*	20TH CENTURY-FOX
WOMEN ON THE INSIDE	*SOBBING VISITOR*	HBO-PRODUCTION
DIEHARD II	*PASSENGER*	20TH CENTURY-FOX

MOTION PICTURE-*FEATURED PLAYER*

ONE GOOD COP	THE CHAMP	DYNAMITE
JESUS SAVES	BIG SHOT	THE MAIN EVENT
THE NIGHT OF THE DOOMED	THE GOD FATHER	GRAND CANYON
DEAD ON	THE LAST BOYSCOUT	MONSTER SQUAD
DIE HARD II	NEW JACK CITY	

TELEVISION

ARCHIE'S PLACE	*FASHION DESIGNER*	CBS-TV

TELEVISION-*FEATURED PLAYER*

QUANTUM LEAP	EQUAL JUSTICE	TWILIGHT ZONE
MATLOCK	FIRST & TEN	BRONX ZOO
DOWNTOWN	ST. ELSEWHERE	TRUE COLORS
L.A. LAW	EDDIE DODD	CIVIL WAR
ROSIE O'NEILL	CONVICTED, A MOTHERS' STORY	

COMMERCIALS

MONEY MAKERS 1990	*QUESTIONER #4*	VIDEO IMAGE PRO
BUD DRY	*SPECTATOR*	SUNSET PRODUCTION

STAGE

FASHION SHOW DIRECTOR - 11 YEARS
TEA ROOMS CONVENTION GARDEN TELEVISION GRAND HOTELS

SINGER

FEATURED RECORDING ARTIST - GOSPEL JAZZ RHYTHM BLUES BALLARDS
MUSICAL SCORE & FEATURE FILM SOUND TRACKS

DANCER

WORLD TOUR W/ LEE CRAVEN
VIP LOUNGES: LOS ANGELES LAS VEG

CONTESTANT

MISS AMERICA BEAUTY CULTURE
MISS BEAUTIFUL EYES & LIPS

TRAINING

ACTOR & DIRECTORS STUDIO: METHOD
LOS ANGELES COMMUNITY COLLEGE: I
MARIE ARTHUR: SINGING - DANCING - D
JOHN ROBERT POWERS: MODELING

PHYSICAL STATISTICS

HEIGHT: 5'8 1/2"	WAIST: 2	
WEIGHT: 145 LBS.	HIPS: 38	
BUST: 36	HAIR: BRO	
BLOUSE: 10/11	HAT: 7	
INSEAM: 27	JACKET: I	
COLLAR: 12	S(II):10	

SPECIAL SKILLS

DANCING, SINGING, MODELING, AEROBIC
SOFTBALL, GOURMET COOKING, PHOTOGRA

👆
Resumé back 8x10

Resumé back 3x5 ☞

MARTEE LaCOMETTE
SAG - AFTRA

Message (310) 969-4897
Pager (213) 969-4897
Calling-in Ser. (818) 969-4897

Hair:	**Dark Blonde**
Eyes:	**Hazel**
Height:	**5'5"**
Weight:	**115 lbs.**
Size:	**4-6**

5. Colleagues

Making movie magic, television shows and commercials is a PEOPLE business. Fifty to 150 crew members are needed to make a feature film; 25-50 for television situation comedies; 15-35 for a ten second commercial. Extras, background actors, atmosphere artists or journey person background actors, as you will be referred to, are generally on every set, and usually on a different set and/or location everyday. The """"JOURNEYPERSON"""" BACKGROUND ACTOR" will display his or her talents wherever and whenever they are needed.

This allows you, the Extra, to exchange inside information about the various projects that are in the development stages, pre-production or in production, (filming currently taking place).

Your fellow Extras are the BEST source for information on other background/acting jobs. The Crew members are also a vital source of upcoming or current projects. They are usually on one specific production anywhere from 10 days to 365 days straight. They do not come in contact with as many people as the """"JOURNEYPERSON"""" BACKGROUND ACTOR." Remember Extras are usually on different sets everyday and they have a lot of time to converse with people. They also have great information about where to get inexpensive wardrobe, make-up, photos, union info, rules and regulations, uniforms and other information you'll find very interesting. It is amazing how much background actors know about what is going on or coming up in regard to future productions.

Keep a good rapport with the serious players. You will be able to spot them in no time. They are actors who look professional. You'll see exactly what I mean. Get to know them even if only to differentiate them from the "pushy-know-nothing-know-it-all-avoid-them-like-the-plague extras".

Have some nice, yet impressive thermoengraved PHOTO business cards printed up for as little as $65.00 for 500. (*See EXTRA ORDER FORM*). Distribute freely.

Always carry spare change. You'll thank me, and so will your colleagues!

V a n n Johnson
Actress Singer Model
SAG/ AFTRA
213 969-4897

Sam Clauder II
Producer/Writer/
Director/Actor
Clauder Creative
Enterprises
(213) 969-4897

Sandra McNeil
SAG/ AFTRA
(818) 508-4974
(818) 969-4897

6. Up-To-Date Information

R EAD, READ, READ. Trade publications are other major ways to stay informed of what may be on the horizon or already in full blown production. The list I have compiled and included in the following pages, should be considered mandatory reading, especially the local newspaper entertainment sections. You do not always have to purchase them, you will find them lying around on all sets. Just ask the owner, most are willing to share. They almost always say yes. Purchasing your own always means you have them. The cost will be about $30.00 per month tax-deductible (see page 254). See the Publishers' Bookshelf section in Chapter 11, for other valuable books and periodicals you will need to soar to the top!

7. Extra Casting Agencies

An Extra Casting Agent is a person who makes his/her income by helping you make yours. The Extra Casting Agent's business is to hire actors and actresses for production companies that need qualified actors to perform in the background of a scene that is filmed or videotaped. Their job is to secure talent for a producer.

Their job as far as you, the background actor is concerned, is to cast & hire you, the Background actors, for work in movies, television and videos. For their efforts they take a percentage of your salary and/or get a fee from the production company that requested the talent. The percentage they get from you varies from 0 to 15%. Make sure you know just how much they want from you up front so there will be no surprises later when you are paid.

When you and an Extra Agent enter into an agreement, you agree with the Agent that they will represent you in getting Extra Work assignments and this agreement is finalized with a contract. They will take your photograph, for a nominal fee, or use the ones you supply them with from your photographer. They will place your photos in their Background Artist file in one of several different categories in which you are classified.

Extra casting directors look for personal characteristics, individual traits and qualities that can be carried into the role. Physical type determines, for the most part, the roles you will be asked to play because these are unchangeable. They begin with your nationality. Then they apply your age and bone structure which are also pretty much unchangeable. Your weight, manner of dress, posture, hair style, health condition, complexion and grooming habits give you great latitude for control.

There is **NO** ideal physical type. Types do exist however, and come under various headings, examples are; **UNDER 30, OVER 30, OVER 18 LOOK YOUNGER, UNDER 18, CHARACTER, ATHLETIC, RUGGED, UPSCALE** etc... It is important to find your type, if only to get yourself in the right category. The specifics of your personal appearance are not individually important to the Casting Director. What matters most is the effect your person and image creates That should be a dynamic one.

The Extra Casting Agencies <u>will</u> get you work! Sometimes they will call you but more often, 90% of the assignments you get will be because you called them or if you are in Hollywood, you had your EXTRA CALLING SERVICE call in for you (*See Tool #8. **Extra Calling-In Services***).

I strongly suggest you personally check out each Extra Casting Agent for <u>yourself</u> before deciding which agencies to register with. For my personal recommendations, look for the STAR (☆) in the NOTE/COMMENT section of each listing.

(l-r) Terry Zarchi, Jerry Conca and Jeff Olan of Rainbow Casting

In Los Angeles, **CENTRAL CASTING/CENEX CASTING** is the biggest and one of the best, with a staff of over twenty casting directors. **Rainbow Casting, Bill Dance Casting, Messenger Associates Casting, T.B.S. Casting, Monica Cooper's M.R. Cooper Casting** and **Prime Casting** are smaller companies in size, with staffs of about four to ten casting directors each. They also are some of the best in Los Angeles and my favorite companies to work for. For music video casting **Hagerman & Associates**, **Creative Image**, **Star Casting**, **Shelia Thompson Casting** and **Prime Casting** are just some of the agencies to be registered with in Los Angeles. Although most extra casting agencies cast music videos those above mentioned agencies cast the majority of the music video projects as well as the feature film and television show projects. See page *190* for the Exclusive complete

BACK TO ONE's Top Ten Picks of The Hottest 1 0 0 Hollywood Extra Casting Agencies 1996.

The Rating is determined by a number of factors, e.g...union wages... non-union wages... full-time agency... part-time agency... daily work.. projects totals, reimbursement for mileage, wardrobe,

Juliette Hagerman
Casting Director & coordinator

hair, interviews or audition... types of shows; feature film, television, music videos, or commercials and infomercials... pay periods, cash jobs... location work or on the sound stages   the talent agents...casting directors... types cast... professionalism and talent relations.

Again, I strongly suggest you check each Extra Casting Agency out for yourself. Call them. Get as much information as you can over the telephone and/or make an appointment if you can and go <u>in</u> to visit them.

Because the more you see them, the more they see you, and the more they see you the more you work!

Be sure to take your valid identification and Social Security card with you. You will need to present them to register. Children must have a valid work permit. Parents read the special section on children extra casting entitled CHILDREN IN ACTION for more detailed information.

Christopher Gray of
Christopher Gray Casting

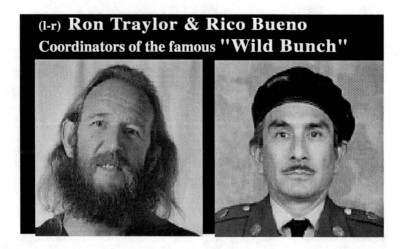

(l-r) **Ron Traylor & Rico Bueno**
Coordinators of the famous **"Wild Bunch"**

All background or extra casting agents such as Hollywood's Annisa Williams Casting, Dixie Webster Casting, AMC Casting, David Anthony's Background Players, First Action Casting need fresh, new faces all the time, especially one of the best kept secrets in Hollywood, casting director Christopher Gray. If they say they don't need your look today they most likely will soon. Keep contacting them. Send a nice note along with acurrent photograph. A friendly telephone call has done the trick for me on hundreds of occasions. If you are booked on a lot for background acting assignments, tell them how much you really appreciate them. If you have not been booked tell them that too, just be tactful and nice about it. Say it with a smile! You'll find the majority of casting directors have professional integrity and really like casting talent in various productions. Treat them respectfully and you'll work all the time!

In Los Angeles speciality characters such as the "Wild Bunch" and ethnic extra casting agents like Betty Dent's "Latin Connection Mgmt", Ron Smith's Celebrity Look-a-Likes and Native American Casting are the agents to register with if you can play the types of characters or

A few of "The Wild Bunch" gather for a *Family Portrait* with C.D., Sandra Alesssi (FRONT CENTER) at casting mixer

ethnic called for on a particular feature film, television, commercial or industrial video production they also cast regular types in roles as well.

For those of you who lives in places other than the major film and video production areas, such as Los Angeles, New York, Chicago, Orlando in the U. S. or

Betty Dent's
Latin Connection Management

Canadian area contact your area Film Commission or Entertainment Bureau from the listing on pages 223-239 for the names of production companies filming in your area.

There are a lot of great background casting companies in other parts of the country and with the 500 channel

Cable TV future which is actually here, there will soon be many other agencies popping up all over.

The commissions are your best source for names and address of production companies who hires the extra casting companies in your local region. The commissions are usually government sponsored or endorsed and the various extra casting agencies around the country and world know this.

The extra casting companies know these commissions will be protecting your rights and the concerns of the production companies from unsavory or unethical practices by agencies so they will treat you professionally when you say how you were referred to that agency.

The commissions have become very necessary to communities because of the economic boost a film production brings to a community.

Establish a good working relationship with someone in the commission's office and the benefits will be great including sometimes the commissions contacting you when they know a production will be coming into the area to film and are in need of talent, both principals and background. They will be able to tell inquiring production companies about the abundance of enthusiastic and qualified persons available for casting from the local area's talent pool. An <u>asset</u> for the commission which could and positively has made in the past, the difference as to whether a film was made there in a location.

It may be necessary to contact them more than once to talk to the right person who will take the time to assist you just be determined and persistent. Know your outcome! I guarantee you will be very successful. Write and tell me of your success stories, it may end up here on the pages of the of Back To One!

We'll see you in the movies!

8. Extra Calling-In Services

It's 4:00 p.m. and you don't have a work assignment for the next day. Logistics are the main problem. You are on a remote location, the location telephone is for production staff and crew only, the nearest public telephone is five miles away, your car is parked two miles away in the opposite direction, what are you to do? Don't Worry, Be Happy, because in Los Angeles you have hired an EXTRA CALLING-IN SERVICE! You've hired them to place calls for you to the Extra Casting Agencies informing the Casting Directors that you are available for an assignment. Your EXTRA CALLING-IN SERVICE has booked you on a background acting work assignment for the next three days on your favorite T.V. show and a commercial on Friday!

In today's fast-paced "HOLLYWOOD EXTRA" world, you cannot get the most, nor the best work assignments when just starting out if you have to call in for work assignments everyday. Besides you waiting on the telephone and feeding it coins, Casting Directors would rather fill a production company's

(l-r) Eden - Laura - Jennifer of ExtraPhone

talent request for 20 people with one telephone call from an EXTRA CALLING-IN SERVICE than to wait for or make 20 calls. Therefore, the EXTRA CALLING-IN SERVICE has become a tremendous liaison of the Extra Casting Agency and especially the Casting Director and you, the background actor. If you want to make the good $$$ that can be made as an Extra, you must have a Calling-In Service.

EXTRA CALLING-IN SERVICES work for you, don't forget that. You will pay them a contracted monthly fee. They call the agencies and attempt to get work assignments for you based on your availability and the casting agent's needs. After dialing in for yourself for a week, you'll agree they're worth double their fee. But never tell them that! Try a particular service for a couple of months. If you find they do not meet your needs, give them notice and contract with a new one. Some EXTRA CALLING-IN SERVICES are better than others. Check around and listen to which Calling Service other Background Actors use.

However, I have personally contracted **one of the best,ExtraPhone** to place calls for me. I work as much as I want, five and sometimes even six and seven days a week, even during hiatus, the so-called "work slow down" periods between television seasons, when feature films and Movie of the Week productions are in high gear. They take my calls for both

Krisha-manager
ExtraPhone

principal and background acting assignments as well as principal roles that I submit for directly from the various trade publications and casting breakdowns as well.

Tell them Cullen sent you and receive $5.00 off your first month's service charge.

My friend uses **<u>DIRECT LINE</u> Calling-In Service** and has been working steadily as well. They treat you like an individual not a number!

Charles Alessi, owner, has also worked as a background actors and is very dedicated to working hard for you. DIRECT LINE and all the other calling in services listed herein will also give you $5.00 off your first month's service.

Monthly service fees for the listed Calling-In services varies from $40.00 -$55.00 per month. **Rapid Casting** and **Valentina's VCM** (*Valentina Casting Management*) offer a interestingly unique concept. They feature a one time fee and then a small percentage based on the work/jobs they obtain for you. Very good especially for people starting out.

I would<u>not</u> recommend you hire a Calling-In Service that does not appear in the listing section, to place your calls. Those listed herein have been thoroughly researched, and are waiting to hear from you.

The service that works for one person may or may not work the same for another person, so check around. **EXTRA CALLING-IN SERVICES** mention here, such as veteran's **Gil Jarmond's "<u>Starting Point</u>"** and a top industry professional **Sandra Reith's " <u>Extra Effort</u>"** listed on page 219 are the best of those available. Tell them Cullen from BACK TO ONE sent you and each will give you an additional $5.00 off your first month service.

Valentina of VCM

9. Thomas Brothers Guide Mapbook

You've gotten your work assignment for the next day production name, call time, wardrobe, check-in person, pay rate and the set location, the place where filming will take place away from the regular studio locations. But you do not know where it is. Just pull out your trusty Thomas Brothers Guide Mapbook, turn to the page and pinpoint the co-ordinate, (point of reference,) e.g. page 42 Co-Ordinates E-2, that the Extra Casting Director will give you or your Extra Calling-In Service. Map out your route and estimate your travel time, and before you can say Taft-Hartley, you're at your work assignment with the perfect wardrobe and a smile on your face, instead of being lost in El Segundo at 7:00 a.m., when you should be in El Monte at 6:30 a.m.

The Casting Director always gives the assignment location calls with the Thomas Brothers Guide Mapbook co-ordinates. If you do not know how to read the mapbook it would be good advice to take 30 minutes to learn. I recommend buying the combination LA/Orange County edition available most everywhere or from us through our Publishers Bookshelf section.

The Thomas Brothers Guide Mapbook is all new for 1996. Featuring new grid page numbers and co-ordinates. They utilize the 911 grid system used by the police, fire and other emergency services. The 1996 Los Angeles/Orange counties Thomas Brothers GUIDE Mapbook is available for only $25.95 from BACK TO ONE (*See EXTRA ORDER FORM*). Most casting call are given with the old Thomas Bros. Mapbook co-ordinates as well.

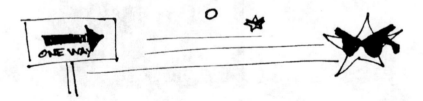

10. Dependable Transportation

T his is an area in which you should be concerned but not panic about. If you don't have a car, can't borrow a car or can't get a ride, the buses go everywhere. Allow enough time to get to your location, taking into consideration delays, traffic congestion and vehicle breakdowns.

If you do own your own car(s), there is a great opportunity to get paid additional money, a Bump, for having it filmed as part of the background scenery or driving by when filming an outdoor street scene.

In Southern California as there are around the country, many companies specialize in placing cars in movies and television shows, especially older, unique, exotic, sporty, luxury, unusual and specialty vehicles. Contact them and register your vehicle today. They can pay up to $125.00 a day just for the use of your vehicle. You can get $10.00 - $30.00 if you are called as a background actors to work with your car in a scene. In Los Angeles contact *Tin Lizzy's* on page 211.

Southern California "SMART TRAVELER" is a one-stop integrated service offering traffic, carpool and mass transit information to everyone.

Call **1-800-COMMUTE** 1-800-266-6883

PRESS 1:   MTA bus and transit

PRESS 2:   Metrolink

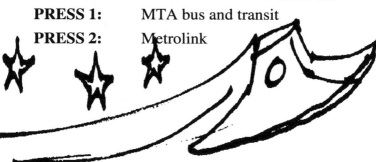

Lights! Cameras! Action!

There you have them, the "TOOLS OF THE TRADE" for "THE HOLLYWOOD EXTRA". With these tools you will be able to make the good $$$$ that can be made as a "HOLLYWOOD" MOVIE EXTRA on your way to super stardom or as a Professional Background Actor or Actress or just for fun the exciting, magical world of movie making!

These tips and tools for success may seem simple, but most good ideas in life are simple and practical. Following through is **EVERYTHING !**

For 10 years I have seen and heard from thousands of people who have used the information to get started with great success . Some have had such phenomenal success that they hadn't the time to think about or prepare their next move and ....

Come up with a plan that fits into your life goals. Anchor it to sound, practical and logical thinking, a well thought-out planning. Making the follow-up visits and telephone calls will gain you a great degree of success no matter where in the country you choose to start.

Hollywood, California is really where the movie making action really is at, and eventually you may want to come here if you live elsewhere especially to further an acting career.

Remember a lot of the great and famous actors and actresses begin their stellar careers as the non-principal performer in a non- speaking role more commonly known as the background actors and actresses and/or extras.

The pay will range from $40.00 for 8 hours (Non-union film) to $250.00 for 8 hours. (Union commercial). Time and half for 8-10 hours and Double time for 10 hours or more. See the specially designed "BACK TO ONE" Pay Rate Schedule for complete information.

On a given day for example... if you work 12.5 hours (which is a typical work day for feature films) at a typical non-union $40.00 base rate, your day's earning will be over $75.00. At the new Screen Actors Guild union $72.00 base rate your day's earnings would be over $135.00. That does not include additional money for wardrobe, use of your vehicle in a scene, mileage or any other special bits.

I have friends who have made over $2,000.00 for four days work on a commercial where they were paid $225.00 for 8 hours. I even have a friend who has made over $1,300.00 per day as an extra. He made almost $10,000.00 in four weeks. Not bad for a little extra work.

Believe me. The jobs are out there and the good $$$$$ is most definitely there for the making. Be there to take it! This book and careful planning will allow you to reach your goals and purpose in the glamorous, exciting and magical entertainment industry. Most importantly, plan your work, then work your plan.

See YOU in the movies!!!

Supplemental Pay Scale and Rate Information

The following information supplements the table on the following page.

PAY SCALE & RATES FOR NON-UNION EXTRAS (FILM AND T.V.)

Minors

$75.00/8 hours ages 6-17 yr.

$75.00/6 hours ages 2-6 yr.

$125.00/4 hours . under 2 yrs.

Stand-ins :

$75.00/8 hrs. plus overtime.

Photo double:

$75.00/8 hrs. plus overtime.

Silent Bits, Hazardous Conditions & Special Abilities:

rates are negotiable.

Saturday & Sunday :

add $10.00 to base rate.

Overtime hours : after eight hours, time and a half; double time after 10th hour.

Interviews & fittings:

$ 10.00.

Special wardrobe, tuxedos, furs, formal, uniforms

$15.00 allowances (non taxable).

Automobile

$15.00 allowance (non taxable).

Mileage $.25 per mile allowance, round trip, (non- taxable) or flat fee.

**PAY SCALE & RATES FOR UNION EXTRAS (FILM & T.V.)

Minors :

$75.00/8 hours ages 6-17.

$75.00/6 hours ages 2-6.

$150.00/4 hours under 2 years.

Stand-ins :

$97.00/8 hours plus overtime,

Photo-double

$97.00/8 hours plus overtime.

Special Abilities: $ 82.00/8 hours.

Saturday: time and a half base rate.

Sunday: double time base rate.

Overtime hours:

after eight hours, time and a half, double time after 12th hour.

*Interviews & fittings:

¼ of base rate (2 hours minimum).

Wardrobe change: $9.00 allowance 1st change, 6.25 (non taxable).

Special wardrobe, tuxedos, furs, formal, uniforms:

$18.00 allowance (non taxable).

Automobile:

$30.00 allowance (non taxable).

Mileage: $.30 per mile allowance, round trip, (non- taxable).

**See S.A.G. Extra Performer Contract digest section for more details.

***Union Extra Players shall not be employed in excess of a total 16 hours, including meals periods, travel time and actual time required to turn in wardrobe or property in any one day of 24 hours. The penalty for violation of the 16 hour rule shall be one day's pay for each hour, or fraction thereof.   *RATES AS OF THIS PRINTING, 02-04-96*

BTO PAY SCALE SCHEDULE

RATES AS OF 02-04-96

**UNION RATES EFFECTIVE 07-01-96

*** Day Player actor minimum union rate EFFECTIVE 07-01-96.

BASE-RATE	0-8 HRS Per/Hr.	9 Hours	10 Hours	11 Hours	12 Hours	13 Hours	14 Hours	15 Hours	16 Hours	GOLD TIME
*** $540	540.00	641.25	742.50	877.50	1,012.50	1,147.50	1,282.50	1,417.50	1,552.50	2,092.50
	67.50	101.25	101.25	101.25	101.25	135.00	135.00	135.00	135.00	540.00
❖ $275	275.50	327.15	378.81	447.68	516.56	585.43	654.30	723.18	792.05	1,067.55
	34.44	51.66	51.66	51.66	51.66	68.87	68.87	68.87	68.87	275.50
$250	250.00	296.88	343.75	406.25	468.75	531.25	593.75	656.25	718.75	968.75
	31.25	46.88	46.88	62.50	62.50	62.50	62.50	62.50	62.50	250.00
$225	225.00	267.19	309.38	351.56	393.75	450.00	506.25	562.50	618.75	675.00
	28.13	42.19	42.19	42.19	42.19	56.25	56.25	56.25	56.25	56.25
$134	134.00	159.13	184.25	217.75	251.25	284.75	318.25	351.75	385.25	519.25
	16.75	25.13	25.13	33.50	33.50	33.50	33.50	33.50	33.50	134.00
$106	106.00	125.88	145.75	172.25	198.75	225.25	251.75	278.25	304.75	410.75
	13.25	19.88	19.88	26.50	26.50	26.50	26.50	26.50	26.50	106.00
** $102	102.00	121.13	140.25	159.38	178.50	204.00	229.50	255.00	280.50	382.50
	12.75	19.13	19.13	19.13	19.13	25.50	25.50	25.50	25.50	102.00
** $79	79.00	93.81	108.63	123.44	138.25	158.00	177.75	197.50	217.25	296.25
	9.88	14.81	14.81	14.81	14.81	19.75	19.75	19.75	19.75	79.00
$72	72.00	85.50	99.00	112.50	126.00	144.00	162.00	180.00	198.00	270.00
	9.00	13.50	13.50	13.50	13.50	18.00	18.00	18.00	18.00	72.00
$50	50.00	59.38	68.75	81.25	93.75	106.25	118.75	131.25	143.75	156.25
	6.25	9.38	9.38	12.50	12.50	12.50	12.50	12.50	12.50	12.50
$40	40.00	47.50	55.00	65.00	75.00	85.00	95.00	105.00	115.00	125.00
	5.00	7.50	7.50	10.00	10.00	10.00	10.00	10.00	10.00	10.00

❖ = AFTRA 5 LINES OR LESS Copyright © 1996 Back To One Publication/Cullen Chambers

For a convenient E-Z Reference 5 panel business card size fold-out of the BACK TO ONE ENTERTAINMENT INDUSTRY TALENT "PAYSCALE AND SCHEDULE with 1996-1997 RATES. Covering movies, television, videos and commercials, that also features SAG-AFTRA supplemental pay rates; such as meal penalty rates, auto use, mileage, wardrobe, personal props and payroll co. address and phone listing. Send $3.00 to Back To One, Payscale Schedule, P.O. Box 753-ps, Hollywood, CA 90078-0753

EXTRA NOTE

Chapter Two

EXTRA BASIC WORKING RIGHTS

EXTRA PLAYER, according to IWC ORDER 12-80, SECTION 2(G), is defined as "any person employed by an employer in the production of motion picture to perform any work, including but not limited to that of a general extra, stand-in, photographic double, sports player, silent bit, or dress extra; or as extras employed in dancing, skating, swimming, diving, riding, driving, or singing; or as extras employed to perform any other actions, gestures, facial expressions, or pantomime."

ON THE JOB YOUR EMPLOYER MUST:

CARRY workers' compensation insurance, at no cost to you, to protect you if you sustain job-related injuries or illness.

FURNISH you an itemized deduction statement at the time your wages are paid. (Wages include regular and overtime pay, commissions, vacation pay and other pay promised by your employer in a written or verbal agreement.) This requirement is also true if your wages are paid in cash.

YOU ARE ENTITLED TO...

RECEIVE the State or Federal minimum wage, whichever is higher.

(Workers in California are covered by one or the

other.) The current minimum wage is $4.25 per hour.

OVERTIME wages for work performed in excess of 8 hours in one day or 40 hours in one work week.

OVERTIME for an extra player on a daily basis is computed at 1 1/2 times the employee's rate of pay for the ninth and tenth work hour, and not less than double (2) time, the extra player's rate of pay for all hours worked thereafter in the same workday.

At least two hours pay is required if you report for work and get less than a half day's work. A meal period of at least 30 minutes for every six hours of work and a rest period of at least 10 minutes for each four hours worked. A variable monetary adjustment is payable to you for each 1/2 hour delay of your meal period.

WHEN YOU LEAVE...

IF discharged, you must be paid immediately and in full all wages due you.

IF you quit without notice, you must be paid all wages due you in full within 72 hours.

IF your employer willfully refuses to pay you within the required time, he may be assessed penalties up to 30 day's wages in addition to the wages he already owes you.

<u>YOU CANNOT BE PENALIZED</u>, discharged or threatened with discharge for making a complaint about unsafe working conditions, for filing a claim for workers' compensation benefits, or for filing a complaint with the Labor Commission.

IF YOU BELIEVE that you are not being treated in accordance with your rights, you may file a complaint with the State Labor commissioner. You will be advised of your rights and obligations. You will be provided assistance in preparing your complaint.

Call the **State of California Labor Department** at **(818) 901-5315 or 901-5312** for the nearest office, or consult your local telephone directory. Ask them to send or go pick-up a copy of the <u>unabridged</u> labor laws concerning background actors. They will be glad to send you a nice wall chart that explains the laws pertaining to background actors rights and privileges. Every background actor should have a copy.

For complaint forms or entertainment related questions

Write or call...

Candy Jennings

State Labor Commission
6105 Van Nuys Blvd. #100
Van Nuys, CA 91401
(818) 901-5484

For questions about wages, discriminations and employment practices call your local:

Fair Employment Practices
(CA 800-884-1684)
Equal Employment Opportunity Commission-
(CA 213 894-1000)

CALIF D.L.S.E. complaint form

STATE OF CALIFORNIA – DEPARTMENT OF INDUSTRIAL RELATIONS
DIVISION OF LABOR STANDARDS ENFORCEMENT
STATE LABOR COMMISSIONER

INITIAL REPORT OR
CLAIM

FOR OFFICE USE ONLY			
TAKEN BY	PROCEEDING NUMBER		ACTION
DATE TAKEN	PROGRAM DO BOFE	SOURCE 1 2 3	IND CODE
FIELD INVESTIGATION REFERRAL			
REFERRING OFFICE		DATE	

PLEASE PRINT ALL INFORMATION

YOUR NAME	SOCIAL SECURITY NO.	NO. TAX EXEMPTIONS
YOUR ADDRESS – NUMBER AND STREET, APARTMENT OR SPACE NO., CITY, ZIP CODE	HOME PHONE NO. ( )	WORK PHONE NO. ( )
KIND OF WORK DONE (OCCUPATION) DATE OF HIRE	CALIFORNIA DRIVER'S LICENSE NO.	DATE OF BIRTH
WORK DONE AT – NUMBER AND STREET, CITY, COUNTY, ZIP CODE	PUBLIC WORKS PROJECT? ☐ YES ☐ NO	WAS YOUR JOB UNION? ☐ YES ☐ NO

AGAINST

NAME OF BUSINESS	EMPLOYER'S NAME	☐ BANKRUPTCY ☐ BUSINESS SOLD ☐ INSOLVENCY
ADDRESS OF BUSINESS (INCLUDE ZIP CODE)		TELEPHONE NUMBER ( )
NAME OF PERSON IN CHARGE TYPE OF BUSINESS	ESTIMATED NO. OF EMPLOYEES:	MINORS EMPLOYED? ☐ YES ☐ NO

WAGES – CONDITIONS OF EMPLOYMENT

RATE OF PAY – PER HOUR, DAY, WEEK OR MONTH (SPECIFY) $	PAID BY PIECE RATE? ☐ YES ☐ NO	DID YOU WORK SPLIT SHIFTS? ☐ YES ☐ NO
TOTAL HOURS WORKED PER DAY: PER WEEK:	PAID OVERTIME? ☐ YES ☐ NO	4 DAY / 10 HOUR WORKWEEK? ☐ YES ☐ NO	IF YES, WRITTEN AGREEMENT? ☐ YES ☐ NO
ARE YOU STILL WORKING FOR THIS EMPLOYER? ☐ YES ☐ NO ☐ QUIT ☐ DISCHARGED ON WHAT DATE?	IF QUIT, DID YOU GIVE 72 HOURS NOTICE? ☐ YES ☐ NO	WERE YOU PAID AT TIME OF DISCHARGE? ☐ YES ☐ NO
HAVE YOU ASKED FOR YOUR WAGES? ☐ YES ☐ NO IF YES, ON WHAT DATE?	CHARGED FOR SHORTAGES? ☐ YES ☐ NO	RECORD OF HOURS WORKED KEPT? ☐ YES ☐ NO
HOW WERE YOU PAID? ☐ BY CHECK ☐ IN CASH GIVEN A DEDUCTION STATEMENT? ☐ YES ☐ NO	UNIFORM / TOOLS REQUIRED? ☐ YES ☐ NO	IF YES, FURNISHED BY EMPLOYER? ☐ YES ☐ NO
MEAL PERIOD: ☐ ON DUTY ☐ OFF DUTY MEALS FURNISHED? ☐ YES ☐ NO IF YES, WRITTEN AGREEMENT? ☐ YES ☐ NO	MEALS FURNISHED: ☐ BREAKFAST ☐ LUNCH ☐ DINNER	
LODGING FURNISHED: ☐ INDIVIDUAL ROOM ☐ SHARED ROOM ☐ APARTMENT	RENTAL VALUE OF APT. TO PUBLIC $	CASH ADVANCES (IF ANY) $

GROSS WAGES CLAIMED (Do Not Deduct Payroll Taxes)

FROM (DATE) 19___	TO (DATE) 19___	NUMBER OF HOURS, DAYS, WEEKS OR MONTHS CLAIMED (SPECIFY)
AT THE RATE OF – PER HOUR, DAY, WEEK OR MONTH (SPECIFY) $	SUB TOTAL ➔	$

BRIEF EXPLANATION OF ISSUES (Use Additional Sheet If Necessary)

	MINUS TOTAL OF CASH OR CREDITS RECEIVED ➔ $
	AMOUNT DUE OR BALANCE CLAIMED ➔ $

I HEREBY CERTIFY that this is a true statement to the best of my knowledge and belief.

MY NAME MAY BE USED IN ANY INVESTIGATION.   ☐ YES   ☐ NO

(Signed) ....   Date ....

Address ....

DLSE 1 (REV. 1 91)   INITIAL REPORT OR CLAIM

Chapter Three

TAFT - HARTLEY ACT OF 1947

The Taft-Hartley Act nullified the old
saying... You have to belong to the union to get
a union acting job... but you cannot get a union
acting job unless you belong to the union.

The TAFT - HARTLEY ACT is the common name for Labor Management Act of 1947. The act was sponsored by Senator Robert A. Taft of Ohio, and Representative Fred A. Hartley, Jr. of New Jersey. It was intended to limit some of the activities of labor unions in the U.S.. It amended the Wagner Act, the National Labor Relations Act of 1935 which had defined unions' rights to organize and bargain with employers. The Taft-Hartley Act outlawed unions to force employees to become members. It forbade unions the closed shop, the practice of hiring only union members and requiring prior union membership as a condition of being hired. It gave the states power to restrict the union shops, in which employees have to join the union after being hired. It required unions to file such information as constitutions and financial statements with the federal government. Taft-Hartley supporters said the act equalized power between union and management. Unions called it a "slave labor law" and tried to have it repealed or amended. The Taft-Hartley Act was passed over the veto of then President Harry S. Truman by Congress. The Landrum Griffin Law, formally the Labor-Management Reporting and Disclosure

Act of 1959, amended certain sections of the Taft-Hartley Act. Thus allowing people who were not in a union to be allowed to work in a "union shop" without being a member of that union first, and also being allowed to join the union after they had gained employment.

> **UNION SHOP:** A condition in which an employer agrees that employees must join a certified union after a period of probation as a condition of employment.
> **OPEN SHOP:** A condition in which an employer hires workers, whether or not they are union members.
> **CLOSED SHOP:** A condition in which an employer agrees to hire only members of a union recognized by contract.
> **FREE-LOADER:** Non-union employees who enjoy without cost the benefits of a contract obtained by dues-paying union members.

The Taft-Hartley Act made it possible for a non-union member aspiring actor to act in a union movie without being a member of the union prior to being cast as a principal (speaking) actor. This makes it possible for an extra to be given lines on the set of a movie by a director, for which the actor will be paid union wages (base rate $504.00/8 hr.) and given an acting contract, along with the privilege of joining the union and receiving residuals or royalties.

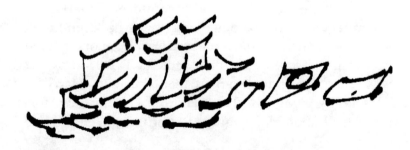

Chapter Four

Screen Actors Guild Extra Performer Theatrical Films And Television Digest

☒ The *Fastest* and *Easiest* way to become eligible to join the Acting Unions is to work 3 days as a Non-Principal Performer/Background Actor/Extra on a S.A.G. union or union-wavier payment voucher!

This is a digest of rates and working conditions applicable to SAG Extra Performers on the West Coast in theatrical motion pictures and television films effective until June 31, 1996 provided by the Screen Actors Guild.

It is as the **Screen Actors Guild Extras Digest** intended, to provide you with a readily available source to answer the frequently asked questions regarding the Extra Performers.

The New York and East Coast Extra Performers rates and conditions sometimes differ from those in the next following pages. If further information is needed concerning specific contract terms, contact your local Guild office (see page 240).

SCREEN ACTORS GUILD

National Headquarters
Museum Square
5757 Wilshire Boulevard
Los Angeles, Ca 90036-3600

☎ Main Switchboard - (213) 954-1600 ☎

☎ **Requirements For Joining- (213) 549-6772** ☎

For a complete listings of the National Headquarters telephone numbers see BTO's Extra Quick & E-Z Reference Phone Directory

S.A.G. EXTRA PERFORMERS 92-95 CONTRACT
SUMMARY THEATRICAL/TELEVISION DIGEST
1. RATES

A. MINIMUM DAILY RATE SCALE (Effective 7/1/95)

General Extra .... $ 72.00
Special Ability Extra... 75.00
Stand-In... 99.00
Choreographed Swimmers and Skaters 244.00

Weekly rates are **five** times the daily rates and shall include a guarantee of **five consecutive** days of employment.

B. DEFINITIONS

➢**General Extra-** Performer of atmospheric business which includes the normal actions, gestures and facial expressions of the Extra Performer's assignment.

➢**Special Ability Extra-** Extra Performer specifically called and assigned to perform work requiring special skill, such as: tennis, golf, choreographed social dancing (including square dancing), swimming, skating, riding animals, driving livestock, non-professional singing (in groups of 15 or fewer), professional or organized athletic sports (including officiating and running), amputees, driving which requires a special skill and a special license (such as truck driving but not cab driving), motorcycle driving (but not bicycle riding), insert work and practical card dealing.

➢**Silent Bit-** The category of Silent Bit has been eliminated as of 7-1-92.

➢**Stand-In-** Extra Performer used as a substitute for another actor for purposes of focusing shots, setting lights, etc., but is not actually photographed. Stand-Ins may also be used as General Extras.

➢**Photographic Double-** Extra Performer who is actually photographed as a substitute for another actor. A General Extra who is required to do photographic doubling shall receive the Special Ability rate.

➢**Day Performer-** A Performer who delivers a speech or line of dialogue. An Extra Performer must be upgraded to Day Performer if given a line, except in the case of "omnies."

➢**Omnies-** Any speech sounds used as general background noise rather than for its meaning. Atmospheric words such as indistinguishable background chatter in a party or restaurant scene.

C. PAYMENTS IN ADDITION TO BASIC DAILY RATE (ADJUSTMENTS)

(1) Hazardous Work

Producer shall notify Extra Performer at time of booking if any rough or dangerous work is involved. If no notice is received, Extra Performer may refuse such work and receive a one-half check or payment for actual hours worked, whichever is greater. However, if other General Extra work is available, Producer may keep Extra Performer to do such work at full rate.

No discrimination shall be permitted against such Extra Performer for such refusal. Extra Performers who accept hazardous work shall be entitled to additional compensation in an amount to be agreed upon between the Extra Performer and the Producer before the performance of such work

It is recommended that the amount of this adjustment be listed on the Extra Performer's daily voucher. Producer will provide immediate access to 'qualified medical personnel' whenever hazardous work is to be performed.

(2) Wet Work/Smoke Work

An Extra Performer required to get wet (including rain work) shall receive an additional $14 unless wearing swimming or surfing gear required for the scene or in the case of a crowd day involving the entire group. An Extra Performer may refuse to get wet unless notified of such work in advance.

Extra Performers working in smoke shall receive an additional $14, except if in the case of a crowd day and the entire group works in smoke at the same time, then no additional pay shall be due. Any Extra Performer not notified of smoke work at the time of call may refuse to perform such work and will receive one-half pay. If an Extra Performer refuses wet or smoke work, the Producer may keep the Extra Performer to perform other General Extra work, if it is available.

(3) Body Make-Up, Skull Cap, Hair Goods, Natural Full-Grown Beard

An Extra Performer required to (1) wear body make-up or oil over more than 50% of the body or over full arms and legs or (2) wear a rubber skull cap, or (3) wear an artificial full beard, "mutton chops," or both goatee and moustache, or (4) wear a natural full-grown beard, or (5) any female Extra Performer required to have body make-up applied to arms, shoulders and chest while wearing a self-furnished low-cut gown shall receive an additional $18 to be added to the basic daily rate.

(4) Haircuts

Any Extra Performer required to get a haircut must be notified in advance at the time of booking. If notice not given, the Extra Performer may refuse the job on arrival without prejudice, but will not be entitled to compensation. Also, a haircut may not be required more than two (2) working days prior to the date of work.

(5) Rehearsals

Rehearsal time is work time, whether on a day prior to filming or on the same day.

(6) Costume Fittings

If on a day prior to work call, payment is one-quarter of daily rate for work call for up to 2 hours; additional time is payable at 2/16 of daily rate for each additional 30 minutes or fraction thereof. If fitted for a production he/she is guaranteed at least one day's pay from that company.

(7) Wardrobe Allowance

Producer may require Extra Performer to report in formal attire (tuxedo, tailcoat or full length formal gown) for which the Extra Performer shall receive $18.00 for maintenance. Producer may require Extra Performer to report in non-formal attire without extra payment. If Producer requires or requests Extra Performer to bring additional complete changes of wardrobe, the Extra Performer shall receive $9.00 per day for the first such complete change and $6.25 per day for each additional change. Payment is for all changes requested, whether used or not. Performer may not be required to leave wardrobe overnight; if Extra Performer agrees to do so, daily wardrobe allowance is paid for each day so held.

(8) Damage to Wardrobe or Property

If any of Extra Performer's personal wardrobe or property is damaged in the course of his/her employment, the Producer shall reimburse him/her for damage or loss, to be paid within two weeks after proof of damage is supplied. Producer would be liable only for property requested by the production company or casting director, as well as personal belongings the Producer might reasonably expect a performer to have on that day - such as a wallet with $20 in it. Any other items that do not fall into the above categories are not covered under this contract; an individual would have to pursue such claims on their own. Please do not bring valuables to the set. If you must, make sure you notify the company and make special arrangements for safekeeping.

2. INTERVIEW FEES

Individually scheduled appointments ---------- 1/4 check
In formal clothes ------------------------ $9 plus 1/4 check
With pet, auto, etc. ------- 1/2 allowance rate + 1/4 check

3. PERSONAL PROPS

A. Extra Performers required to furnish the following shall receive the indicated additional payments:

1) Pets, Personal Accessories - Allowances Per Day:
Pets $23.00
Golf Clubs - set w/ bags 12.00

Tennis Racquet 5.00
(no additional pay if paid for tennis outfit)
Luggage 5.50
Camera 5.50
Skiis and poles 12.00

2) **For props not listed above, the Extra Performer must negotiate a fee at time of booking.**

3) **Autos, Etc. - Allowances Per Day:**
Auto $30.00
Trailer 19.00
Bicycle 12.00
Moped 15.00
Motorcycle 35.00
Police Motorcycle 50.00
Skate/Skateboard 5.50

B. Automobile - Allowance of $.30 per mile round trip, computed from Producer's base to location within studio zone. (In Los Angeles, if no Producer's base, mileage is computed from the corner of Beverly Boulevard and La Cienega.)

4. SIXTEEN HOUR VIOLATION

One day's pay for each hour (or fraction thereof) beyond 16 hours. Meal breaks and paid travel time are included in calculating 16 hours. An Extra Performer employed in excess of 16 hours in any one day of 24 hours shall receive this additional amount except in circumstances beyond the control of the Producer. Production considerations or conditions are not considered to be beyond Producer's control.

5. MEAL PERIODS

Meal period must be at least 1/2 hour but not more than one hour in duration (and is not counted as part of paid work time.) A 12 minute "grace" is permitted; however, if camera is rolling in middle of a take after the grace period, the Producer may complete that one take.

A non-deductible (N.D.) breakfast may be served to synchronize performers and crew's meal times. The next meal shall be served six hours from the end of the N.D. breakfast.

When crew members' meal period is shorter than that of Extra Performers', crew members may be served before Extra Performers are served.

Meal Period Violations

First 1/2 hour of delay or fraction thereof $7.50
Second 1/2 hour of delay or fraction thereof 10.50
Each additional 1/2 hour of delay or fraction thereof 12.50

An Extra Performer who does not receive a meal break within the first 6 hours after time of call shall receive the above meal penalties. Other meal breaks are due within 6 hours after the end of the previous meal break. The meal break may be as short as 30 minutes but no more than 1 hour (meal break time is not counted as part of work time). Only one meal break may be counted within the first 8 hours of work.

Meal Allowance

Whenever the Producer supplies meals or other food or hot drinks or pays any money for meals to the cast and crew, Producer shall supply the same to all Extra Performers. "Meal" means an adequate, well-balanced serving of a variety of wholesome, nutritious foods. Snacks such as hot dogs or hamburgers shall not constitute a meal.

6. OVERTIME

The regular work day is eight (8) consecutive hours (excluding meal periods.) The 9th, 10th, 11th and 12th hours are payable at time-and-a-half in tenths of an hour (6 minute units).

Work beyond the 12th hour is payable at double-time in tenths of an hour (6 minute units).

<u>How to compute</u>

Time-and-a-half: One-eighth of basic daily wage* 0. 15 equals time-and-a-half per 6 minute unit.

Example: One-eighth of $65.00* 0.15 = $1.21 per 6 minute unit.

Double Time: Basic daily wage divided by 40 equals double time per 6 minute unit.

Example: $65.00 divided by 40 = $1.62 per 6 minute unit.

7. WARDROBE

A. Allowance

Producer may request performer to report in normal attire without additional payment.

1st complete change	**$9.00 per day**
Each additional change	**6.25 per day**
Formal attire	**18.00 per day**

Payment is for all changes requested, whether used or not. Performer may not be required to leave wardrobe overnight; if Extra Performer agrees to do so, daily wardrobe allowance paid for each day so held.

B. Removal

Wardrobe removal time shall be counted as work time for all purposes including computation of overtime, unless wardrobe is supplied by the Extra Performer. The Extra Performer shall be dismissed as soon as his/her wardrobe or property is turned in.

C. Non-Normal Wardrobe

Extra Performers may not be required to report in out-of-season, period dress, or in other non-normal wardrobe.

8. SIXTH AND SEVENTH DAY, AND HOLIDAYS WORKED

The regular studio workweek shall consist of any five (5) consecutive days out of any seven (7) consecutive days, commencing with the first of such five (5) days. However, the five (5) consecutive day requirement shall be deemed satisfied where, on commencing employment, the Extra Performer is assigned to a schedule that calls for him/her to work, for example, on Monday and Tuesday, with Wednesday and Thursday as the regular days off, and is followed by work on Friday through the following Tuesday.

Holidays

New Year's Day, President's Day, Good Friday, Memorial Day, Independence Day, Labor Day, Thanksgiving Day, the day after Thanksgiving Day, and Christmas Day shall be recognized holidays. If any of the above holidays fall on the 6th day of the work week, the preceding day shall be considered the holiday and if a holiday falls on the 7th day, the following day shall be considered the holiday, except that on overnight locations, 6th day holidays will be recognized on that 6th day.

Provisions for Holidays Not Worked
Studio employment: Allowance of one (1) day's pay at straight time if the Extra Performer is employed by Producer the day before and the day after any of the above named nine (9) holidays.

Overnight Location Employment
Allowance of one (1) day's pay at straight time.
Provisions, for Holidays Worked
Double daily wage.

Overtime premium payments shall not be compounded or pyramided and shall be paid at the highest applicable premium rate only.

9. CROWD WORK

Minimum number of Registered Extras before Non-Registered persons be may be employed on same day:

Features 30

Television 15

10. NUDITY

Extra Performer must be notified in advance of required nudity. Set must be closed and no still photography permitted without Extra Performer's prior written consent.

If not notified, Extra Performer may refuse to work and shall receive full day's pay.

11. REST BREAKS

When working on a theatrical or TV production, Extra Performers are entitled to at least a five minute break during each hour of actual rehearsal or shooting. If shooting or rehearsing a scene of a continual nature, such rest breaks may be at least ten minutes for every two hours of said work. Our experience is that contractual breaks are not always given in a timely manner. When working on a set where there is no SAG field representative and breaks are not being given in accordance with the contract, the Extra Performer should advise the SAG office, on the same day if possible, or speak to the assistant director or production assistant.

12. WORKING IN A HIGHER CLASSIFICATION

If any part of the day is worked at a higher rate than at which the Extra Performer was called for to work, the higher rate shall apply to the entire day.

13. CALLBACKS

If the Extra Performer is established in the film so that he/she cannot be replaced and if the Producer requires his/her services on the following work day and notifies the Extra Performer of this by 5 P.M., the Extra Performer shall report for the following work day. If the Extra Performer performs as a Special Ability Extra and is given a callback, the Special Ability rate must be offered for the callback. If not, the Extra Performer shall be free to accept other employment rather than the callback.

If callback is cancelled by 4:30 P.M.., there is no payment due.

14. AVAILABILITIES AND BOOKINGS

Example: A casting director calls you and says, "There is a two-day shoot next Monday and Tuesday; are you available?" And you reply "yes" and are told to call back on Sunday for details. When you call you are given all the necessary information (time, place, wardrobe) for Monday, but Tuesday is not mentioned. At this point you should ask "Am I booked for Tuesday?" Many casting directors would like to give the impression that the Extra Performer is obligated to hold the second day, but this is not true. If you specifically ask whether or not you are booked you can avoid losing any other potential work. Asking for availability does not obligate either the actor or the Producer.   Availabilities are not bookings.

15. CANCELLATIONS

The Extra Performer is entitled to a full day's pay for a work call cancellation except if due to illness in principal cast, fire, flood, or other similar catastrophe or national emergency. In the event of such cancellation the Extra Performer will be entitled to a half-check. If the Extra Performer is notified of such cancellation before 6:00 P.M. of the work day previous to the work date, the Extra Performer will not be entitled to the half check.

16. WEATHER PERMIT CALLS

The Extra Performer must be advised at the time of booking that a call is "weather permitting" and the type of weather required for the scene. If such a call is cancelled or postponed due to unsuitable weather, a half day's pay shall be due. Producer may require up to 4 hours of work for rehearsal, etc., but performer may not be recorded or photographed. Producer cannot request the Extra Performer to call in the early morning hours of the following day for a possible "weather permitting call. If Extra Performer is held for more than 4 hours, an additional one-half check is due.

17. PAYMENT REQUIREMENT

The Extra Performer will be paid by check to be mailed by the Thursday following the week of employment (except Saturday, Sunday or Holidays).

Late payment damages will be assessed at $3.00 per day (excluding Saturday, Sunday & Holidays) without cut-off.

18. TRAVEL/TRANSPORTATION

When an Extra Performer is required to report at any studio zone location. Producer shall furnish transportation to the Extra Performer or, at Producer's option, may require Extra Performer to report at such location in which latter case Producer will allow mileage of $.30 per mile computed between the studio and the zone location. The Producer shall have the right to require the Extra Performer to report (subject to the same mileage allowance between the studio and the pick-up point).

Extra Performers shall be dismissed at the place of reporting. If Performer transport the Extra Performer, this shall be counted as work time, payable in tenths of an hour and shall be considered in computing overtime, if any.

19. SANITARY PROVISIONS

The following shall be provided:

(a) Pure drinking water.

(b) A seat for each Extra Performer.

(c) A stretcher or cot to be used as a stretcher.

(d) Separate dressing rooms for actors of each sex.

(e) Separate dressing rooms for children of each sex.

(f) Adequate provisions for proper and safe keep ing of Extra Performer's clothes.

(g) Adequately clean and sanitary, individually-screened toilet facilities. Toilet paper, soap and paper towels or individual towels. Sanitary napkins must be obtainable.

(h) Reasonable protection against severe climate conditions such as heat cold, rain and snow. Also, reasonable protection for Extra Performer required to wear out-of-season wardrobe.

Extra Performer may refuse to change wardrobe if not provided with a place of privacy and comfort. Dressing rooms with adequate lighting to be provided. Buses are not considered acceptable places to change. Buses used as holding areas must have lights and proper seasonal climate control. Violations subject to grievance or Cooperative Committee, at the Guild's option.

20. AGENT'S FEE

Extra Performers employed at scale shall not be required to pay commission to an agent. Any agent's fee shall be borne by the Producer.

- (a) No Extra Performer shall be hired due to personal favoritism.
- (b) Rotation of work shall be established to such rea son able degree as may be possible and practical.
- (c) Producer will not hire an Extra Performer who is currently on the payroll of the Producer or any of its

hiring, casting or payroll agencies, except upon written waiver by the Guild.

● (d) No fee, gift or other remuneration shall be de manded or accepted by any person having authority to hire, employ or direct services of Extra Performers.

● (e) Non-discrimination: Producer will make every effort to cast Extra Performers belonging to all groups in all types of roles, having regard for requirements of and suitability for the role so the American scene may be realistically portrayed.

Producers agree not to discriminate based on geographic residence. Violations subject to grievance or Cooperative Committee at the Guild's option.

21. REMINDER OF PROFESSIONAL CONDUCT FOR PROFESSIONAL PERFORMERS

In order to be recognized by others as a professional performer and to protect the dignity of the entire acting profession, members are advised of the following guidelines:

☑(1) Always carry your paid-up SAG card or receipt of payment from the Membership Department.

☑(2) Make sure that you arrive on the set on time, with required outfits and/or props. Production companies have the right to dismiss without payment any performer who is not on time. It is better to arrive early than to report late.

☑(3) Be courteous and attentive.

☑(4) Remember: Fill out your contract or voucher with care, making sure all information appears on all copies. Keep your own records of hours worked, meal breaks, etc. Make sure you note all wardrobe and props supplied at the request of Producer.

☑(5) Bring along some busy work. Part of working

sometimes requires hours of idleness on the set. Remember: Down time on the set is still considered work time

☑**(6)** Never leave the set without getting approval from the Assistant Director.

☑**(7)** Smoke only in designated areas. This is a matter of courtesy to your fellow performers.

☑**(8)**The professional performer is always prepared to take down the reporting location, date and time of a call, as well as the required wardrobe.

☑**(9)** Once you are hired, you have been hired until released by the production company. In short, do ask not to leave early and do not leave early.

☑**(10)** Notify casting director of potential conflicts caused by other bookings immediately.

22. UNION SECURITY

If the professional Extra Performer owes dues to the Guild at the time of employment, or if the performer is considered a *"**must-join**," the Producer may be liable to pay liquidated damages to the Guild in the amount of $522.00. *"**Must-joins**" are performers who are not SAG members but have worked under SAG jurisdiction more than 30 days prior to this new work call.

For additional information see the complete 1995 SAG Extra Performers Agreement or contact your local Screen Actors Guild.

23. EXTRA PERFORMERS INFORMATION

Question: *If I work on a film and the meal is not catered, do I get a meal allowance?*

Answer: You are entitled to whatever the crew gets. If the crew gets a meal allowance, you are entitled to the same.

Question: *If I volunteer a line as an Extra Performer, doesn't that entitle me to an upgrade to Day Performer?*

Answer: If you think a scene would be further enhanced by dialogue, you can ask if that's what the director wants. Let him/her make that determination. Otherwise, a volunteered line cannot be considered as a basis for an upgrade. If you simply add the dialogue yourself without approval, the Guild will not pursue a claim on your behalf, even if your line remains in the final version of the film.

Question: *Can anything be done if a casting director has not hired me for a long time to perform work as an Extra Performer?*

Answer: The collective bargaining agreement reads: 'Rotation work shall be established to such reasonable degree as may be possible and practicable.

Also, please keep in mind that SAG is not a hiring hall and cannot guarantee employment to its members.

Question: *What obligation do I have to a casting director who asks for my availability for certain days?*

Answer: An availability inquiry is not a booking. You should advise the casting director if you are available on the dates specified. However, if you are not definitely booked, you have no obligation to keep those days available if you get another offer of employment. A hold is a booking. In order to be clear about whether you are booked and the company is obligated to pay you in the event of a cancellation, you should ask the question, "Is this a booking?"

SAG RULE ONE:
No Non-union work!

Guild Rule One requires that no member shall work as an actor for any producer who is not signed to a Guild contract. No matter who offers you an acting job in the Guild's field - producer, talent agent, casting director or friend - it is **YOUR** obligaion and responsibility to make certain that the producer wishing to employ you is a SAG Signatory. Always telephone the nearest guild office to check a producer's SAG status. The Guild's staff is always happy to provide this important information.

WORK   UNION   -   LIVE   BETTER

SCREEN ACTORS GUILD

Hollywood

AFTRA
TIPS ON GETTING AN AGENT

Let's face it, trying to get an agent is no day at the beach (unless, of course, you happen to run into one there). There are hundreds of talent agencies of various types and sizes out there. Finding the one agent that is right for you is a formidable task. It involves dedication, persistence... and a game plan!

TARGETING AGENTS

Determine what your interests and needs are. Then target those agencies on the AFTRA franchised agency list who indicate they represent your type and the field you are interested in. The agents on this list are signed to AFTRA's Regulations Governing Agents (Rule 12-B). This means they are licensed by the State of California and are accountable to AFTRA.

There are publications for sale at such theatrical bookstores as Samuel French and Larry Edmunds which provide information on the background of the talent agencies in the Los Angeles and Orange County areas. Be sure to check with the unions to verify that the agency is union franchised. Remember, AFTRA members are required to sign only with a franchised agent.

To find out the clients of a particular agency you can check the client list at the Academy Players Directory.

Ask your performer friends which agent they are with and see if they can put in a word for you with their agent, or refer you to another reputable agent.

GET INVOLVED

Performers often find agents through friends and fellow performers. Get involved with activities that will put you in touch with other performers, such as workshops and AFTRA membership meetings, casting showcases, rap sessions, and special seminars.

Agents want experience. Many agents will consider taking on new clients only if they have a strong theatrical background. Get involved in a play or a showcase and send invitations to your targeted agents. Many agents periodically attend plays and showcases to scout new talent.

Even without an agent, there are things you can do to get jobs on your own.

SUBMIT APPROPRIATELY

All resumés are not created equal. Tailor your resumé to the specific area of representation in which you are interested (i.e., if you are looking for a commercial agent, list your commercials credits first.) Always keep your resumé current, and remember to include all union affiliations.

Submit appropriate photos. Commercial agents require different types of photos from theatrical agents. If you have a film or tape of yourself you may want to submit it either in addition to or in lieu of a photo.

An audio demo tape should generally not exceed 3 minutes. The purpose of the tape is to display your style, quality and range.

Always send your submission to a specific person at the agency. Indicate in your cover letter that you are seeking representation and state why you would like to be represented by them.

Keep notes of the agents you submitted your pictures and resumé to, as well as the date of submission and any response or comments they may have had.

INTERVIEW YOUR AGENT

Now that you've got that interview, make the most of it. If you've done your homework you'll already know his/her reputation in the industry, connections, background, possibly some clients. But it is a good idea to check these out again. Ask questions. INTERVIEW YOUR AGENT. Your agent works for you and you work for your agent. The ideal relationship will be satisfying and beneficial for both parties.

SPECIAL NOTE REGARDING CHILDREN

Parents, please bear in mind that this industry is highly competitive. It's physically and emotionally demanding on everyone, but particularly so on children. It is advised not to get children involved unless they really want to get involved, and unless you are willing to devote the great deal of time and effort necessary to your child's career. If so, take full responsibility by reading all contracts and documents thoroughly and familiarizing yourself with special regulations and laws that apply to children.

BREAK A LEG!

AFTRA 10 POINTS

1 In accordance with a rule adopted by the National Board of AFTRA, members may not sign any r e p r e s e n t a t i o n agreements with Agents unless such agent is franchised with AFTRA. Non-franchised agents are not authorized to negotiate for or procure employment in AFTRA's fields.

2 No agent may charge or collect a higher rate of commission than ten percent (10%). In order to receive commission on scale payments Agents must negotiate your fee, including all overtime and rehearsal, above minimum scale or minimum scale plus ten percent except in the Broadcast/Industrials where commission may be taken on scale payments for persons other than singers, dancers, and extras.

3 Commission is payable separately on each engagement fee. Separate engagements may not be lumped together ;for the purpose of computing commissions.

4 AFTRA Agents are required to use the Standard AFTRA Exclusive Agency Contract when signing for services within AFTRA's fields.   A copy must be filed with AFTRA and a copy given to you. If your contract is not filed with AFTRA within a specified it may be held to be invalid.

5 If you do not wish one agent to represent you in all of AFTRA's fields, consult your local AFTRA office as to how your AFTRA's fields, consult your local AFTRA office as to how your AFTRA contract may be limited to enable you to be represented by other agents.

TO REMEMBER

6 Agents franchised with AFTRA may not request fees for registration, headshots, portfolios, or as a condition to procure employment. Nor may they instruct clients to use a specific photographer. The choice of photographer is up to the waist and cannot be a condition upon which agency representation is based.

7 Pursuant to AFTRA's Regulations Governing Agents, you are entitled to submit a written request to your Agent, once every four weeks, for information on what efforts the Agent has rendered on your behalf regarding auditions and procuring employment.

8 All payments for your services should be made directly to you unless you have given written authorization for payments to be sent to your agent or some other person. Such authorization will remain in effect until rescinded by you in writing. Please read all check author- izations and contracts carefully before signing or initialing.

9 When you have signed an exclusive representation agreement with an agent you may be released from it or terminate it under specific conditions set forth in the AFTRA Regulations Governing Agents.

10 When terminating an AFTRA Exclusive Agency Contract you must send a letter of termination to the Agent and a copy of the letter to AFTRA. The letter must include your name (and any a.k.a.'s), address, social security number, the name of the agency being terminated, and any new agency you may have. Please be very specific.

☹ TO TERMINATE ☹
STANDARD AFTRA EXCLUSIVE AGENCY CONTRACT

UNDER RULE 12-B

From time to time AFTRA Members who are not receiving satisfactory representation from agents with whom they have Exclusive Agency contracts, inquire how they may terminate such agreements. In all cases of termination by the performer, the following procedures apply as provided ion Pgh six (6) of the AFTRA Exclusive Agency Contract:

☐1. In any ninety-one (91) day period before serving termination notice;

☐2. If you are not employed, being paid, or entitled to be paid for fifteen (15) days, work in AFTRA's field or any other entertainment branch for which this agent is authorized by written contract to represent you;

☐3. And you are not working under a written contract guaranteeing you employment for at least one program each week for thirteen (13) consecutive weeks;

☐4. Or do not have such a written contact under which you will begin working within forty-five (45) days;

☐5. Or do not have such a written contract beginning no later than October 15—if you are terminating in Aug. or Sept.

☐6. And you are not working under a written contact guaranteeing you employment for at least one (1) television program every other week in a cycle of thirteen (13), broadcast on an alternate week basis, or eight (8) within thirty-nine (39) weeks on a one (1) show per month basis;

☐7. And you do not have a contract guaranteeing you compensation of $20,000.00 in the next one hundred eighty-two (182) days for performances in radio, television or phonographic recordings;

☐8. Or do not have a contract guaranteeing you compensation of $25,000.00 in the next one hundred eighty-two (182) days for performances in any entertainment field for which this agent represents you;

☐9. You are not physically/mentally incapable of performing;

❑**10.** And you are available for calls at your customary compensation and conditions (commensurate with your prestige and usual standards);

❖You may terminate your Exclusive Agency Contract by simply notifying your agent in writing (with a copy sent to AFTRA).

❖Keep the following points in mind: (Ninety-one (91) days are computed on this basis):

❖-Two and one-half (2 1/2) days counted for each television broadcast except during June, July or August, when each day's employment in the television broadcasting field counts as three and three-fourths (3 3/4) days;

❖-One (1) day counted for each radio broadcast and transcribed program except during June, July or August, when each day's employment in the television broadcasting field counts as three and three-fourths (3 3/4) days;

❖-One (1) day counted for each master phonograph record; But if your television performance exceeds three (3) days (including show day) or you have exclusivity in excess of three (3) days (including show day) the 91-day period is extended by the number of television days in excess of three (3) days.

Likewise, you do not count days:

❖During which you have formally declared yourself unavailable;

❖Or are incapacitated;

❖Or are at work in an entertainment field in which your agent does not represent you;

❖Or are at work in an entertainment field in which your agent does not represent you; do count:

❖The period of guaranteed employment specified in an actual written bona fide offer of employment (at your customary salary, usual terms and commensurate with your prestige) which you refuse; or a broadcast for which you are paid even when you do not perform.

Chapter Five

CHILDREN IN ACTION

Children find background acting very exciting, financially rewarding and big fun! Knowledge and follow through on the parents' part will make for a nice trust fund for your son's or daughter's future education and/or career. Make sure your child has stamina, talent and the ability to take simple directions from the Director while under your watchful eye. Most Directors who work with children really enjoy doing so. Children really do make for an interesting workday.

Don't pressure your child into show business. I repeat, "Do not force your child to perform in show business." If they find it intriguing, great. If not now they may want to later. Don't ruin what could be the most memorable experience in their lives by being an overbearing "Stage Parent."

The new California Children Labor Laws, which are the most protective laws of its kind in the country, has no rules regarding "STAGE PARENTS." However their 60 page booklet and addendum does cover everything a parent should know about child labor laws. Ask your local D.L.S.E. (Department of Labor Standards Enforcement) to send you a copy of the laws.

I have summarized the following laws with the help of Rhona Jepsea (818) 501-6468, Kenneth B. Wolin (213) 655-2886, studio teachers and Affordable Studio Teachers' Association (213) 662-9787, an Association of Studio Teachers, Nurses, Baby Wranglers and Guardians.

Summary of The New California Child Labor Laws

ENTERTAINMENT WORK PERMIT- All minors must have a valid work permit and bring it with them to the job site. They must maintain a C average. The employer must have a permit to employ on file with the D.L.S.E.. Blanket permits may be granted for large groups of minors such as baseball teams, marching bands, classroom etc. Permits can be obtained at the addresses listed on page 59.

PARENTS OR GUARDIANS- Must be within sight or sound for all minors under the age of 1 year old.

BABIES- For babies 15 days to 6 weeks a nurse and a studio teacher must be provided for every 10 babies.

EMANCIPATION- Regulations are fully applicable to emancipated minors except for minors 14-17 years of age who have obtained a high school proficiency certificate.

MATERIALS- School age minors are required to bring books, assignments, paper and writing utensils from regular school. Employers are required to provide adequate school facilities (i.e. tables, chairs, etc.).

STUDIO TEACHERS/WELFARE WORKERS- A Studio Teacher/Welfare Worker must be provided for the education of all minors (up to 18 years) and has the responsibility for caring and attending to the health, safety, and morals for all minors under 16 years of age. A Studio Teacher must be certified by the D. L. S. E.

MINORS PER STUDIO TEACHER - 1 to 10 on school days and 1 to 20 on non-school days.

REST AND RECREATION- The rest and recreation periods vary with the age of the child see WORK AND

SCHOOL HOURS FOR MINORS SCHEDULE for details.

MEAL PERIOD- A minor cannot work for more than 6 hrs. without a meal period of no less than 1/2 hour.

TRAVEL TIME- Studio to location to studio counts as part of a minors work day. (To minimize loss of work hours children should report directly to a local location.) When on a distant location with overnight a grace period of 45 minutes each way from "hotel" to shoot location is not counted towards work time.

TURN AROUND- Twelve hours must elapse between minors dismissal and next day call time or school start time otherwise minor must be schooled at employers place of business.

EXTENSIONS- Request must be submitted in writing to the D.L.S.E. 8 hours in advance.

WAIVERS- Minors 14-18 may work up to eight hours a day for a maximum of two consecutive days with permission from school authorities.

Work And School Hours For Minors

WORK DAY-Between 5 AM & 10 PM on nights before school days. 5 AM & 12 AM on nights before non-school days.

OUTSIDE OF CALIFORNIA- California Laws are fully applicable when taking minors out of the state including the use of a California Certified Studio Teacher. Out of state minors working in California must also adhere to Title 8 and must obtain a California Entertainment Work Permit.

CA. Department of Labor Standards Enforcements:

Valley office: 6150 Van Nuys Blvd., Suite 100, Van Nuys, CA 91402 (818) 901-5312 or (818) 901-5315.

The **HOLLYWOOD SCREEN PARENTS ASSO-CIATION** is a personal support, resource referral and information network by and for parents of children and teens who work in the film, T.V., commercial and print industry. The HSPA's first resources directory, Screen Parents Bookshelf, is a comprehensive 32 page booklet created from their growing Parent Library of books, audio and videotapes. It contains other items of interest to families of gifted/talented kids and teens, covering a wide spectrum of resources, including bookstores and mail order outlets where these products can be purchased. The Screen Parents Bookshelf directory may be ordered at a discount on the EXTRA ORDER FORM or contact **Barbara Schiffman at (818) 955-6510**, she'll be glad to help you out!

The **GREEN BOOK** is a summary of Title 8, the rules and regulations for employment of minors in the entertainment industry. For a copy of the **GREEN BOOK** send a self-addressed business envelope with two first class stamps for each book to: **The GREEN BOOK, 9101 Sawyer St., L.A., CA 90035**

STATE OF CALIFORNIA
Department of Industrial Relations
Division of Labor Standards Enforcement

THIS IS NOT A PERMIT

APPLICATION FOR PERMISSION TO WORK IN
THE ENTERTAINMENT INDUSTRY

Name of Child				Professional Name, if applicable		
Permanent Address				Temporary Address, if applicable		
School Attending						Grade
School Address						

Mo/Day/Year of Birth	Sex M F	Height	Weight	Hair Color	Eye Color
/ /					

STATEMENT OF PARENT OR GUARDIAN: *It is my desire that an Entertainment Work Permit be issued to the above named child. I will read the rules and regulations governing such employment and will cooperate to the best of my ability in safeguarding his or her educational, moral and physical interests.*

Name of Parent or Guardian (Print or type)	Signed

DLSE-277 (Rev. 3-86)

APPLICATION FOR CHILDRENS WORK PERMIT
FRONT

SCHOOL RECORD

Name of Minor _____ Birthdate ___ / ___ / ___ Grade _____

Attendance _____ Scholarship _____ Health _____
(State whether "Satisfactory" or "Unsatisfactory" for each.)

I certify that the above named minor meets the school district's requirements with respect to age, school record, attendance and health.

Remarks: _____

School _____

School Address _____ School Telephone _____

Signed _____ Title _____ Date _____

Remarks: _____

Name of Doctor (Please type or print) _____

Address _____ Telephone _____

Complete the following only if instructed to do so.

I hereby certify that I have carefully examined, in my opinion, he/she is/is not physically fit to be employed in the production of motion pictures and television.

Signed _____ M.D.   Date _____

Remarks: _____

APPLICATION FOR CHILDRENS WORK PERMIT
REAR

Chapter Six

EXTRA ETIQUETTE

The accepted behavior before and on the set. The do's and the dont']s for the background artist. Following these guidelines will assure you high regards and professional treatment on the movie or television set. Take them seriously for they will pay off in a big way.

1 Always have a pen and paper to write down the information given to you about your assignment. Do not try to remember it. It is better to ask until you get it right than have incorrect information.

2 Have the proper wardrobe, look the role, have the right equipment, have transportation, be able to work under the conditions on the scene before you accept the assignment.

3 Arrive on time to the location, preferably 20 to 30 minutes before your call time. The extra time you allow to get to your location will give you breathing room in case something unexpected happens en route. You may also need additional time to walk to the set, or wait for shuttle vans if the parking location is distant from the set location.

4 If you see you are going to be more than 15 minutes late, **STOP AND CALL** the emergency number you have been given. Explain to them your situation.

5 Lay your wardrobe out the night before so you won't be running around frantic in the mornings. This helps take off the morning pressures and will allow for that much desired extra sleep time.

6 Take at least two additional changes of your wardrobe for each outfit you are asked to bring. Don't wear bright bold strips, or freaky colors and styles unless told to do so. Always bring appropriate underclothes and socks or stockings. Wear what you've been asked to wear and you'll do fine.

7 Bringing the following to the set will make for a good day; a good book/newspaper, a pen and writing paper, spare change, in case you need to use the telephone, a small folding chair, a quiet game or hobby. Some people bring small radios, televisions, or computer games, use your discretion. Remember you are there to WORK and must be attentive to the Director and the Assistant Director (A.D.)

8 NEVER, NEVER take the following... cameras, alcohol, drugs, friends or relatives, large TV or radios.

9 Check in immediately with the person you have been told to do so with. (This is usually when you are given your payment voucher).

10 Fill out your voucher completely and correctly. This is your time card. If you are unsure how, ask for assistance.

11 Check in with the wardrobe department when you are instructed to do so. Wear the appropriate wardrobe and mention any special bit that you are to perform to the A.D. and to the wardrobe and property (props) persons as soon as possible. Take care of business before donuts and coffee. Be Smart.

12 Always be where the A.D./Set Coordinator instructs you to be. If you must leave that area for any reason inform that person first then expedite your return.

13 Do not touch any equipment unless instructed do so.

14 Do not talk to crew people to the point where you keep them from doing their assigned task.

15 When on location, allow the crew to eat all meals first unless instructed to do differently. They must eat quickly so that they can set-up the after meal period shots. There will be plenty of food for everyone. If not they will pay you!

16 Return all props and wardrobe as you received them when you are finished. Tell the appropriate person if something breaks or is torn so it can be repaired.

17 Never look into the camera unless told to do so.

18 Pick up after yourself and ask others to do the same.

19 When on the set, if you listen, you learn!

20 Always carry yourself as a professional. Someone is always watching you and evaluating your professionalism. They may be the person who can select you for the specialty parts which could result in a bump or even a day player's contract!

21 Do not depend on craft services to feed you all the time or assume that you'll always get free breakfast from the catering wagon. Pack a little snack or bring some fruit and nuts to ease your before lunch hunger pangs.

22 Never call the casting director on a production line or at home unless personally asked to do so;

Thank you Janet!

Chapter Seven

WHO'S WHO ON THE SET

In addition to principal and background talent, a number of people will be on each set with various duties and responsibilities. This section is designed to acquaint you with the departments they represent. While on the set ask one of each of the following crew members to give you a one or two line description of what their duties and responsibility are and write it in the space provided. It's a great way to break the ice and you may be amazed how much they are willing to talk to you about their position.

PRODUCTION STAFF

Director - Interprets the story given to him into a visual medium. He tells a story using a technical and mechanical process. He determines the shots and angles the camera will photographically record the action.

First Assistant Director - Assists the director to capture and maintain the mood, continuity and action of the storyline. Works closely with the production manager and camera crew setting up the next scene/shot that the director wants to record.

Second Assistant Director - Assists the director by summoning talent and crew to the set. Keeps records of the films' over-all production schedule. On some productions handles background talent or Extras!

Second Second Assistant Director - On larger production projects assists the Second A.D. in all duties.

Third Assistant Director - On larger productions assists the second second A.D. Sometimes referred to as a Production Assistant.

Location Scout - Searches and secures various places for the scenery or background that will be filmed in a certain scene. A place that will help recreate and enhance the mood and/or look of a scene that is in the storyline. They usually secure locations that are away from the studio lot.

Script Supervisor

CAMERA DEPARTMENT

Cinematographer/Director Of Photography
Camera Operator
First Assistant Camera
Second Assistant Camera
Still Photographer

SET OPERATION

Key Grip
Second Grip
Crane Operator
Dolly Grip
Craft Services
Painter
Prop Maker
Special Effects Coordination
First Aid/Nurse

SOUND

Sound Mixer
Boom/Mike Operator
Cable Person
Playback Machine & Operator
Video Assist Operator

WHO'S WHO ON THE SET PAGE 105

PROPERTY

Property Person
Assistant Property Person
Set Dresser
Production Designer
Art Director
Set Decorator
Lead Man
Assistant Art Director
Wrangler

WARDROBE

Costume Designer
Assistant Costume Designer
Wardrobe Supervisor
Men's Costumer
Women's Costumer
Set Costumer

MAKE-UP

Make-Up Person
Assistant Make-Up Person
Body Make-Up Person
Hair Stylist
Assistant Hair Stylist

ELECTRICAL

Gaffer
Second Electrician
Lamp Operators
Assistant Electrician
Rigging Gaffer

POLICE & FIRE

Fire Control Officer
Fire Warden Location
Whistle Person
Set Security Person
City Police
Studio Police
Motorcycle Officer

PRODUCTION STAFF

Producer
Unit Production Manager
Production Office Coordinator
Assistant Production Office Coordinator
Production Secretary
Office Production Assistant
Production Auditor
Assistant Auditor
Location Manager
Assistant Location Manager
Production Assistants
Director's Assistant

CATERER

Caterer
Caterer Assistants

TRANSPORTATION

Transportation Coordinator
Transportation Co-Captain
Camera Truck
Electric Truck
Construction Truck
Limousine Driver(s)
Crew Cabs
Grip Truck
Prop Truck
Special F/X Truck
Set Dressing
Wardrobe/Make-Up Truck
Room Trailers
Cast Trailers
Honey Wagon
Picture Car Truck

Chapter Eight

SET-TALK

Words or phrases used on movie or television sets, describing certain actions, movements, people, places and things is "set-talk". It can be intimidating to those who have limited motion picture production experience. Have no fear... I have briefly explained over 250 of the most commonly used terms. Once on the set, you'll pick-up the jargon and the vernacular before the Director calls "CUT".

ACTION: The verbal cue indicating the camera is rolling and physical scene action is set to take place. What the director calls out to begin all principal acting on a set.

A.D.: The Assistant Director. Short for Assistant Director, The First A.D., hardly ever leaves the Director's side. He tells you your action in a scene. The Second A.D. will also tell you what to do as well, he/she will usually be whom you check in & out with and have the most contact with.

AD LIB: Dialogue delivery without relying on a prepared script, also called Improvisation.

ADR: Additional (or Automatic) Dialogue Replacement. Sometimes erroneously called "looping".

AEA: Actors' Equity Association; often called simply "Equity".

AFI: The American Film Institute.

AFM: American Federation of Musicians.

AFL-ClO: The American Federation of Labor/Congress of Industrial Organizations.

AFTRA: The American Federation of Television & Radio Artists.

AGMA: The American Guild of Musical Artists.

AGVA: The American Guild of Variety Artists.

ALL-AMERICAN LOOK: Middle-American appearance; a.k.a. "White Bread", "P&G" look.

AMPTP: Alliance of Motion Picture and Television Producers.

ART DIRECTOR: Person who conceives and designs the sets, usually on a commercial.

ATA: The Association of Talent Agents.

AUDITION: A tryout for a film or TV role, usually in front of a casting director for which a reading is required.

AVAIL: A courtesy situation extended by an agent to a producer indicating that a performer is available to work a certain job. Avails have no legal or contractual status.

BACK TO ONE: Starting from your first position of action in a scene. The title of this book!

BACKGROUND *ACTOR/PERFORMANCE/PLAYER*: Extras, atmosphere, non-principle performers. Extras are commonly referred to as background. In a scene however, background refers to the action that the extras will need to make.

BACK-UP: A performer hired to work only if the designated principal doesn't perform satisfactorily.

BEAUTY SHOT: On TV soap operas, the shot over which the credits are rolled.

BEST BOY: In films, the assistant to the Electrician.

BILLING: The order of the names in the titles or opening credits of a film, video or TV show.

BIO: A resumé in narrative form for a printed program or press release.

BLOCKING: Planning the movement in a scene. The planned physical movements by actors in a scene.

BOOKING: A firm commitment to a performer to do a specific job.

BOOM: An overhead microphone, usually on an extended pole.

BREAKAWAY: A prop or set piece which looks solid but shatters or "breaks" easily.

BREAKDOWN: A detailed listing and description of roles available for casting in a production.

BUMP: Money given for performing a certain action on camera in a scene, over and above you base wage. This is very good.

BURY: To hide someone or something out of sight in a scene.

BUYOUT: An offer of full payment in advance in lieu of residuals, when the contract permits.

C**ALLBACK:** Any follow-up interview or audition. To be instructed to come back to work on a certain day, usually the next day.

CALL SHEET: Production term for daily listing of schedule, scenes and cast required. A printed schedule of the day's work that is to be filmed and the people, place, and things needed.

CALL TIME: The actual time you are needed on the set.

CAMERA LEFT & CAMERA RIGHT: The direction of which to look or to proceed when facing the camera, Camera left is your right.

CASTING DIRECTOR: The producer's representative responsible for auditioning and casting performers for consideration by the director and or producer.

CATTLE CALL: A general audition for roles where many people turn out looking for the part. A mob scene; often an "open call."

CHANGES: Clothing and costumes to be worn.

CLOSE-UP (CU): Camera term for tight shot of the general area of the head and shoulder.

COLD READING: Unrehearsed reading of a particular part of a scene, usually at auditions.

COMMISSION: Percentage of a performer's earnings paid to agents and manager for acting and/or vocal services rendered.

COMPOSITE: A series of photographs on one sheet representing an actor's different looks.

CONFLICT: Status of being paid for services in a commercial for one advertiser, thereby contractually preventing performing services in a commercial for a competitor.

COPY: The script for a commercial or voice over.

CRAFT SERVICES: On-set catering.

CRANE SHOT: A camera shot raised over or above the set or the action.

CRAWL: Usually the end credits in a film or TV shot which "crawl" up the screen.

CREDITS: Performance experience listed on a resumé: also, opening optical with lettering characters scrolling across the opening scene of a film or a TV show.

CUE: Hand signal by the Stage Manager.

CUTAWAY: A short scene between two shots of the same person, showing something other than that person.

CLAPBOARD: A mini chalkboard that has the name of the production, director, producer. It is used to keep records of what scene is being filmed and makes a clapping sound to tell the person who put the pieces of film together where to start the sound.

COLD READING: While working as an extra you are asked to read some lines of a character because the director needs your type for something added to a scene.

CONTINUITY: Matching everything you did in a previous scene so it looks exactly like it happened the first time you did it.

CROSS: The movement the extra makes in front of the camera when the scene is being filmed.

CUT: What the Director calls out to Stop all principal acting on a set.

CUT & HOLD: What the director calls out to stop all principal action. Freeze in this position until told to release.

CUE: A signal (nonverbal or verbal) from the director to start your action.

DAILIES: Screening of footage before it is edited.

DAY PLAYER: An actor hired by the production to play a certain role generally for one day only, rather than on a longer term contract.

DAYTIME DRAMA: A daily daytime dramatic television show with an ongoing theme, commonly referred to as Soap Operas because of the soap companies that originally sponsored them in the early days of T.V..

DEALER COMMERCIAL: A national commercial produced and paid for by a national advertiser and then turned over to local dealers to book air time, usually with the dealer's tag added on.

DEMO TAPE: An audio or video tape that agents use for audition

CLINT EASTWOOD
OVERNITE SENSATIONS
ACTORS WHO WERE EXTRAS?
CLINT EASTWOOD

purposes.

DGA: Directors Guild of America.

DIALECT: A distinctly regional or cultural sound.

DIALOGUE: The scripted words exchanged by Performers.

DIRECTOR: The coordinator of all artistic and technical aspects of any production.

DOLLY: Camera movements forward and backward.

DOUBLE: A performer who appears in place of another performer, i.e. as in a stunt.

DOWNGRADE: Reduction of a performer's on-camera role from principal to extra.

D.P.: Director of Photography or Cinematographer.

DRESS THE SET: Add such items to the set as curtains, furniture props, etc.

DRIVE-ON PASS: In Los Angeles, a pass to drive onto and park on a studio lot.

DROP-PICKUP: A contractual situation where a performer is laid off and rehired on the same production.

DUPE: A duplicate copy of a film or tape; also, a dub.

EIGHTEEN, 18-TO-PLAY-YOUNGER: Legally 18 years of age, but can be convincingly cast as a younger person.

ELECTRICIAN: Crew chief responsible for lighting.

EMANCIPATED MINOR: A child by a judge, who has been given the status of a legal adult.

EMPLOYER OF RECORD (EOR): The company responsible for employment and for taxes and unemployment benefits.

EQUITY: Actors' Equity Association.

ESTABLISHED: Having been filmed in a certain position in a

previous scene.

Equity WAIVER: In Los Angeles, 99-seat (or less) theatres which are otherwise professional, over which Equity has waived contract provisions under certain conditions.

EXCLUSIVITY: Achieved by virtue of performing as a principal in a commercial. During the contractual period of payment, the advertiser has exclusive right to the Performer's work likeness and image with regard to competitive products.

EXECUTIVE PRODUCER: Person responsible for funding the production.

EXHIBIT A: That portion of the AFTRA Network Code pertaining to Prime Time television work which generally parallels the SAG Basic Television Agreement.

EXT. (Exterior): A scene shot outside.

EXTRA: The background movement players, commonly referred to as background, background artist, atmosphere. Background talent, used only in non-principal roles.

FICA: Social Security taxes (Federal Insurance Corporation of America).

FIRST TEAM: Principal actors and actresses.

FIELD REP: AFTRA or SAG staff member who ensures contractual compliance on sets.

FIRST REFUSAL: A non-contractual courtesy situation extended to producers by agents on behalf of performers, giving the producer the "right" to decline to employ the performer before the performer accepts a conflicting assignment.

FIVE OUT OF SEVEN: A rearrangement of the five days of a work week.

FIXED CYCLE: For commercials, an established 13-week period for which the advertiser pays a holding fee to retain the right to use

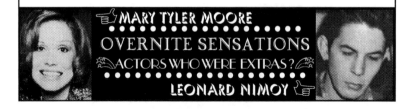

the performer's services, likeness and image in a previously pro-duced advertisement.

FLIPPER: Easily removed false teeth for children, used for cos-metic purposes.

FORCED CALL: A call to work less than 12 hours after dismissal on the previous day.

FOREGROUND: The area in front of the camera lens, between a principal actor, actress or object.

FOREIGN REPLAY: A fee paid for reruns outside the U.S..

4-As: Associated Actors and Artistes of America; umbrella organi-zation for AFTRA, SAG and other performers' unions.

FRANCHISED AGENT: A talent agent approved by AFTRA or SAG to solicit and negotiate employment for their members.

FREE-LANCING: Working through more than one franchised agent rather than signing exclusively with any one agent. Also, working for multiple employers as a performer, distinguished from permanent employment at a radio/TV station or network.

FX (Effects): Slang word used for special effects.

GAFFER: In film, a crew member who places lighting and electrical equipment and instruments.

G.E.D.: General Equivalency Diploma , high school graduate equivalency test.

GLOSSY: A shiny photofinishing process.

GOFER: An errand runner, who "goes for this and goes for that.

GOLDEN TIME: Overtime after the 16th hour for theatrical talent.

GRIP: A crew member who grab and moves things on the set, e.g... set furniture pieces or props.

GUARANTEED BILLING: Position of work credit in the place-ment at the head or end of a theatrical production specifically

negotiated by agent.

HAND MODEL: A performer whose hands are used in a shoot, or used to double for someone else.

HEAD SHOT: A still photo, usually 8" x 10", showing head and shoulders.

HEALTH & RETIREMENT (or Pension & Health)**PAYMENT:** An additional amount of money paid by the employer to cover employee benefits under union contracts.

HIATUS: Time during which a TV series is out of actual production.

HOLD (On Hold): A contractual obligation for a Performer to be available for work.

HOLDING FEE: Set payment by an advertiser to retain the right to use a performer's services, image or likeness on an product exclusion basis.

HONEY WAGON: A truck or towed vehicle containing one or more dressing rooms, and or production offices and mobile restrooms.

HOT SET: Hands Off! This is a set that has been used or has been prepared for use and is <u>NOT</u> To Be Disturbed.

IATSE: International Alliance of Theatrical Stage Employees.

INDUSTRIAL: Non-broadcast, often educational, films or tapes.

INSERTS: Shots, usually close-ups of hands or close business, inserted into previously shot footage.

INT. (Interior): A scene shot indoors.

"IN" TIME: The actual call time or start time; also, return time from a break.

LIFT: Process of taking a sequence from one commercial to create all or part of another commercial. Sometimes called a "mechanical lift".

LIQUIDATED DAMAGES: Monetary penalties imposed on an employer when contract provisions are violated.

LOCATION: Any place where a set is not on a studio sound stage.

LONG SHOT (LS): A camera shot which captures the whole of a scene, usually including the performer's full body.

LOOPING: An in-studio technique matching, synchronizing voice to picture.

MARK: A predetermined place you should be or proceed to when the action in a scene begins.

MEAL PENALTY: A set fee paid by the producer for failure to provide meals or meal breaks as specified by the contract.

MONOLOGUE: A solo Performance by an actor.

MOS (Mit Out Sound/Motion Only Shot)**:** Any shot without dialogue or sound.

M.O.W.: Movie of the Week.

NABET: National Association of Broadcast Employees and Technicians.

NATIONAL COMMERCIAL: A commercial produced for use throughout country.

NETWORK CODE: In AFTRA the contract covering network programming.

NIGHT PREMIUM: A 10% surcharge for work performed after 8:00 P.M..

OFF-CAMERA (OC or OS)**:** Dialogue delivered without being on screen.

ON A BELL: A request by the Director to the sound man to turn on a bell to alert everyone that filming is about to begin and <u>Silence is Golden!</u>

OPEN CALL: An interview situation open to anyone qualifying

with the physical attributes of a character or part.

OUT CLAUSE: Section of a contract allowing the performer to terminate agreement under certain circumstances.

OUT OF FRAME: An actor is outside the camera range.

"OUT" TIME: The actual time after which you have changed out of wardrobe and are released.

OVERDUBBING: In studio singing or voice work, the process of laying a new soundtrack over an old one.

OVERTIME (OT): Work extending beyond the contractual work day.

PA.: Production Assistant, an entry-level producer position.

PAN: A camera shot which sweeps from side-to-side.

PANTOMIME: Mouthing words in a scene when there is dialogue being recorded as the action takes place.

PAYMASTER: An independent talent payment service acting as the employer of record and signatory for the producer.

PAY OR PLAY: A job for which an actor is guaranteed to be paid regardless of actual work.

PER DIEM: Set fee paid by producer on location shoots to compensate performer for expenditures and for meals not provided by the producer.

PRINCIPALS: The people who have speaking lines, special bit or stunts in a scene.

PHOTO DOUBLE: To be photographed as the principal actor in a scene when the actor face or look is not necessary.

PRINT: When the director has filmed a scene and wants to look at it later for possible inclusion in the finished movie. This is a good sign he will usually move ahead to the next scene.

P&G: Performers who have a clean-cut, all-American look as commonly favored by Proctor & Gamble for its commercials or soap operas.

PHOTO DOUBLE: An actor cast to perform on camera in place of the regular actor usually from the back or at a distance.

PICK UP: An added take because of a some type of problem with a scene or camera shot.

PILOT: The first or maiden show introducing the characters and series situations for a potential TV serial or series.

"POPPING" or PLOSIVE A vocal term to describe the sudden release of blocked-in air causing a popping sound on the mike; The letters p,b,t,d,k,g.c.

POV SHOT: Point-of-View shot; camera angle from the Perspective of one actor.

PREPPY TYPE: An Eastern prep school-casual appearance.

PRESENTATION REEL: See Demo Tape.

PRIME TIME: Network programming aired 8-11 P.M. Eastern and Pacific time zones, (7-10 P.M.. in Central Mountain-time zone.

PRINCIPAL: A Performer with lines or special business which advances the story.

PRODUCER: Often called the Line Producer; the person responsible for the day-to-day decision-making on a production.

PROFICIENCY TEST: An advance placement test taken by high school students to achieve high school graduation equivalence without dropping out of school.

PROPS: Easily moved object, such as furniture and fake rocks used in the scene or as part of the set.

PSA: Public Service Announcement.

QUOTE: An actor's most recent salary figure used by agents in

negotiations.

RATINGS: Public surveys used to measure the number of TV viewers or radio listeners.

REGIONAL COMMERCIAL: For airing only in certain regions.

REHEARSAL: Running through the scene without the camera actually filming the action to work out any unknown action, mistakes or movement or for last second directions or instructions.

RELEASE: In commercials, termination of use of a commercial.

RELEASE LETTER: Written dismissal of a talent agent, as required by Unions.

RERUN: Rebroadcast of a TV program; in commercials, often called "reuse".

RESIDUAL: The fee paid to a performer for rebroadcast of a commercial, film or TV Program.

RESUMÉ: List of credits, usually attached to an 8 x 10 or composite.

REWRITE: Changes in the script, often using color-coded pages.

RIGHT-TO-WORK STATES: Those states which do not honor certain union provisions.

ROLLING: Camera and sound are in motion and the action is ready to be filmed.

RUNNING /REOCCURRING PART: In TV series, a recurring role.

SAG: Screen Actors Guild.

SCALE: Minimum payment for services under Union contracts.

SCALE + 10: Minimum payment plus 10% to cover the agent's commission, required in some jurisdictions for agents to receive commissions.

SCREEN TEST: A filmed performance of a short scene to confirm how an actor performs on camera; increasingly applied to taped

tests.

SCRIPT: The written form of a screenplay, teleplay, radio or stage play.

SCRIPT SUPERVISOR: The crew member assigned to record all changes or actions as the production proceeds.

SDI: State Disability Insurance, required insurance the producer must have to compensate performers and crew in case of an on set disabling accident or injury.

SECOND TEAM/STAND-IN: The people who substitute for the principal actor and actress when they are not needed, such as when lighting or camera blocking is being done by the production crew. This is a premium extra position!

SEGUE: In film or tape editing, a transition from one shot to another.

SESSION FEE: Payment for initial performance in a commercial.

SET: An indoor location, often constructed on a sound stage.

SPECIAL BUSINESS: Special action that you are asked to perform that can and is vital to the action in a scene. You are usually given a bump, sometimes you must ask for the bump.

SFX: Sound Effects.

SIDES : Sample pages or scenes from a script, used for auditions.

SIGHT-AND-SOUND: Parent's right under Union contracts to be within sight of their child performer at all times.

SIGNATORY: An employer who has agreed to produce under the terms of a union contract.

SILENT BIT: A piece of work without lines featured by the camera.

SINGLE CARD: A credit in a film or TV show in which only one performer's name appears.

SIT COM: Situation comedy; an episodic TV comedy, produced on a soundstage.

SLATE: A small chalkboard and clapper device, used to mark and identify shots on film for editing' also the process of verbal identification by a performer in a taped audition (e.g., Slate your name!).

SOAP: Soap opera or daytime drama.

SOUNDTRACK: The audio portion of a film or TV production.

SPECIAL BUSINESS: Specially directed action by an extra player.

SPOT: A commercial message, usually booked at random.

SSDC: Society of Stage Directors and Choreographers.

STAGE MANAGER: The person who oversees the technical aspects of an in-studio production.

STAGE RIGHT: To the Performer's right side, to the audience's left side. Likewise, Stage Left is to the Performer's left, the audience's right.

STATION 12: At SAG, the office responsible for clearing SAG members to work.

STATION 15: At SAG, the office responsible for clearing signatory producers.

STANDARD UNION CONTRACT: The standard format/contract approved by the Unions and offered to performers prior to the job.

STANDARDS & PRACTICES: The network TV censorship departments.

STAND-INS: Extra players used to substitute for featured players, usually for purposes of setting lights.

"STICKS": Slate or clapboard.

STORYBOARD : A pictured rendering of the sequential dialogue and action in a production of film T.V. or commercial.

STUDIO: A building, recording room or sound stage which accommodates film or TV Production.

STUDIO TEACHER: Set teacher or tutor, hired to provide education to working young performers; also responsible for enforcing Child Labor Laws and minors' provisions in the Union contracts.

STUNT COORDINATOR: The person in charge of designing and supervising the Performance of stunts and hazardous activities.

STUNT DOUBLE : A specially trained performer who actually performs stunts in place of a principal player.

SUBMISSION: An agent's suggestion to a casting director for a role in a certain production for the agents client.

SWEETENING: In singing/recording, the process of adding additional voices to previously recorded work.

SYNDICATION : Selling TV programs to individual stations rather than to network.

TAFT-HARTLEY ACT: A federal statute which allows 30 days after first employment before being required to join a union.

TAG: An introduction or ending to a commercial or TV show to identify a the sponsor or production company's or dealer, address, phone number, etc.

TAKE: The clapboard indication of a shot "taken" or printed.

TAKE 5: The announcement of periodic five minute breaks.

TELEPROMPTER: The brand name of a device which enables a broadcaster to read a script while looking into the camera lens.

TEST MARKET: Airing of a commercial in one area to determine response.

TIGHT SHOT (Go In Tight): Framing of a shot with little or no

space around the central figure(s) or feature(s); usually a close-up.

THEATRICAL: TV shows or feature film work, as opposed to commercials.

3/4" TAPE : Industrial quality video tape; requires special tape deck.

TIME & 1/2: Overtime Payment of 1 1/2 times the hourly rate.

TRADES: Newspapers and periodicals featuring entertainment news and information.

TRAILER: A mobile production facility. A series of excerpts or "clips" film clippings, used to promote a film or TV show.

TRUCKING: A camera move, involving shifts side to side.

TURNAROUND: The specified number of hours between dismissal one day and call time the next time.

TV-Q: An industry barometer of audience recognition.

TWO-SHOT: A camera framing of two persons.

TYPECASTING (Typed): Categorizing performers based on their "look".

UNDER 5 (U-5): In AFTRA contracts, a speaking role having 5 lines or less.

UNDERSTUDY: A performer hired to do a role only if the hired featured player is unable to perform.

UP STAGE: The area located at the back of the stage. Down Stage is the area in front of the Performer. Also to draw attention to oneself at the expense of a fellow performer.

UPGRADE: Acknowledgment by a Producer that a player hi red as an extra has Performed Principal work, resulting in Principal Payment.

USE CYCLE: Any 13-week period during which a commercial is actually aired;used to determine payment schedule for residuals and

KEN WAHL
OVERNITE SENSATIONS
ACTORS WHO WERE EXTRAS?
KEN WAHL

often differing from holding cycle.

VOICE-OVER (VO): Also OS; off-camera dialogue.

WAIVERS: Board-approved permission for deviation from the terms of a contract.

WALK-ON: A very brief role.

WALLA WALLA: Background noises, also known as rhubarb.

WARDROBE: The clothing a performer wears on camera in a scene.

WARDROBE ALLOWANCE: A maintenance fee paid to on-camera talent for the use (and dry cleaning) of talent's own clothing.

WARDROBE FITTING: A paid session held prior to production to prepare a performer's costumes.

WGA: Writers Guild of America.

WILD SPOT: A commercial which is contracted to air on a station-by-station basis, rather than by network.

WILD TRACK: Soundtrack having no direct relationship to the picture.

WORK PERMIT: A legal document required to allow a child to work, issued by various state or local agencies.

WRAP: What the director calls out when the days' filming is completed. A very, very good thing. Finishing principal photography on a production.

ZED CARD: A composite, usually 5" x 7", used for or print work or modeling.

ZOOM: A camera technique with a special lens to adjust the depth of a shot accomplished without moving the camera.

Chapter Nine

WARDROBE

I've had hundreds of background actors and actresses, especially those new to the extra business, call me late at night in a panic asking me, "I was booked on a job today, what shall I wear?" My response is always "Clothes, I hope!" I do not say that to be sarcastic, I say it to drive home a very important point. We all wear clothes almost every day. Most of us get dressed 365 days a year, and have been since our parents started dressing us funny (smile). Why should dressing for a background acting assignment be any different? Actually it is easier. You don't have to make decisions about what kind of clothing to wear because the production company has hired someone specifically to tell you.

One of the numerous responsibilities of the wardrobe person, is to outfit background actors with guidelines for wardrobe they will need you to bring or wear in a scene. Sometimes you will be outfitted and/or they will outfit you from their production wardrobe collection (wardrobe that has either been bought and/or rented for that particular scene/show.) A good complete wardrobe is the biggest single you can control to guarantee yourself consistent background acting jobs. Casting agents cast extras based on physical characteristics and wardrobe, and not always in that order. See actor Don Balalio, who also sometimes does background work, the man of 1,000 faces collage on the following page. You will see the importance of good character looks and a wide collection of wardrobe, some were supplied. Actress Lorraine Montgomery's varied wardrobe and wig collection has landed her many choice speciality bits roles including one of my favorite, Quentin Tarantino's "White Man's Burden" with John Travolta and Harry Belafonte (see photo below without wig).

Actress **Lorraine Montgomery**
(l) Lorraine as one of her many character with wig and wardrobe.

Don Balalio
The Man Of 1,000 Faces

The guidelines for wardrobe are:

1   SEASON- Winter, Spring, Summer, Fall.

2   TIME OF DAY- Early morning, Noontime, Evening, Night.

3   STORYLINE LOCATION - The city, area or country in or "out of this world" where the story takes place e.g... New York, Los Angeles, London, Vietnam, Dallas, San Francisco, Tokyo, Lima Ohio, Portland Oregon, Seoul Korea, Milwaukee Wisconsin, Saudi Arabian Desert, Wenatchee Washington, Washington, D.C., etc.

4   ECONOMIC STATUS OF CHARACTER Upper class\ Middle class\ Lower-middle class\ Lower class\ Homeless.

5   PROFESSION OF CHARACTER Doctor, lawyer, businessperson, waiter, policeperson, homemaker, customer rep, athlete, salesperson, blue collar, office worker, construction worker, fireman, nurse, news reporter/journalist, school crossing guard, etc.

6   STYLE OF DRESS - Upscale, business, casual, downscale, sporty, formal, risque, exotic, erotic, punk, street, etc.

7   TYPE OF ACTION TAKING PLACE Watching a ball game, shopping in a mall, walking/ crossing the street, patron in restaurant, working in an office building, courtroom, reporting a press conference, dancing in a nite club, fighting a fire, etc.

Do Not Wear
WHITE, BLACK, RED, BRIGHT
COLORS or LOUD PRINTS

The only time these wardrobe selections are allowed is when your casting director <u>asks</u> specifically for them.

Always bring three complete changes with accessories: shoes, ties, handbags, etc.

Always arrive dressed and ready to shoot. Hair and makeup should be done at home, unless asked differently. There is often not time or a place to change, and the production company forms a first impression of you when you show up for work. You look bad and make the casting agency look bad when you show up in shorts for a formal call.

Be sure that your clothes are clean and pressed, with no rips or stains. (There are exceptions eg.. bag ladies, bums, winos, etc.)

Use your imagination. Bring props to complete your character, i.e., sunglasses, books, shopping bags, briefcases, roller skates, etc.)

The wardrobe changes on the following pages are often used. It is a good idea to pick up a few of these at a thrift store so that you will make yourself available for more parts.

NEVER ACCEPT A JOB THAT REQUIRES SPECIFIC WARDROBE THAT YOU <u>DO NOT</u> HAVE!!!

On the following pages are some professional Hollywood" actor and actress friends and colleagues who from time to time choose to work in background acting roles for various reasons (*the fun, the excitement, the money and the chance at a possible principal speaking role upgrade, which happens a lot, is the true essence of each of their varied replies if you were to ask me*). Most of those who perform both principal speaking roles and background acting parts are in the **Top 20%** of

UNIQUE

SAG   **ERL** Ψ   ARTIST-MODEL-ACTOR

money-makers union card carrying members in the Hollywood acting community. Top **20%**. The real day to day money-making movie maker professional actors and actresses in New York also perform in the background. There is great opportunity and good money to be made and a varied wardrobe is one of the vital elements to being a frequently requested background actor. Besides the wardrobe is tax deductible when you wear them *for work-related* purpose only.

E X O T I C

ELISHA of CHOICE

SAG AFTRA   MODEL ACTRESS

⚞ SPECIFIC WARDROBE ⚟

Blue Collar:

Men- Chino or khaki work pants and shirts (dark brown green, navy, khaki color), Levi or Lee jeans (no designer jeans), T-shirts (no logos), heavy work shoes and boots, muscle shirts, caps, jean jackets, Pendleton shirt jackets, bandanna handkerchiefs.

Women- Polyester slacks or pant suits, floral print

B L U E

C O L L A R

&

U N I F O R M S

SAG   **Michael Lofgren**   AFTRA

Brad Bradbury
BLUE COLLAR

Nancy Register
CLEANING LADY

Ron Traylor
TRUCK DRIVER

Fran Avery
DOMESTIC

Donna Marcou
WAITRESS

Drew Orecchio
WAITER

Toni Perrotta
DINER WAITRESS

Jerry Wallace
WORKER

Rico Bueno
MILITARY GUARD

Cheryl Felton
Military Dress Uniform

Josef Hill
COMBAT SOLDIER

R.H. Stahchild
Hollywood Hype

GOOD GUYS BAD GUYS

Barry Lotterman

SAG

AFTRA

**Ron Traylor
BIKER**

tops, halter tops, ban-
dannas and scarves over
hair, hip length polyester
vests, aprons, house
dresses, polyester floral
print dresses, sweaters,
ponchos, work shoes,
waitress uniforms, Levi
and Lee jeans no de-
signer jeans.

Cops/Firemen:
Black lace-up shoes, black
socks and white T-shirt.

Waiter/Bartender:
Black dress pants, black
dress shoes, black socks,
and a white shirt or blue
button down.

**Gil
STREET GANG**

**Dutch
MOTORCYCLE GANG**

GOOD BAD UNDERCOVER?

Maurice Lewis SAG

**Rico Bueno
Colunbian Kingpin**

**Brad Bradbury
SHERIFF**

**Merita Valenti
BIKER CHIC**

**Ron Simmons
DETECTIVE**

**Ginger Tyne
NURSE**

**Veronica Reeves
SCRUB NURSE**

Nurse:
White lace-up or loafer-type shoes and white hose. Be sure to give your correct size, saves you embarrassment if the uniform assigned to you does not fit.

Orderlies:
White pants, white undershirt, white long sleeve shirt, black belt plain-toe white shoes. (Sometimes white tennis shoes will work, but please ask first.)

Stewardess:
Plain low heel black, navy, or nude pumps.

Pilots:
Black lace-up shoes, black pants, black belt, black socks and white shirt.

DOCTORS & NURSES

Claude Oatts

SAG AFTRA MODEL

Upscale Business:

Men - Two and three piece conservative suits (usually dark; possibly pin-stripped), solid long sleeve dress shirt (usually off white or soft pastel), nice silk or knit ties, dress shirt to match your suit. (Be sure that the tie and lapel width are contemporary.) Other possibilities are sport coats and slacks, check with the casting director on these alternatives. Polyester is rarely/never acceptable in this category.

UPSCALE

Octogenarian **'Poppa Brown'** Chambers

**Carolyn Rivers
UPSCALE**

**Lisa Marie Stagno
UPSCALE**

**Josef Hill
UPSCALE TRENDY**

**Cynthia Noritake
TRENDY**

General look should be well groomed and clean shaven.

Women- Nice conservative suits or dresses (linens, wools, and silks), dress shoes, hosiery, conservative jewelry. Outfits should be tailored and well fitted. Nothing outlandish, tight fitting, low cut or suggestive. No loud prints or stripes and no miniskirts.

General look should be neat and well groomed. Hair and makeup should be conservative.

Drew Orecchio
UPSCALE SUIT

Ginger Tyne
UPSCALE SUIT

Claude Oatts
UPSCALE CASUAL

Chuck Loch
UPSCALE SPORTS

Cheryl Felton
UPSCALE CHIC

Josef Hill
UPSCALE TRENDY

Barbara Matlin
UPSCALE CASUAL

Formal Dress: Men - Black tuxedo coat with contemporary lapels, black tuxedo pants, white or off white tuxedo shirts, black cummerbund, black dress shoes and socks. Top coats with tails and shirts with ruffles are only used in contemporary projects. While being dressed in a tuxedo, you want to be well groomed: hair trimmed and styled and clean shaven. You will be given a $10.00-30.00 bump for a tuxedo. *Women* - Formal floor length evening gowns evening bags and shoes evening wrap. Do not bring cocktail length dresses or evening pants unless it is okayed by the casting

F O R M A L

Tracey Poreé

**Al Wilbanks
FORMAL**

**Sarah Kane
FORMAL**

**Juanita Arneaud
FORMAL**

**Michael Moorehead
FORMAL**

director. You may be asked to bring furs. Be sure that they are real furs and are in good shape. (You will get a $10.00-$30.00 bump for the furs.)

Chiffons, velvets, silks, satins, velveteens, sateens, brocades, and beaded dresses look best according to the season. Bright colors and lames must be cleared with the casting director. When you are buying formal gowns, try to find something in a pastel or a rich deep jewel colors eg.. emerald, sapphire and ruby. Black and/or white dresses are seldom asked for but keep one close at hand. With all of the men in black and white, the ladies add the life and **color** to the scene.

Jewelry, shoes and handbags as well as scarves and wraps should be formal as well and truly compliment your attire. Bring appropriate accessories to complete your outfit. You will get a $10.00-$30.00 bump for formal wear.

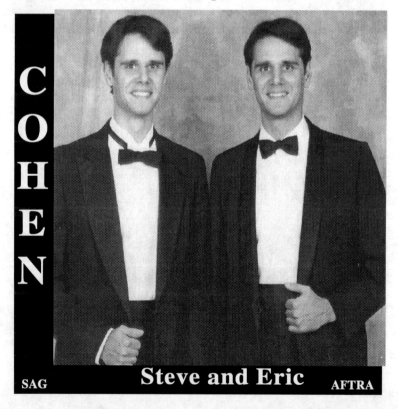

COHEN

SAG   **Steve and Eric**   AFTRA

Winter Weather:

Men and Women- Full length overcoats (with or without linings to go over suits. Dress length overcoats and capes, hats, scarves, gloves, mittens, umbrellas, earmuffs and boots. Fabrics should be heavy; wools, tweeds, and flannels. Layers and accessories sell a winter look.

W I N T E R

W E A R

SAG

Les Pollack

AFTRA

George Hill
WINTER JACKET

Cynthia Noritake
LEATHER COAT

Drew Orecchio
SKI BUM

Jerry Wallace
WINTER OVERCOAT

Business: Men and Women -Suits, two piece or three piece. Dark colors and earthtones are preferred, black, blue, brown gray and pin-striped. White shirt/blouse, blue button down with a matching tie and kerchief or other appropriate neckwear for women. Accent with accessories, glasses, brief case, umbrella eg...as though you were going to a very special day in court.

B
U
S
I
N
E
S
S

SAG **Sylvia Anderson** AFTRA

Jules Koenigsberg
BUSINESS

Tracey Poreé
BUSINESS

Neil Eisman
BUSINESSMAN

Kathleen Sandoval
UPSCALE

Frank Trevino
SINGLE-BREASTED

Aixa Maldonado
SUIT and BLOUSE

Nella Nielson
SUIT w/ TIE-SCARF

Rene Beard
DOUBLE-BREASTED

Preppie: Men and Women-Khaki or navy pants and skirts, solid color pastel button down shirts, short sleeve Izod/Polo shirts, V-neck and crew neck solid colored sweaters worn over shirts and under sport coats or tied around shoulder, new and worn Levi or new designer blue jeans, windbreakers, canvas espadrille shoes, ribbon headbands, canvas or leather handbags and conservative jewelry.

T R E N D Y

Kaye Shoemaker
UPSCALE TRENDY

Maurice Lewis
UPSCALE TRENDY

Debbie Rock
STREET TRENDY

Drew Barten
ROCKER TRENDY

Kathleen Sandoval
CASUAL TRENDY

Kinnette Michelle
CALIF TRENDY

LaVelle Davenport
SUMMER TRENDY

Felipe
COWBOY TRENDY

Maurice Lewis
BUSINESS TRENDY

Cynthia Noritake
CASUAL TRENDY

Alan Bates
PREPPIE TRENDY

Carolyn Rivers
UPSCALE TRENDY

TRENDY CHIC

SAG

Casual: *Men and Women-* Pants and tops that you feel most comfortable wearing is the general rule of thumb when choosing a casual wardrobe. Something you would wear at an outdoor event or walking around casually shopping. Could include sports coats and sweaters, jackets and vest. Easy does it!

CASUAL TRENDY

SAG   **Charlotte Crowley**   AFTRA

Steve & Eric Cohen
LEATHER & T-SHIRT

Gary James
UPSCALE CASUAL

Katy Sumerland
CASUAL w/ VEST

Alan Bates
LAYERED CASUAL

Kaye Shoemaker
SWEATERSUIT

Lacy
CALIFORNIA COOL

Martee LaComette
CASUAL JACKET

George Hill
CASUAL SWEATER

Kim Dunn
CASUAL

Kristine Halverson
AEROBICS

Nancy Register
TENNIS PLAYER

Nella Nielson
DANCER

Jules Koenigsberg

SPORTS & ATHLETIC

Neil Eisman
BICYCLIST

Alphonso Jones
BOXER

Tony Piccino
TENNIS

LaVell Davenport
ATHELETE

Western: *Men-* Basically blue collar look for men with more emphasis on western cut shirts, western boots, cowboy hats, plaids and flannel. Also add western cut suits, rodeo belt buckles, silver and turquoise jewelry, fringed shirts, chaps, suede jackets, and bolero string tie.

WESTERN & OLD WEST

R.C. Bates
MOUNTAINMAN

Dave Sales
NATIVE AMERICAN

Ron Traylor
COWBOY

R.C. Bates
PROSPECTOR

Women - Blossomy long cotton print dress with simple patterns, hat/bonnets and tie up boot type shoes or same as western wear for the men. Add denim skirts (knee length or mini) and split skirts.

Wayne Miller
COWPOKE
SAG   AFTRA

Actor **Ron McFarlin** as a towns

:rson on a Hollywood old western town set.

AFTRA

SPECIALITY COSTUMES & BUMS

Kiyoko Yamaguchi

SAG   AFTRA

**Les Pollack
TOURIST**

**Al Verdun
SPINSTER**

**Mick Lehr
70's HIPPIE**

**Steve & Eric Cohen
CLOWNING**

**Harriet Walker
CHOIR**

**Jerry Wallace
PRIEST**

**R.C. Bates
RABBI**

NINJA

Bums, Winos, Bag Ladies and Scumbags:
Men and Women - Anything torn, old, and ragged looking. It should also not be clean looking.

A
W
A
R
D
W
I
N
N
I
N
G
L
O
O
K
S

SAG   **R. C. Bates**   AFTRA

These guidelines will give you enough information to put you in mind of the type of wardrobe that you have immediate access to, whether your own personal or something readily borrowed. Most of the wardrobe requests are of the types and styles of clothing that you already have.

Sometimes you will need to purchase an item or two, when that happens do what most background actors do, Thrift shop, Salvation Army, Goodwill, or garage sales if time allows.

IT'S A WRAP   818 567-7366
3315 MAGNOLIA BLVD., BURBANK,CA

Consult your local telephone book for stores in your area under the headings: CLOTHING -USED, THRIFT SHOPS, UNIFORMS, GOODWILL, CHURCH CENTERS, SALVATION ARMY, Movie & TV Show Clothes Liquidators eg.. It A Wrap & Studio Wardrobe, etc.. When you do not have the time use good common sense when purchasing an item.

Do not spend $100.00 for an item that you may only wear once. However if you find where you may be able to use it for future background jobs and it is a bargain.
Go For It!

STUDIOWARDROBE
818 508-7762. 3953 LAUREL GROVE AVE.,
STUDIO CITY, CA.

R EMEMBER the prepared background artist brings at least two, preferably three additional changes of wardrobe to the set. Sometimes you are asked to bring more. You should bring a selection of different fabrics, colors, style, patterns and designs that are in the overall description of the kind of wardrobe asked for by the wardrobe person.

Don't bring a California winter outfit for a show that takes place in the winter in New York City. Be smart. Use good fashion sense when asked to bring a selection. You are projecting your image as well and it should be at least, a good one.

If time allows watch television shows the night before and pay close attention to the wardrobe worn by background people on several shows that have a similar wardrobe requirement as the show that you have been booked on.

With a little planning and experience, you will be selecting your wardrobe without second guessing your judgement. Always remember, if you listen carefully to the request given out by the wardrobe person to the casting agent and ask the right questions you will become an expert at what kind of wardrobe and accessories to bring. I can tell right away by the show what the wardrobe requirement may be. In a short time you will too. Keep it pressed and neat by bringing it in a garment bag or dry cleaners clothing bag. If in a pinch use a clean new trash bag as I sometimes do. Always look your very best and you'll do great!

Chapter Ten

BACKGROUND ACTING

THE FIVE SECOND ACTOR
The Art of Acting for the Background
by
Cullen Chambers

The #1 "trick" to background acting is do what ever would be natural in that situation or circumstance for you. If you have no experience in that particular situation or circumstances simply follow the directions of the director. The director will give you a certain action to perform in a scene and tell you when to do it. You will notice sometimes they do not give directions to certain background actors. This is usually because the director has worked with those background actors before and is aware of those background actor's knowledge of making crosses, walking in front of the cameras, and doing "business," acting as though they were really doing what would be naturally done in that particular scene if it were in "real life."

It is the directors goal to have you make the action look real and to be knowledgeable of the technical limitations of film-making at the same time. Sometimes the directors may ask you to do an action that may seem unreal, this is usually to fulfill a technical necessity. He, the director, knows what he/she is looking for and may need you to "cheat" the action to make the scene look real.

Follow their directions to the letter and you will do fine. If you don't or won't he will usually get someone who will.

If at anytime you do not hear the directions clearly or do not fully understand what action the director has directed you to do exactly, ask, it is professional to ask them to repeat themselves, it is very unprofessional not to ask and do something wrong. Be smart, listen, listen, listen. Listen to the directors when they are talking. What they are saying is vitally important. You can not listen and talk at the same time as the director. Listen well and you will do fine. Always remember, film-making is a cooperative effort, the director wants you to get it right!

Study the sections titled "EXTRA ETIQUETTE" and "EXTRA SETTALK" thoroughly and you will be well informed when it comes to understanding the film-making jargon that the directors will be speaking. Remember be or rather **ACT**, natural!

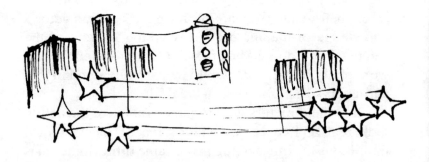

Chapter Eleven

BUMPS:
When and How to Ask for One

A bump is just that... a move forward, swelling of your paycheck caused by performing a certain action that is above and beyond what was normal activity for a background actor. This comes as a result of displaying a special ability... sewing a garment... riding a bicycle... lifting a heavy object... driving a car... etc, performing a "silent bit"... directly interacting with a principle character; e.g. handing them a flower... opening the door... waiter serving them food... restraining the principle... etc, or working under adverse or hazardous conditions... smoke... rain... cold... mountainous... dusty... on the waters edge... ice... snow... near deep hole or cliff edge... etc.

The tip or trick of getting a bump is putting yourself in a position to be asked to do specialty acting. By having it listed on your resumé, registration profile card, informing the casting director or the Assistant Director on the actual set, of your skills and experiences regarding the action that will be taking place. Another way is to stay aware of the upcoming scenes by paying close attention to discussions and eavesdropping on conversations between production staff and crew concerning future setups. I have been in the right place hundreds of times to benefit from my special espionage-type listening skills!

The ultimate secret to getting a bump is to ask for one. Do not demand, request, claim, sue, press for, impose upon, insist, dictate, badger, push, petition and definitely not nag or whine for a bump. Simply ask. You will stand a greater chance of getting it also by having the knowledge of what may constitute as a bump and not asking when you know it doesn't deserve special compensation. This is a skill you will acquire as you become more experienced. I receive 90 % of the bumps I ask for, it may not always be as much as I would have asked for (I'm working on that) but it was much more than I would have received had I not asked at all. Most of all be patient with the Assistant Director, he/she is one of the few people who is always doing something on the set. Select a semi-quiet time to approach him/her about the bump adjustment. By waiting five extra minutes I received a $50.00 bump adjustment while the other "Pushy, Won't Wait Extras" did not receive a bump at all for the same action I performed.

IMPORTANT: *The information on bumps does necessarily pertain to non-union background players participating in a commercial.*

EXTRA NOTE

Chapter Twelve

EXTRA! EXTRA!
This section contains
**EXTRA SPECIAL
INFORMATION**
to keep **YOU** rising to
the **TOP!**

DIRECTORY LISTINGS
Phone numbers and addresses for your
convenience.

PROMOTIONAL SERVICES
Just what you need to "beef up" your
act.

ORDER FORMS
Quick and easy ways to get the job
done.

AND MORE . . . .

AFTRA TV SHOW

from the AFTRA TELEVISION SHOW SHEET AS OF January 09, 1996

AFTRA OFFICE	**(213) 461-8111**
AFTRA SHOWCASE	**(213) 467-8702**
AFTRA CASTING LINE	**(213) 461-1377**

THE MAILING ADDRESS IS THE FACILITY WHERE THE PROGRAM TAPES UNLESS OTHERWISE INDICATED.

THIS IS DESIGNED FOR AFTRA MEMBERS TO ASCERTAIN WHICH SHOWS FALL UNDER AFTRA'S JURISDICTION

AFTRA Representatives assigned to show

TELEVISION DEPARTMENT .. Ext. 256
ASST. EXEC. DIR./TV DEPT. JOAN HALPERN (JH) .... Ext. 223
LAUREN BAILEY (LB) .... Ext. 225   JEAN FROST (JF) .... Ext. 222
KATHY EWERS (ICE) .... Ext. 226   FRANK MESSINEO (FM) Ext. 224
CHRISTINA HAGSTROM (CVH .... Ext. 227
ROB BROWN (RB) (INTERACTIVE MEDIA) .... Ext. 219

DRAMATIC SERIALS (SOAP OPERAS)

BOLD AND BEAUTIFUL (KE)

Bell-Phillip TV Prod. ...... (213) 853-2345
All Casting: Christy Dooley ..... No phone calls
Submit Pictures & Resumés c/o CBS
Include your membership number on your picture and resumé
(Tapes CBS TV City)

GENERAL HOSPITAL (FM)

ABC .... (310) 557-7777
Principal Casting:
Mark Teschner .... (310) 557-5542
Extra Casting: Lisa Snedeker
Casting Call in Number. (310) 520-CAST
M-F 11:30-12:30
Pictures & Resumés c/o ABC-Prospect
(Tapes ABC Prospect)

DAYS OF OUR LIVES (CVH)

Corday Productions .... (818) 972-0918
Fran Bascom .... (818) 972-8339
3400 Riverside Drive, Suite 652
Burbank, CA 91505
Extra Casting:
Linda Poindexter .... (818) 972-0973
Casting Call in Number: (818) 972-0971
3400 Riverside Drive, Suite 778
Burbank, CA 91505
(Tapes NBC Burbank)

THE YOUNG AND THE RESTLESS (KE)

Columbia Pictures TV ... (213) 852-2345
Principal & Five Lines or Less:
Jill W. Newton .... No phone calls
Extra Casting:
Gail Camacho .... No phone calls
All casting c/o CBS
Submit Pictures & Resumés
(Tapes CBS TV City)

PRIMETIME/NETWORK
EXHIBIT A SITUATION COMEDIES

THE FRESH PRINCE OF BEL-AIR (LZ)

NBC Productions .... (818) 840-7500
Principal Casting:
 Lisa Miller .... (818) 760-6064
Extras: Central Casting - Steve Spiker
Females: .... (818) 562-2813
Males: .... (818) 562-2807
(Tapes NBC. Studios, Stage 11)

ROSEANNE (LB)

Carsey-Werner Co .... (818) 760-5135
Principal Casting:
Karen Vice .... No phone calls
Extras Casting: Central Casting
Females .... (818) 562-2813
Males .... (818) 562-2807
(Tapes CBS/MTM Studios)

GRACE UNDER FIRE (CVH)

The Carsey-Werner Co.(818) 760-6064
Principal Casting:
Liberman & Hirschfeld . No phone calls
5979 West 3rd. St., Suite 204,
Los Angeles, CA 90036
Extras Casting: Central Casting
Females:: .... (818) 562-2813
Males: .... (818) 562-2807
(Tapes CBS-MTM Studios, Stage 14)

DRAMATIC SYNDICATED PROGRAMS SIT-COM

CALIFORNIA DREAMS (FM)

NBC Productions .... (818) 840-2250
Principal Casting:
Robin Lippin .... No Phone Calls
Extras: Central Casting -Shannon Dunn

Females .... (818) 562-2813
Males .... (818) 562-2807
(Tapes NBC Studios)

CLEGHORNE! (LB) WB-TV

20th Century Fox TV .... (310) 760-6064
10201 W. Pico Blvd.
Los Angeles, CA 90035
Principal Casting:
Monica Swann .... No phone call
Extras: Central Casting- Steve Spiker
Females:: .... (818) 562-2813
Males: .... (818) 562-2807
(Tapes Fox Television Center)

FIRST TIME OUT (CVH) WB-TV

ELP Communications .. (310) 280-7087
Principal Casting:
Patricia Nolan .... No phone call
Extras: Central Casting -Helen Mayer
Females:: .... (818) 562-2813
Males: .... (818) 562-2807
(Tapes Culver Studios)

HANG TIME (LB) NBC

NBC Prods. .... (818) 850-6570
330 Bob Hope Drive
Burbank, CA 91523
Principal Casting:Lisa Miller
Extras: Central Casting -Steve Spiker
Females:: .... (818) 562-2813
Males: .... (818) 562-2807
(Tapes Sunset Gower Studios)
(ON HIATUS)

MARRIED WITH CHILDREN (CVH)

ELP Communications .. (213) 460-7505
Principal Casting: Vicki Rosenberg &
Terri Tunder .... No phone calls
Extras Casting: Central Casting

Females .... (818) 569- 5155
Males .... (818) 569-5140
(Tapes Sony Studios, Stage 28)

MARTIN (DC)

Home Box Office, Inc ... (818) 777-7800
Principal Casting
Kim Williams Castng .. No Phone Calls
4063 Radford Ave., Ste. 109,
Studio City, CA 91604
Extras: Natalie Johnson Casting
(310) 418-2019
(Tapes Universal Studios, Stage 31)

SIMON (LB) WB-TV

Montrose Productions
9336 West Washington Blvd.
Culver City, CA 90232
Casting: Tammy Billik .... No calls
Extras: Central Casting -Tony Hobb
(Tapes Culver Studios)

HYPERNAUTS (JF)

Hypernauts Prod. Co., Inc
28165 Crocker Ave.
Valencia, CA 91355
Principal: Fern Champion/Mark Paladini
 No phone calls
Extras: Central Casting
Females:: .... (818) 562-2813
Males: .... (818) 562-2807

RIMBAS ISLAND (LB)

HAC-MFP Prods, Inc
303 No. Glen Oaks, 4th Floor
Burbank, CA 91502
Casting: Marcia Goodman .... No calls
Tapes V.P.S. Studios .. (213) 464-2473

SAVED BY THE BELL THE NEW CLASS

NBC Productions .... (818) 840-2250
Principal Casting:Robin Lippin
Extra Casting:CENEX Casting
Females .... (818) 562-2825
Males .... (818) 562-2819
(Tapes NBC Studios)

REALITY & ENTERTAINMENT/ NEWS PROGRAMS

AMERICA'S MOST WANTED(JF)

STF PRODUCTIONS ... (202) 895-3102
5151 Wisconsin Ave, N.W. 2
Washington, D.C. 20016
(Tapes Various locations U.S.)

ENTERTAINMENT TONIGHT (KE)

Paramount Television
5555 Melrose Avenue .. (213) 956-4900
Los Angeles, CA 90038
(Tapes Paramount)

EXTRA (KE)

TTT West Coast Inc., .. (818) 840-4444
1840 Victory Boulevard
Glendale, CA 91523
Casting: TBA
(Tapes Various Locations)

EXTREMISTS (KE)

Extremist Prods. Inc., .. (714) 821-7337
10351 Santa Monica Blvd., Suite 200
Los Angeles, CA 90025
(Tapes Various Locations)

HARD COPY (KE)

Paramount Television .. (213) 956-5808
5555 Melrose Ave. Studios E & G
Los Angeles, CA 90038
(Tapes Paramount)

LIFESTYLES W/ ROBIN LEACH & SHARI BELAFONTE (KE)

Lifestyles Prods. (818) 846-0030
3400 Riverside Drive, 6th Floor
Burbank, CA 91505
(Tapes Various Locations)

OTHER SIDE (FM)

Four Point Entertainment(213) 850-1600
3575 Cahuenga Blvd., West
Los Angeles, CA 90068
(Reality Talk Series)

PUZZLE PLACE (KE)

Lancit Prods. .... (213) 953-5282
4401 Sunset Blvd.
Los Angeles, CA 90232
Principal Casting: Bob Morones (213)
953-5657
(Tapes KCET Studios)

RESCUE 911 (ICE)

CBS/Katy Film Productions Inc. . (213) 466-7594
c/o Arnold Shapiro Productions, Inc.
1438 N. Gower St., Bldg. #48,
Los Angeles, CA 90028
(Tapes Various in the U.S.A.)

BASIC CABLE

E! ENTERTAINMENT TV (LZ)

E! Entertainment TV .... (213) 956-4900
5670 Wilshire Blvd.
Los Angeles, CA 90038

VARIETY & NON-DRAMATIC PROGRAMS

AMERICA'S FUNNIEST HOME VIDEOS (FM)

Cara Productions c/o
Vin Di Bona Productions(310) 442-9804
12233 W. Olympic Blvd., Ste. 160,
Los Angeles, CA 90065
All Casting: Susan Jacobs ...... No calls

MAD-TV (CVH)-FOX

Girl Group Productions (213) 993-5393
c/o Ren-Mar Studios
846 N. Cahuenga Blvd., Bldg A, Rm 217
Los Angeles, CA 90038
Principal Casting: Julie Mossberg & Jill
Anthony .... No calls
Extras Casting: Rich King - Axium
Casting (818) 557-2980
(Tapes Ren-Mar Studios & Various Locations)

NIGHTSTAND (FM)

Big Ticket Pictures (213) 634-5200
c/o Empire Studios
1854 Empire Avenue
Burbank, CA 91504
All Casting: Coralyn Wahlborg-Knopp
(ON HIATUS)

BASIC CABLE

MASTERS OF THE MAZE (JF)

Kline & Friends (818) 760-5947
11415 Canton Drive
Studio City, CA 91504
(Tapes CBS Studios Center)

PAY TV:

SHOWTIME NIGHTTIME (LB)

Kline & Friends (818) 760-5947
11415 Canton Drive
Studio City, CA 91504
(Tapes CBS Studios Center)

TALK SHOWS

THE GEORGE & ALANA SHOW (JK)

George & Alana, Inc. .
(213) 468-5000
6230 Sunset Blvd.
Los Angeles, CA 90028
(Tapes Sunset- Gower Theatre)

LATE LATE SHOW W/ TOM SNYDER (KE)

Worldwide Trousers Co
(213) 852-7900
c/o CBS TV CITY.
7800 Beverly Blvd.
Los Angeles, CA 90036
Talent Exec.: Carole Propp
(Tapes CBS TV City)

LATER WITH GREG KINEAR (CVH)

NBC Productions
(818) 840-7500

Talent Exec.:Lillian Mizrahi & Vicki Frank

MIKE & MATY (FM)

Valleycrest Prods. .... (213) 871-8292
500 South Buena Vista Ave.
Burbank, CA 91521
(Tapes Hollywood Center Studios)

DENNIS MILLER LIVE (FM)

Happy Family Prods. ... (213) 852-4495
7800 Beverly Blvd.
Los Angeles, CA 90036
Casting: Michelle Dévoe-No Phone Call
(Tapes NBC Burbank)

THE TONIGHT SHOW WITH JAY LENO (CVH)

NBC Productions .... (818) 840-4444
Co-Producer/Talent Executive: Tori
Pelligrino
(Tapes NBC-Burbank)

GAME SHOWS

AMERICAN GLADIATORS (FM)

Four Point Entertain. ..... 213) 850-1600
3575 Cahuenga Blvd. W. #600
Los Angeles, CA 90068

GLADIATORS 2000 (FM)

Four Point Entertain. ..... 213) 850-1600
3575 Cahuenga Blvd. W. #600
Los Angeles, CA 90068
-ON HAITUS-

JEOPARDY (KE)

Quadra Productions ..... (310) 280-8855
10202 Washington Blvd.
Culver City, CA 90230
 (Tapes Sony Studios, Stage 10)

THE PRICE IS RIGHT (KE)

Jonathan Goodson Partners,LLC (213) 965-6500
5750 Wilshire Blvd., Suite. 475 WEST
Los Angeles, CA 90036-3697

TRIVAL PURSUIT (LB)

Martindale Hillier Prod.
(818) 502-5550
1330 S. Glendale Ave.
Glendale, CA 91205,
(TapesOakridge TV Studios- Glendale)
-ON HAITUS-

WHEEL OF FORTUNE (KE)

Quadra Productions .
(818)972-7931
9860 Wilshire Blvd.,
Beverly Hills, CA 90210
 (Tapes CBS TV CENTER)

BASIC CABLE:

FAMILY CHALLENGE (KE)

Woody Fraser Enterprises, Inc
(818) 502-4800
2220 Colorado Avenue
Santa Monica, CA 91504
(Tapes Glendale Studios)

FREE FOR ALL (FM)

Fun House Productions
(213) 960-2599
1040 No. Las Palmas
Hollywood, CA 90038
(Tapes KTLA)

QUICK SILVER (FM)

Fun House Prods.
(213) 960-2599
1040 No. Las Palmas
Hollywood, CA 90038
(Tapes KTLA)

WILD ANIMAL GAMES (FM)

Woody Fraser Enterprises, Inc
(818) 502-4800
2220 Colorado Avenue
Santa Monica, CA 91504
(Tapes Glendale Studios)

LOCAL PROGRAMS

KABC (FM)
(310) 557-7777
Monday Night Live
(Tapes ABC Prospect)
KCAL TV (KE)
(310) 460-5086
TOONTOWN KIDS
(213) 460-5086
1 Hour Children's Series
All Casting: Marilyn Kagan
(Tapes KCAL)
KCOP (CVH)
(213) 851-1000
L.A. Kids
(Tapes KCOP)
KNBC (CVH)
(818) 840-4444
TODAY IN L.A.
(Tapes NBC Burbank)
KTLA (LB)
(213) 460-5 500
PACESETTERS
WEEKEND GALLERY

(Tapes KTLA)
KTTV (LB)
(213) 462-7111
MIDDAY SUNDAY
SIGN OF THE TIMES
(Tapes Fox TV)

PRINCIPAL CASTING ONLY

CALLAHAN HEIGHT
4741 Laurel Canyon Blvd.
Suite 104
No. Hollywood, CA 91607

CHAMPION CASTING
1040 N. Las Palmas,
Bldg. 27, Room 118
Hollywood, CA 90038

EILEEN KNIGHT CASTING
4063 Radford Ave., Ste. 109
Studio City, CA 91604

LIEBERMAN-HIRSCHFELD
Meg Lieberman, Marc Hirschfeld
6979 W. 3rd St., Ste. 204,
Los Angles, CA 90036

RICK MILLIKAN CASTING
Rick Millikan/ Stacy Wise
10201 W. Pico Blvd., Bldg 75
Los Angles, CA 90035

EXTRAS AND FIVE LINES OR LESS PERFORMERS

The phone numbers listed as "Recorded Casting Information" under each casting company is information on all shows cast by that particular company. Some jobs may not be covered by AFTRA or another union.

Before accepting work, always verify that it is a union job. You may ask the company if the job is union and which union it is being produced under. If the show name is not announced on the recording, ask the company for the show name and union status.

Always verify with the AFTRA office that the show is indeed an AFTRA covered show. Contact the Television Department for information.

COMPANY CASTING THE ABOVE AFTRA SHOWS
CENEX CASTING
CENTRAL CASTING

BACK TO ONE
CULLEN CHAMBERS
TOP 10 PICKS
OF THE
HOTTEST 100
HOLLYWOOD
EXTRA CASTING AGENCIES
1 9 9 6

1. CENTRAL/CENEX CASTING............... **(page 197)**

2. RAINBOW CASTING .... **(page 207)**

3. BILL DANCE CASTING .... **(page 195)**

4. M.R. COOPER CASTING .... **(page 203)**

(TIE) T.B.S. CASTING .... **(page 210)**

6. MESSENGER ASSOCIATES .... **(page 204)**

7. PRIME CASTING .... **(page 206)**

8. ANNA MILLER CASTING .... **(page 193)**

9. LATIN CONNECTION CASTING ... **(page 202)**

10. STAR CASTING................................. **(page 209)**

(TIE) WEBSTER CASTING .... **(page 211)**

HONORABLE MENTIONS	COMMERCIALS/ MUSIC VIDEO	CHILDREN
1. AXIUM (page 194)	**1.** PRODUCERS (page 207)	**1.** ACADEMY KIDS MGMT (page 192)
2. NAT JOHNSON (page 205)	**2.** IDELL JAMES (page 201)	**2.** SCREEN CHILDREN'S AGENCY (page 208)
3. LANE Model &Talent (page 202)	**3.** SUNSET (page 209)	**3.** JEAN PAGE MGMT (page 206)
4. CHRIS GRAY (page 198)	**4.** HAGERMAN & (page 201)	**4.** PRIME CASTING (page 206)
5. WILD BUNCH (page 212)		
6. XTRAS CASTING (page 196)		
7. CAST OF 1000's (page 196)		
8. DENNIS HANSEN (page 199)		

HOLLYWOOD Extra Casting Agents

(Effective January 09, 1996)

The following listing of Hollywood Casting Agencies is current as we go to press. The information was gathered directly from the agents and/or our vast information network. The agencies have assured us that the fees listed will be honored to people who register with a copy of **"Back To One"** in hand. **If any listed agency charges you a higher fee, contact us <u>immediately</u>.**

From time to time agencies change policies, dates and times of registration, and sometimes ownership. Be sure to telephone them first to verify their current requirements and then please call us at

(213) 969-4897

Rating Guide

☆☆☆☆☆ = Must sign-up

☆☆☆☆ = Should sign-up

☆☆☆ = Worthwhile sign-up

☆☆ = Why not sign-up

☆ = If you must

If there is no ☆ please check out the agency for yourself.
-- Not enough data to rate. --

☐ACADEMY KIDS MANAGEMENT

VINELAND STUDIO**S**   **THOMAS BROS GUIDE: PG:** 23 **CO-ORD:** E-4
4942 VINELAND AVE SUITE 103   **1996 EDITION: PG:** 563   **CO-ORD:** A-3
NO. HOLLYWOOD CA 91601

TELEPHONES
INFO: 818 769-8091
WORK LINES: (Men):   **(Women):**
HOT LINE: **PAYROLL:**

FEES
REGISTRATION: $0.00   **PHOTO:** $0.00   **MONTHLY:** 0%

METHOD OF REGISTRATION
PHONE: No   **MAIL PHOTO/RESUMÉ:** No
PHOTO SIZE & QUANTITY: 3"X5": 0   **4"X6":** 2 **8"X10":** 0
WALK-IN: No   **APPOINTMENT:** ONCE A MONTH

REGISTRATION	VISITATION	
Every Six Weeks	**DAYS:** By Appt	**TIMES:** By Appt

EXTRAS

UNION: Yes	**NON-UNION:** Yes	**STAND-IN:** Yes	**PHOTO-DOUBLE:** Yes
FULL SERVICE: Yes	**FILM:** Yes	**TELEVISION:** Yes	
COMMERCIALS: Yes	**VIDEO:** Yes	**PRINT:** Yes	
ADULT: No	**YOUTH/CHILDREN:** Yes		

PRINCIPALS

UNION: Yes	**NON-UNION:** Yes	**PHOTO-DOUBLE:** Yes	**STUNTS:** No
FULL SERVICE: Yes	**FILM:** Yes	**TELEVISION:** Yes	
COMMERCIALS: Yes	**VIDEO:** Yes	**PRINT:** Yes	
ADULTS: No	**YOUTH/CHILDREN:** Yes		

NOTES/COMMENTS: GREAT! YOU SEE SOME OF THEIR CLIENTS, EVERYDAY
DADDY DEAREST, DISNEY, LEGAL TO LOOK YOUNGER FOR EXTRA WORK ONLY.
LOTS OF PRINCIPAL. CALL OR SEND SELF ADDRESS S.A.S.E. ALONG W/ A NOTE
ABOUT THE CHILD FOR FOR MORE DETAIL

RATING: ☆ ☆ ☆ ☆ ☆

☐ACTOR'S REPETOIRE BANK

18034 Ventura Blvd. 291   **THOMAS BROS GUIDE: PG:** 21 **CO-ORD:** C-2
Encino CA 91316   **1996 EDITION: PG:** 561   **CO-ORD:** A-3

TELEPHONES
INFO: 818 996-0505
WORK LINES: (Men):   **(Women):**
HOT LINE: **PAYROLL:**

FEES
REGISTRATION: $20.00   **PHOTO:** $0.00   **MONTHLY:** 0%

METHOD OF REGISTRATION
PHONE: No   **MAIL PHOTO/RESUMÉ:** Yes
PHOTO SIZE & QUANTITY: 3"X5": 1   **4"X6":** No **8"X10":** 1
WALK-IN: No   **APPOINTMENT:** No

REGISTRATION		VISITATION	
DAYS: No	**TIMES:** No	**DAYS:** No	**TIMES:** No

EXTRAS

UNION: Yes	**NON-UNION:** Yes	**STAND-IN:** Yes	**PHOTO-DOUBLE:** Yes
FULL SERVICE: No	**FILM:** Yes	**TELEVISION:** Yes	
COMMERCIALS: Yes	**VIDEO:** Yes	**PRINT:** No	
ADULT: Yes	**YOUTH/CHILDREN:** No		

PRINCIPALS

UNION: Yes	**NON-UNION:** Yes	**PHOTO-DOUBLE:** No	**STUNTS:** Yes
FULL SERVICE: No	**FILM:** Yes	**TELEVISION:** Yes	
COMMERCIALS: Yes	**VIDEO:** Yes	**PRINT:** No	
ADULTS: No	**YOUTH/CHILDREN:** No		

NOTES/COMMENTS: SUBMIT PHOTO FOR CONSIDERATION

RATING: ☆ ☆ ☆

❑ALLISON & ASSOCIATES CASTING

6960 Vesper Ave., #12   **THOMAS BROS GUIDE: PG:** 34 **CO-ORD:** B-3
Van Nuys Ca 91405   **1996 EDITION: PG:**   **CO-ORD:**

TELEPHONES

INFO: 818 782-3676
WORK LINES: (Men):   **(Women):**
HOT LINE: **PAYROLL:**

FEES

REGISTRATION: $10.00   **PHOTO:** $5.00   **MONTHLY:** 0%

METHOD OF REGISTRATION

PHONE: No   **MAIL PHOTO/RESUMÉ:** Yes
PHOTO SIZE & QUANTITY: 3"X5": 5   4"X6": 0 8"X10": 3
WALK-IN: No   **APPOINTMENT:** Only

REGISTRATION   **VISITATION**
DAYS: By Appt   **TIMES:** 10a-7p   **DAYS:** By Appt.   **TIMES:**

EXTRAS

UNION: Yes   **NON-UNION:** Yes   **STAND-IN:** Yes   **PHOTO-DOUBLE:** Yes
FULL SERVICE: Yes   **FILM:** Yes **TELEVISION:** Yes
COMMERCIALS: Yes   **VIDEO:** Yes   **PRINT:** Yes
ADULT: Yes   **YOUTH/CHILDREN:** No

PRINCIPALS

UNION: Yes   **NON-UNION:** Yes   **PHOTO-DOUBLE:** Yes   **STUNTS:** No
FULL SERVICE: Yes   **FILM:** Yes **TELEVISION:** Yes
COMMERCIALS: Yes   **VIDEO: Yes**   **PRINT:** Yes
ADULTS: Yes   **YOUTH/CHILDREN:** No

NOTES/COMMENTS: CAST FOR PROMOS FOR FILM & T.V. TRAILERS & COMMER-
CIALS. MOST RECENT PROJECTS: "TIME AFTER TIME", "WHEN TIME RAN OUT",
"HOLLYWOOD WALK OF FAME".

RATING: ☆ ☆ ☆

❑AMC - ANNA MILLER CASTING

P.O. Box 66   **THOMAS BROS GUIDE: PG:** 34 **CO-ORD:** C-3
Sunland CA 91041   **1996 EDITION: PG:** 593   **CO-ORD:** E-4

TELEPHONES

INFO: 213 957-4696
WORK LINES: (Men):   **(Women):**
HOT LINE: 213 960-7994   **PAYROLL:**

FEES

REGISTRATION: $20.00   **PHOTO:** $5.00   **MONTHLY:** 0%

METHOD OF REGISTRATION

PHONE: No   **MAIL PHOTO/RESUMÉ:** Yes
PHOTO SIZE & QUANTITY: 3"X5": 2   4"X6": 0 8"X10": 5
WALK-IN: Yes   **APPOINTMENT:** No

REGISTRATION   **VISITATION**
DAYS: monthly by appt. **TIMES:**   **DAYS:**   **TIMES:**

EXTRAS

UNION: Yes   **NON-UNION:** Yes   **STAND-IN:** Yes   **PHOTO-DOUBLE:** Yes
FULL SERVICE: Yes   **FILM:** Yes   **TELEVISION:** Yes
COMMERCIALS: Yes   **VIDEO:** Yes   **PRINT:** Yes
ADULT: Yes   **YOUTH/CHILDREN:** Yes

PRINCIPALS

UNION: Yes   **NON-UNION:** Yes   **PHOTO-DOUBLE:** Yes   **STUNTS:** Yes
FULL SERVICE: Yes   **FILM:** Yes   **TELEVISION:** Yes
COMMERCIALS: Yes   **VIDEO:** Yes   **PRINT:** Yes
ADULTS: Yes   **YOUTH/CHILDREN:** Yes

NOTES/COMMENTS: PAST PROJECTS INCLUDE: SEPARATE LIVES,   "TERMINA-
TOR 2 ", REVENGE OF THE NERDS, AND MOW- CONFESSIONS & HYPNOTIC, NINJA
KID II. SEPARATE LIVES CONTACT: ANNA .

RATING: ☆ ☆ ☆ ☆ ☆

☐ AXIUM CASTING

4001 W. ALAMEDA AVE, SUITE 301   **THOMAS BROS GUIDE: PG:**   **CO-ORD:**
BURBANK , CA 91505   **1996 EDITION: PG:**   563   **CO-ORD:** D-3

TELEPHONES

INFO: 818 557-2997
WORK LINES: (Men): 310 789-4444   **(Women):** 310 789-4474
HOT LINE: 818 557-2980   **PAYROLL:**

FEES

REGISTRATION: $10.00   **PHOTO:** $0.00   **MONTHLY:** 0%

METHOD OF REGISTRATION

PHONE: No   **MAIL PHOTO/RESUMÉ:** No
PHOTO SIZE & QUANTITY: 3"X5": 0   **4"X6":** 0   **8"X10":** 0
WALK-IN: Yes   **APPOINTMENT:** No

REGISTRATION		VISITATION	
DAYS: T & TH	**TIMES:** 10-12P	**DAYS:** T & TH	**TIMES:** 10-12P

EXTRAS

UNION: Yes   **NON-UNION:** Yes   **STAND-IN:** Yes   **PHOTO-DOUBLE:** Yes
FULL SERVICE: Yes   **FILM:** Yes   **TELEVISION:** Yes
COMMERCIALS: Yes   **VIDEO:** Yes   **PRINT:** Yes
ADULT: Yes   **YOUTH/CHILDREN:** Yes

PRINCIPALS

UNION: Yes   **NON-UNION:** Yes   **PHOTO-DOUBLE:** Yes   **STUNTS:** Yes
FULL SERVICE: Yes   **FILM:** Yes   **TELEVISION:** Yes
COMMERCIALS: Yes   **VIDEO:** Yes   **PRINT:** Yes
ADULTS: Yes   **YOUTH/CHILDREN:** Yes

NOTES/COMMENTS: MOST RECENT CREDITS, HOW TO MAKE AN AMERICAN QUILT, THE ICE CREAM DIMENSION.

RATING: ☆☆☆☆☆

☐ BACK TO ONE/HOLLYWOOD CASTING

P.O. Box 753   **THOMAS BROS GUIDE: PG:**   **CO-ORD:**
Hollywood Ca 90078-0753   **1996 EDITION: PG:**   **CO-ORD:**

TELEPHONES

INFO:
WORK LINES: (Men):   **(Women):**
HOT LINE: **PAYROLL:**

FEES

REGISTRATION: $0.00   **COMPUTER IMAGING FEE:** $20.00   **MONTHLY:** 0%

METHOD OF REGISTRATION

PHONE: No   **MAIL PHOTO/RESUMÉ:** Yes
PHOTO SIZE & QUANTITY: 3"X5": 4   **4"X6":** 0   **8"X10":** 2
WALK-IN: No   **APPOINTMENT:** **

REGISTRATION		VISITATION	
DAYS: Mail Only	**TIMES:** No	**DAYS:** No	**TIMES:** No

EXTRAS

UNION: Yes   **NON-UNION:** Yes   **STAND-IN:** Yes   **PHOTO-DOUBLE:** Yes
FULL SERVICE: Yes   **FILM:** Yes   **TELEVISION:** Yes
COMMERCIALS: Yes   **VIDEO:** Yes   **PRINT:** Yes
ADULT: Yes   **YOUTH/CHILDREN:** Yes

PRINCIPALS

UNION: Yes   **NON-UNION:** Yes   **PHOTO-DOUBLE:** Yes   **STUNTS:** Yes
FULL SERVICE: Yes   **FILM:** Yes   **TELEVISION:** Yes
COMMERCIALS: Yes   **VIDEO:** Yes   **PRINT:** Yes
ADULTS: Yes   **YOUTH/CHILDREN:** Yes

NOTES/COMMENTS: WILL CALL WHEN NEEDED. TAFT-HARTLEY IS A GREAT POSSIBILITY! SPECIALIZE IN UNIQUE, COMMERCIALS, INDUSTRIAL & EDUCATIONAL. PHOTOS POSTED ON WORLD WIDE WEB ON BACK TO ONE WEB PAGES AND VIA E-MAIL

RATING: ☆☆☆☆

❑B.J. CASTING

3439 Cahuenga Blvd. West
Studio City Ca 90068

THOMAS BROS GUIDE: PG: 23	**CO-ORD:** E-2
1996 EDITION: PG: 563	**CO-ORD:** B5

TELEPHONES

INFO: 213 851-7881
WORK LINES: (Men):   **(Women):**
HOT LINE: **PAYROLL:**

FEES

REGISTRATION: $20.00   **PHOTO:** $0.00   **MONTHLY:** 0%

METHOD OF REGISTRATION

PHONE: No   **MAIL PHOTO/RESUMÉ:** Yes
PHOTO SIZE & QUANTITY: 3"X5": 2   **4"X6":** 0 **8"X10":** 0
WALK-IN: Yes   **APPOINTMENT:** Yes

REGISTRATION   VISITATION

DAYS: M-F   **TIMES:** 11a-6p   **DAYS:** Call   **TIMES:**

EXTRAS

UNION: Yes   **NON-UNION:** Yes   **STAND-IN:** Yes   **PHOTO-DOUBLE:** Yes
FULL SERVICE: Yes   **FILM:** Yes **TELEVISION:** Yes
COMMERCIALS: Yes   **VIDEO:** Yes   **PRINT:** Yes
ADULT: Yes   **YOUTH/CHILDREN:** Yes

PRINCIPALS

UNION: Yes   **NON-UNION:** Yes   **PHOTO-DOUBLE:** Yes   **STUNTS:** Yes
FULL SERVICE: Yes   **FILM:** Yes **TELEVISION:** Yes
COMMERCIALS: Yes   **VIDEO:** Yes   **PRINT:** Yes
ADULTS: Yes   **YOUTH/CHILDREN:** Yes

NOTES/COMMENTS: ONLY ACCEPTS SERIOUS ACTORS. ALSO HAS TALENT MGT. DIVISION. SAG NO FEE. CREDITS- SPRING FEVER USA, MASTER OF MENACE

RATING: ☆☆☆☆

❑BILL DANCE CASTING

3518 W. Cahuenga Blvd. 210
Los Angeles Ca 90068

THOMAS BROS GUIDE: PG: 24	**CO-ORD:** B-6
1996 EDITION: PG: 563	**CO-ORD:** B-6

TELEPHONES

INFO: 213 878-1131
WORK LINES: (Men):   **(Women):**
HOT LINE: **PAYROLL:**

FEES

REGISTRATION: $15.00   **PHOTO:** $0.00   **MONTHLY:** 0%

METHOD OF REGISTRATION

PHONE: No   **MAIL PHOTO/RESUMÉ:** No
PHOTO SIZE & QUANTITY: 3"X5": 1   **4"X6":**   **8"X10":**
WALK-IN: No   **APPOINTMENT:** No

REGISTRATION   VISITATION

DAYS: M-Thur   **TIMES:** 12p   **DAYS:** No   **TIMES:**

EXTRAS

UNION: Yes   **NON-UNION:** Yes   **STAND-IN:** Yes   **PHOTO-DOUBLE:** Yes
FULL SERVICE: Yes   **FILM:** Yes **TELEVISION:** No
COMMERCIALS: Yes   **VIDEO:** Yes   **PRINT:** Yes
ADULT: Yes   **YOUTH/CHILDREN:** No

PRINCIPALS

UNION: No   **NON-UNION:** No   **PHOTO-DOUBLE:** No   **STUNTS:** No
FULL SERVICE: No   **FILM:** No   **TELEVISION:** No
COMMERCIALS: No   **VIDEO:** No **PRINT:** No
ADULTS: No   **YOUTH/CHILDREN:** No

NOTES/COMMENTS: SAG NO FEE. CREDITS-Sgt. Bilko, Devil In A Blue Dress, Congo, Mortal Combat

RATING: ☆☆☆☆☆

☐ CAST OF THOUSANDS

4011 W. Magnolia
Burbank, Ca 91050

THOMAS BROS GUIDE: PG: **CO-ORD:**
1996 EDITION: PG: 533   **CO-ORD:** D-7

TELEPHONES

INFO: 818 955-9995
WORK LINES: (Men): 818 955-8419   **(Women):** 818 955-8498
HOT LINE: **PAYROLL:**

FEES

REGISTRATION: $10.00   **COMPUTER IMAGING FEE:** $0.00 cash **MONTHLY:** 5%

METHOD OF REGISTRATION

PHONE: No   **MAIL PHOTO/RESUMÉ:** No
PHOTO SIZE & QUANTITY: 3"X5": 1   **4"X6":**   **8"X10":**
WALK-IN: Yes   **APPOINTMENT:** No

REGISTRATION	VISITATION
DAYS: T **TIMES**: 2p - 5p	**DAYS**: TU **TIMES**: 2p - 5p

EXTRAS

UNION: Yes   **NON-UNION:** Yes   **STAND-IN:** Yes   **PHOTO-DOUBLE:** Yes
FULL SERVICE: Yes   **FILM:** Yes   **TELEVISION:** Yes
COMMERCIALS: Yes   **VIDEO:** Yes   **PRINT:** Yes
ADULT: Yes   **YOUTH/CHILDREN:** Yes

PRINCIPALS

UNION: Yes   **NON-UNION:** Yes   **PHOTO-DOUBLE:** Yes   **STUNTS:** Yes
FULL SERVICE: Yes   **FILM:** Yes   **TELEVISION:** Yes
COMMERCIALS: Yes   **VIDEO:** Yes   **PRINT:** Yes
ADULTS: Yes   **YOUTH/CHILDREN:** Yes

NOTES/COMMENTS: Credits include NIXON, WESTSIDE WALTZ, THE JUDDS Mini-Series, A WALK IN THE CLOUD, TENDERFOOT. WILL ACCEPT UNSOLICITED PHOTOS

RATING: ☆☆☆

☐ CASTING WORKS LA

1317 N. San Fernando Blvd. Suite 326
Sherman Oaks, Ca 91403

THOMAS BROS GUIDE: PG: **CO-ORD:**
1996 EDITION: PG: 563   **CO-ORD:** H-1

TELEPHONES

INFO: 818 556-6218
WORK LINES: (Men):   **(Women):**
HOT LINE: **PAYROLL:**

FEES

REGISTRATION: $0.00   **COMPUTER IMAGING FEE:** $0.00 cash **MONTHLY:** 5%

METHOD OF REGISTRATION

PHONE: No   **MAIL PHOTO/RESUMÉ:** No
PHOTO SIZE & QUANTITY: 3"X5": 1   **4"X6":**   **8"X10":**
WALK-IN: No   **APPOINTMENT:** No

REGISTRATION	VISITATION
DAYS: M,W,F **TIMES**: 10a-11³⁰a	**DAYS**: TU,THU **TIMES**: 11¹⁵a-12¹⁵p

EXTRAS

UNION: No   **NON-UNION:** No   **STAND-IN:** No   **PHOTO-DOUBLE:** No
FULL SERVICE: No   **FILM:** No   **TELEVISION:** No
COMMERCIALS: No   **VIDEO:** No   **PRINT:** No
ADULT: No   **YOUTH/CHILDREN:** No

PRINCIPALS ONLY

UNION: Yes   **NON-UNION:** Yes   **PHOTO-DOUBLE:** Yes   **STUNTS:** Yes
FULL SERVICE: Yes   **FILM:** Yes   **TELEVISION:** Yes
COMMERCIALS: Yes   **VIDEO:** Yes   **PRINT:** Yes
ADULTS: Yes   **YOUTH/CHILDREN:** Yes

NOTES/COMMENTS: WILL ACCEPT UNSOLICITED PHOTOS FROM NEW FACES.
CREDITS INCLUDE : THE POET, LEADERSHIP 200, RABIT BROWN AND THE LAST OF THE BLUES

RATING: ☆☆☆☆☆

☐ CENEX CASTING

1700 W. Burbank Blvd.   **THOMAS BROS GUIDE: PG:** 24 **CO-ORD:** C-2
Burbank Ca 91506   **1996 EDITION: PG:**   563   **CO-ORD:** E-3

TELEPHONES
INFO: 818 562-2800
WORK LINES: (Men):   **(Women):**
HOT LINE: **PAYROLL:**

FEES
REGISTRATION: $0.00   **COMPUTER IMAGING FEE:** $20.00 cash **MONTHLY:** 5%

METHOD OF REGISTRATION
PHONE: No   **MAIL PHOTO/RESUMÉ:** No
PHOTO SIZE & QUANTITY: 3"X5":   **4"X6":**   **8"X10":**
WALK-IN: Yes   **APPOINTMENT:** No

REGISTRATION	VISITATION
DAYS: M,W,F **TIMES:** 10a-11³⁰a	**DAYS:** TU,THU **TIMES:** 11¹⁵a-12¹⁵p

EXTRAS
UNION: Yes   **NON-UNION:** Yes   **STAND-IN:** Yes   **PHOTO-DOUBLE:** Yes
FULL SERVICE: Yes   **FILM:** Yes **TELEVISION:** Yes
COMMERCIALS: Yes   **VIDEO:** Yes   **PRINT:** Yes
ADULT: Yes   **YOUTH/CHILDREN:** Yes

PRINCIPALS
UNION: No   **NON-UNION:** No   **PHOTO-DOUBLE:** No   **STUNTS:** No
FULL SERVICE: No   **FILM:** No   **TELEVISION:** No
COMMERCIALS: Yes   **VIDEO:** No **PRINT:** No
ADULTS: No   **YOUTH/CHILDREN:** No

NOTES/COMMENTS: CENEX IS THE LARGEST NON-UNION & AFTRA CASTING
AGENCY. PRINCIPAL S.A.G. COMMERCIALS. WILL ACCEPT UNSOLICITED PHOTOS

RATING: ☆ ☆ ☆ ☆ ☆

☐ CENTRAL CASTING

1700 Burbank Blvd.   **THOMAS BROS GUIDE: PG:** 24 **CO-ORD:** C-2
Burbank Ca 91506   **1996 EDITION: PG:**   563   **CO-ORD:** E-3

TELEPHONES
INFO: 818 562-2700
WORK LINES: (Men): 818 562-2707   **(Women):** 818 562-2713
HOT LINE: 818   **PAYROLL:**

FEES
REGISTRATION: $0.00   **COMPUTER IMAGING FEE:** $20.00   **MONTHLY:** 0%

METHOD OF REGISTRATION
PHONE: No   **MAIL PHOTO/RESUMÉ:** No
PHOTO SIZE & QUANTITY: 3"X5":   **4"X6":**   **8"X10":**
WALK-IN: Yes   **APPOINTMENT:** No

REGISTRATION	VISITATION
DAYS: TU,THU **TIMES:** 2p-3:30p	**DAYS:** A-L Tu, M-Z Th **TIMES:** 9³⁰a-10³⁰a

EXTRAS
UNION: Yes   **NON-UNION:** Yes   **STAND-IN:** Yes   **PHOTO-DOUBLE:** Yes
FULL SERVICE: Yes   **FILM:** Yes **TELEVISION:** Yes
COMMERCIALS: Yes   **VIDEO:** Yes   **PRINT:** Yes
ADULT: Yes   **YOUTH/CHILDREN:** No

PRINCIPALS
UNION: **NON-UNION:**   **PHOTO-DOUBLE:**   **STUNTS:**
FULL SERVICE: **FILM:**   **TELEVISION:**
COMMERCIALS: **VIDEO:**   **PRINT:**
ADULTS: **YOUTH/CHILDREN:**

NOTES/COMMENTS: THE LARGEST EXTRA CASTING AGENCY IN ENTERTAINMENT
HISTORY. VISITITATION IS LIMITED TO ONCE A MONTH FOR PAID UP UNION
MEMBERS.

RATING: ☆ ☆ ☆ ☆ ☆

☐ CHRISTOPHER GRAY CASTING

1538 N. HAYWORTH Ave. Suite: 6
Los Angeles Ca 90046

THOMAS BROS GUIDE: PG: **CO-ORD:**
1996 EDITION: PG: 593   **CO-ORD:** B-4

TELEPHONES

INFO: 213 850-7114
WORK LINES: (Men):   **(Women):**
HOT LINE: 213 656-6599   **PAYROLL:**

FEES

REGISTRATION: $0.00   **PHOTO:** $10.00   **MONTHLY:** 0%

METHOD OF REGISTRATION

PHONE: No   **MAIL PHOTO/RESUMÉ:** Yes
PHOTO SIZE & QUANTITY: 3"X5":   **4"X6":** No **8"X10":** No
WALK-IN: No   **APPOINTMENT:** ONLY

REGISTRATION   VISITATION

DAYS: APPT ONLY **TIMES:** APPT   **DAYS:** No   **TIMES:** No

EXTRAS

UNION: Yes   **NON-UNION:** Yes   **STAND-IN:** Yes   **PHOTO-DOUBLE:** Yes
FULL SERVICE: Yes   **FILM:** Yes **TELEVISION:** Yes
COMMERCIALS: Yes   **VIDEO:** Yes   **PRINT:** Yes
ADULT: Yes   **YOUTH/CHILDREN:** Yes

PRINCIPALS

UNION: Yes   **NON-UNION:** Yes   **PHOTO-DOUBLE:** Yes   **STUNTS:** Yes
FULL SERVICE: Yes   **FILM:** Yes **TELEVISION:** Yes
COMMERCIALS: Yes   **VIDEO:** Yes   **PRINT:** Yes
ADULTS: Yes   **YOUTH/CHILDREN:** Yes

NOTES/COMMENTS: RECENT PROJECTS INCLUDE WORK ON KAZAM, DEATH BENEFITS, TUSKEGEE AIRMEN, LOST HIGH, LEAVING LOS VEGAS W/ NICHOLAS CAGE

RATING: ☆ ☆ ☆ ☆ ☆

☐ CREATIVE IMAGE

6363 Wilshire Blvd. 500
Los Angeles Ca 90048

THOMAS BROS GUIDE: PG: 42 **CO-ORD:** E1
1996 EDITION: PG: 633   **CO-ORD:** A2

TELEPHONES

INFO: 213 655-9505
WORK LINES: (Men):   **(Women):**
HOT LINE: **PAYROLL:**

FEES

REGISTRATION: $20.00   **PHOTO:** $0.00   **MONTHLY:** 0%

METHOD OF REGISTRATION

PHONE: No   **MAIL PHOTO/RESUMÉ:** Yes
PHOTO SIZE & QUANTITY: 3"X5": 1   **4"X6":** 1 **8"X10":** 1
WALK-IN: No   **APPOINTMENT:** Yes

REGISTRATION   VISITATION

DAYS: No   **TIMES:** No   **DAYS:** No   **TIMES:** No

EXTRAS

UNION: Yes   **NON-UNION:** Yes   **STAND-IN:** Yes   **PHOTO-DOUBLE:** Yes
FULL SERVICE: Yes   **FILM:** No   **TELEVISION:** Yes
COMMERCIALS: Yes   **VIDEO:** Yes   **PRINT:** Yes
ADULT: Yes   **YOUTH/CHILDREN:** Yes

PRINCIPALS

UNION: Yes   **NON-UNION:** Yes   **PHOTO-DOUBLE:** Yes   **STUNTS:** No
FULL SERVICE: Yes   **FILM:** No   **TELEVISION:** Yes
COMMERCIALS: Yes   **VIDEO:** Yes   **PRINT:** Yes
ADULTS: Yes   **YOUTH/CHILDREN:** Yes

NOTES/COMMENTS: CONTACT TANYA.

RATING: ☆ ☆ ☆ ☆ ☆

☐DAVID ANTHONY'S BACKGROUND PLAYERS

30 Raymond Ave. # 211   **THOMAS BROS GUIDE: PG:**   **CO-ORD:**
Pasadena CA 91103   **1996 EDITION: PG:**   **CO-ORD:**

TELEPHONES

INFO: 213 243-1974
WORK LINES: (Men): 818 683-2528   **(Women):** 818 683-2529
HOT LINE: **PAYROLL:**

FEES

REGISTRATION: $5.00   **PHOTO:** $0.00   **MONTHLY:** 0%

METHOD OF REGISTRATION

PHONE: No   **MAIL PHOTO/RESUMÉ:** Yes
PHOTO SIZE & QUANTITY: 3"X5": 1   **4"X6":** 0 **8"X10":** 1
WALK-IN: No   **APPOINTMENT:** Only

REGISTRATION   VISITATION

DAYS: By Appt   **TIMES:** By Appt   **DAYS:** By Appt   **TIMES:** By Appt

EXTRAS

UNION: Yes   **NON-UNION:** Yes   **STAND-IN:** Yes **PHOTO-DOUBLE:** Yes
FULL SERVICE: Yes   **FILM:** Yes   **TELEVISION:** Yes
COMMERCIALS: Yes   **VIDEO:** Yes   **PRINT:** Yes
ADULT: Yes   **YOUTH/CHILDREN:** Yes

PRINCIPALS

UNION: Yes   **NON-UNION:** Yes   **PHOTO-DOUBLE:** Yes   **STUNTS:** Yes
FULL SERVICE: Yes   **FILM:** Yes   **TELEVISION:** Yes
COMMERCIALS: Yes   **VIDEO:** Yes   **PRINT:** Yes
ADULTS: Yes   **YOUTH/CHILDREN:** Yes

NOTES/COMMENTS: New casting service with experienced casting director. A unique casting service.

RATING: ✰ ✰ ✰ ✰

☐DENNIS HANSEN CASTING

8829 National Blvd. Suite #33   **THOMAS BROS GUIDE: PG:**   **CO-ORD:**
Culver City, CA 90232   **1996 EDITION: PG:**   **CO-ORD:**

TELEPHONES

INFO: 213 558-4870
WORK LINES: (Men):   **(Women):**
HOT LINE: **PAYROLL:**

FEES

REGISTRATION: $13.00   **PHOTO:** $0.00   **MONTHLY:** 0%

METHOD OF REGISTRATION

PHONE: No   **MAIL PHOTO/RESUMÉ:** Yes
PHOTO SIZE & QUANTITY: 3"X5": 1   **4"X6":** 1 **8"X10":** 1
WALK-IN: No   **APPOINTMENT:** Yes

REGISTRATION   VISITATION

DAYS: No   **TIMES:** No   **DAYS:** No   **TIMES:** No

EXTRAS

UNION: Yes   **NON-UNION:** Yes   **STAND-IN:** Yes **PHOTO-DOUBLE:** Yes
FULL SERVICE: Yes   **FILM:** Yes   **TELEVISION:** Yes
COMMERCIALS: Yes   **VIDEO:** Yes   **PRINT:** Yes
ADULT: Yes   **YOUTH/CHILDREN:** No

PRINCIPALS

UNION: Yes   **NON-UNION:** Yes   **PHOTO-DOUBLE:** Yes   **STUNTS:** No
FULL SERVICE: Yes   **FILM:** Yes   **TELEVISION:** Yes
COMMERCIALS: Yes   **VIDEO:** Yes   **PRINT:** Yes
ADULTS: Yes   **YOUTH/CHILDREN:** No

NOTES/COMMENTS: CASTS MANY MAJOR ACTION ADVENTURE AND COMEDY MOTION PICTURES. BUT GOOD TAFT-HARTLEY POTENTIAL.

RATING: ✰ ✰ ✰ ✰ ✰

☐ FIRST ACTION CASTING

1174 Canto Place   **THOMAS BROS GUIDE: PG:**   **CO-ORD:**
Studio City CA 91604   **1996 EDITION: PG: 562**   **CO-ORD:** H-7

TELEPHONES

INFO: 818 754-0960
WORK LINES: (Men):   **(Women):**
HOT LINE: **PAYROLL:**

FEES

REGISTRATION: $30.00 N-U **PHOTO:** $5.00   **MONTHLY:** 0%

METHOD OF REGISTRATION

PHONE: No   **MAIL PHOTO/RESUMÉ:** Yes
PHOTO SIZE & QUANTITY: 3"X5": 2   **4"X6":** 0   **8"X10":** 5
WALK-IN: Yes   **APPOINTMENT:** YES

REGISTRATION		**VISITATION**	
DAYS: M-F	**TIMES:** 11a-3p	**DAYS:**	**TIMES:**

EXTRAS

UNION: Yes   **NON-UNION:** Yes   **STAND-IN:** Yes   **PHOTO-DOUBLE:** Yes
FULL SERVICE: Yes   **FILM:** Yes   **TELEVISION:** Yes
COMMERCIALS: Yes   **VIDEO:** Yes   **PRINT:** Yes
ADULT: Yes   **YOUTH/CHILDREN:** Yes

PRINCIPALS

UNION: Yes   **NON-UNION:** Yes   **PHOTO-DOUBLE:** Yes   **STUNTS:** Yes
FULL SERVICE: Yes   **FILM:** Yes   **TELEVISION:** Yes
COMMERCIALS: Yes   **VIDEO:** Yes   **PRINT:** Yes
ADULTS: Yes   **YOUTH/CHILDREN:** Yes

NOTES/COMMENTS: DIAGNOSE MURDER, CYBER KIDS, DEADLY GAMES, TRIGGER HAPPY. MENTION BACK TO ONE RECEIVE $10.00 DISCOUNT OFF REGISTRATION FEE.

RATING: ☆ ☆ ☆ ☆

☐ FRANZ PIERRE CASTING

P.O. Box 7971   **THOMAS BROS GUIDE: PG:**   **CO-ORD:**
Culver City, Ca 90233   **1996 EDITION: PG:**   **CO-ORD:**

TELEPHONES

INFO:
WORK LINES: (Men):   **(Women):**
HOT LINE: **PAYROLL:**

FEES

REGISTRATION: $0.00   **PHOTO:** $0.00   **MONTHLY:** 0%

METHOD OF REGISTRATION

PHONE: Yes   **MAIL PHOTO/RESUMÉ:** MAIL ONLY
PHOTO SIZE & QUANTITY: 3"X5": 2   **4"X6":** 0   **8"X10":** 2
WALK-IN: No   **APPOINTMENT:** No

REGISTRATION		**VISITATION**	
DAYS: By Appt	**TIMES:** By Appt	**DAYS:** No	**TIMES:** No

EXTRAS

UNION: Yes   **NON-UNION:** Yes   **STAND-IN:** Yes   **PHOTO-DOUBLE:** Yes
FULL SERVICE: Yes   **FILM:** Yes   **TELEVISION:** Yes
COMMERCIALS: Yes   **VIDEO:** Yes   **PRINT:** Yes
ADULT: Yes   **YOUTH/CHILDREN:** No

PRINCIPALS

UNION: Yes   **NON-UNION:** Yes   **PHOTO-DOUBLE:** Yes   **STUNTS:** No
FULL SERVICE: Yes   **FILM:** Yes   **TELEVISION:** Yes
COMMERCIALS: Yes   **VIDEO:** Yes   **PRINT:** Yes
ADULTS: Yes   **YOUTH/CHILDREN:** No

NOTES/COMMENTS: GREAT TAFT-HARTLEY POTENTIAL. CAST A LOT OF TV, FILM AND COMMERCIALS. DOES A LOT OF UNIQUE PROJECTS! MAIL ONLY

RATING: ☆ ☆ ☆ ☆

❑ HAGERMAN & ASSOCIATES CASTING

505 S. Beverly Dr. Suite 315   THOMAS BROS GUIDE: PG: CO-ORD:
Beverly Hills CA 90212   1996 EDITION: PG: 632   CO-ORD: G-3

TELEPHONES
INFO: 310 285-7765
WORK LINES: (Men):   (Women):
HOT LINE: PAYROLL:

FEES
REGISTRATION: $20.00   PHOTO: $0.00   MONTHLY: 0%

METHOD OF REGISTRATION
PHONE: No   MAIL PHOTO/RESUMÉ: Yes
PHOTO SIZE & QUANTITY: 3"X5": 1   4"X6":0   8"X10": 1
WALK-IN: No   APPOINTMENT: Yes

REGISTRATION   VISITATION
DAYS: See Notes   TIMES: No   DAYS: No   TIMES: No

EXTRAS
UNION: Yes   NON-UNION: Yes   STAND-IN: Yes   PHOTO-DOUBLE: Yes
FULL SERVICE: No   FILM: No   TELEVISION: No
COMMERCIALS: Yes   VIDEO: Yes   PRINT: Yes
ADULT: Yes   YOUTH/CHILDREN: No

PRINCIPALS
UNION: NON-UNION: PHOTO-DOUBLE: STUNTS:
FULL SERVICE: FILM: TELEVISION:
COMMERCIALS: VIDEO: PRINT:
ADULTS: YOUTH/CHILDREN:

NOTES/COMMENTS: PHOTO MUST BE SUBMITTED FIRST. CALL FOR DATE & TIME
OF TWICE MONTHLY REGISTRATION. **DOES A LOT OF MUSIC VIDEOS. GREAT
PAY, FUN ASSIGNMENTS. CAST MUSIC VIDEOS FOR MANY TOP MUSIC GROUPS**

RATING: ✩ ✩ ✩ ✩ ✩

❑ IDELL JAMES CASTING

626 Santa Monica Blvd. #315   THOMAS BROS GUIDE: PG: 40 CO-ORD: F-6
Santa Monica Ca 90401   1996 EDITION: PG: 671   CO-ORD: D-2

TELEPHONES
INFO: 310 394-3919
WORK LINES: (Men):   (Women):
HOT LINE: 310 394-3919   PAYROLL:

FEES
REGISTRATION: $0.00   PHOTO: $20.00   MONTHLY: 0%

METHOD OF REGISTRATION
PHONE: No   MAIL PHOTO/RESUMÉ: Yes
PHOTO SIZE & QUANTITY: 3"X5": 2   4"X6": 2   8"X10": 2
WALK-IN: No   APPOINTMENT: Yes

REGISTRATION   VISITATION
DAYS: No   TIMES: No   DAYS: No   TIMES: No

EXTRAS
UNION: Yes   NON-UNION: No   STAND-IN: Yes   PHOTO-DOUBLE: Yes
FULL SERVICE: No   FILM: No   TELEVISION: No
COMMERCIALS: Yes   VIDEO: Yes   PRINT: Yes
ADULT: Yes   YOUTH/CHILDREN: No

PRINCIPALS
UNION: NON-UNION: PHOTO-DOUBLE: STUNTS:
FULL SERVICE: FILM: TELEVISION:
COMMERCIALS: VIDEO: PRINT:
ADULTS: YOUTH/CHILDREN:

NOTES/COMMENTS: CONTACT PHOTOGRAPHER RICH HOGAN 213 467-2628 FOR
PHOTOS.

RATING: ✩ ✩ ✩ ✩ ✩

LANE MODEL AND TALENT AGENCY

14071 Windsor Place THOMAS BROS GUIDE: PG: **23** CO-ORD: **D2**
Santa Ana Ca 92705 1996 EDITION: PG: CO-ORD:

TELEPHONES
INFO: 714 731-1420
WORK LINES: (Men): (Women):
HOT LINE: PAYROLL:

FEES
REGISTRATION: $0.00 PHOTO: $0.00 MONTHLY: 0%

METHOD OF REGISTRATION
PHONE: No MAIL PHOTO/RESUMÉ: Yes
PHOTO SIZE & QUANTITY: 3"X5": 0 4"X6": 0 8"X10": 1
WALK-IN: No APPOINTMENT: No

REGISTRATION VISITATION
DAYS: Call TIMES: Call DAYS: Call TIMES: Call

EXTRAS
UNION: Yes NON-UNION: Yes STAND-IN: Yes PHOTO-DOUBLE: Yes
FULL SERVICE: Yes FILM: Yes TELEVISION: Yes
COMMERCIALS: Yes VIDEO: Yes PRINT: Yes
ADULT: Yes YOUTH/CHILDREN: Yes

PRINCIPALS
UNION: Yes NON-UNION: Yes PHOTO-DOUBLE: Yes STUNTS: Yes
FULL SERVICE: Yes FILM: Yes TELEVISION: Yes
COMMERCIALS: Yes VIDEO: Yes PRINT: Yes
ADULTS: Yes YOUTH/CHILDREN: Yes

NOTES/COMMENTS: MAIL COMPOSITE, ZED CARD OR HEADSHOT WITH
S.A.S.LG.E. MUST HAVE EXPERIENCE. SEEKING BI-LINGUAL TALENT OF ALL
AGES. SUBMIT V.O. TAPE AND DEMO TAPE IF AVAILABLE. CONTACT: GRACE

RATING: ☆☆☆☆

☐ LATIN CONNECTION

1426 No. Avenue 55 THOMAS BROS GUIDE: PG: 36 CO-ORD: B-1
Los Angeles Ca 90042 1996 EDITION: PG: 595 CO-ORD: B-1

TELEPHONES
INFO: 213 257-9748
WORK LINES: (Men): (Women):
HOT LINE: PAYROLL:

FEES
REGISTRATION: $0.00 PHOTO: $0.00 MONTHLY: 10%

METHOD OF REGISTRATION
PHONE: No MAIL PHOTO/RESUMÉ: Yes
PHOTO SIZE & QUANTITY: 3"X5": 1 4"X6": 0 8"X10": 1
WALK-IN: No APPOINTMENT: Only

REGISTRATION VISITATION
DAYS: Call TIMES: Call DAYS: No TIMES: No

EXTRAS
UNION: Yes NON-UNION: Yes STAND-IN: Yes PHOTO-DOUBLE: Yes
FULL SERVICE: Yes FILM: Yes TELEVISION: Yes
COMMERCIALS: Yes VIDEO: Yes PRINT: Yes
ADULT: Yes YOUTH/CHILDREN: Yes

PRINCIPALS
UNION: Yes NON-UNION: Yes PHOTO-DOUBLE: Yes STUNTS: Yes
FULL SERVICE: Yes FILM: Yes TELEVISION: Yes
COMMERCIALS: Yes VIDEO: Yes PRINT: Yes
ADULTS: Yes YOUTH/CHILDREN: Yes

NOTES/COMMENTS: ALSO VOICE-OVERS. CONTACT: BETTY DENT, PERSONAL
MGR. BY APPOINTMENT ONLY. NEW REGISTRANTS CALL AFTER 7:30 P.M.. VERY
GOOD AGENCY TO WORK FOR. SPECIALIZE IN MARIACHI BAND, FLAMENCO &
FOLKLOCRIO DANCERS AND PIANO PLAYERS

RATING: ☆☆☆☆☆

☐ M & J MANAGEMENT

P.O. Box 1913
San Gabriel, CA 91776

THOMAS BROS GUIDE: PG: CO-ORD:
1996 EDITION: PG: CO-ORD:

TELEPHONES
INFO: 818 286-4008
WORK LINES: (Men):   (Women):
HOT LINE: PAYROLL:

FEES
REGISTRATION: $0.00   PHOTO: $0.00   MONTHLY: 0%

METHOD OF REGISTRATION
PHONE: No   MAIL PHOTO/RESUMÉ: Yes
PHOTO SIZE & QUANTITY: 3"X5": 2   4"X6": 0 8"X10": 2
WALK-IN: No   APPOINTMENT: Only

REGISTRATION   VISITATION
DAYS: Call   TIMES: Call   DAYS: No   TIMES: No

EXTRAS
UNION: Yes   NON-UNION: Yes   STAND-IN: Yes   PHOTO-DOUBLE: Yes
FULL SERVICE: Yes   FILM: Yes   TELEVISION: Yes
COMMERCIALS: Yes   VIDEO: Yes   PRINT: Yes
ADULT: No   YOUTH/CHILDREN: Yes

PRINCIPALS
UNION: Yes   NON-UNION: Yes   PHOTO-DOUBLE: Yes   STUNTS: No
FULL SERVICE: Yes   FILM: Yes   TELEVISION: Yes
COMMERCIALS: Yes   VIDEO: Yes   PRINT: Yes
ADULTS: No   YOUTH/CHILDREN: Yes

NOTES/COMMENTS: SPECIALIZE IN CHILDREN. NEWBORNS TO 18 YEARS.
REGISTRATION ONCE PER MONTH FOR NEW CLIENTS.

RATING: ☆ ☆ ☆ ☆

☐ M.R. COOPER CASTING

P.O. Box 461614
Los Angeles, CA 90046

THOMAS BROS GUIDE: PG: CO-ORD:
1996 EDITION: PG: CO-ORD:

TELEPHONES
INFO: 213 613-1565
WORK LINES: (Men):   (Women):
HOT LINE: 213 845-4750   PAYROLL:

FEES
REGISTRATION: $0.00   PHOTO: $20.00   MONTHLY: 0%

METHOD OF REGISTRATION
PHONE: No   MAIL PHOTO/RESUMÉ: Yes
PHOTO SIZE & QUANTITY: 3"X5": 0   4"X6": 0 8"X10": 1
WALK-IN: No   APPOINTMENT: Yes

REGISTRATION   VISITATION
DAYS: TIMES: DAYS: TIMES:

EXTRAS
UNION: Yes   NON-UNION: Yes   STAND-IN: Yes   PHOTO-DOUBLE: Yes
FULL SERVICE: Yes   FILM: Yes   TELEVISION: Yes
COMMERCIALS: Yes   VIDEO: Yes   PRINT: Yes
ADULT: Yes   YOUTH/CHILDREN: Yes

PRINCIPALS
UNION: Yes   NON-UNION: Yes   PHOTO-DOUBLE: Yes   STUNTS: Yes
FULL SERVICE: Yes   FILM: Yes   TELEVISION: Yes
COMMERCIALS: Yes   VIDEO: Yes   PRINT: Yes
ADULTS: Yes   YOUTH/CHILDREN: Yes

NOTES/COMMENTS: EXCELLENT PEOPLE. ESTABLISHED COMPANY W/ VERY
EXPERIENCED CASTING DIRECTORS. GOOD TAFT HARTLEY POTENTIAL. VERY
HOT! RECENT CREDITS: BLACK PANTHER, COSMIC SLOP, TANG, CROSSROADS
CAFE, NED & STACY AND TALES FROM THE HOOD. T.V. SERIES:, FRIDAYS

RATING: ☆ ☆ ☆ ☆ ☆

☐ MAGIC CASTING

1660 Cougar Ridge Rd.
Buetton, CA 93463

THOMAS BROS GUIDE: PG: CO-ORD:
1996 EDITION: PG: CO-ORD:

TELEPHONES
INFO: 805 688-3702
WORK LINES: (Men):   (Women):
HOT LINE: PAYROLL:

FEES
REGISTRATION: N-U $10.00, SAG - $10.00   PHOTO: $0.00 MONTHLY: 0

METHOD OF REGISTRATION
PHONE: Yes   MAIL PHOTO/RESUMÉ: Yes
PHOTO SIZE & QUANTITY: 3"X5": 1   4"X6": 0 8"X10": 1
WALK-IN: No   APPOINTMENT: No

REGISTRATION   VISITATION
DAYS: NO   TIMES: NO   DAYS: NO   TIMES: NO

EXTRAS
UNION: Yes   NON-UNION: Yes   STAND-IN: Yes PHOTO-DOUBLE: Yes
FULL SERVICE: Yes   FILM: Yes   TELEVISION: Yes
COMMERCIALS: Yes   VIDEO: Yes   PRINT: Yes
ADULT: Yes   YOUTH/CHILDREN: Yes

PRINCIPALS
UNION: Yes   NON-UNION: Yes   PHOTO-DOUBLE: Yes   STUNTS: Yes
FULL SERVICE: Yes   FILM: Yes   TELEVISION: Yes
COMMERCIALS: Yes   VIDEO: Yes   PRINT: Yes
ADULTS: Yes   YOUTH/CHILDREN: Yes

NOTES/COMMENTS: Please call for specific registration procedure.

RATING: ☆ ☆ ☆ ☆

☐ MESSENGER ASSOCIATES CASTING

P.O. BOX 2380
TOLUCA LAKE, CA 91601

THOMAS BROS GUIDE: PG: 23 CO-ORD: D-4
1996 EDITION: PG: 563   CO-ORD: C-4

TELEPHONES
INFO: 818 995-3575
WORK LINES: (Men): 818 760-3783   (Women): 818 760-3696
HOT LINE: PAYROLL: 818 755-4750

FEES
REGISTRATION: $0.00   COMPUTER IMAGING FEE: $20.00 N-U

METHOD OF REGISTRATION
PHONE: No   MAIL PHOTO/RESUMÉ: Yes
PHOTO SIZE & QUANTITY: 3"X5": 4   4"X6": 0 8"X10": 2
WALK-IN: No   APPOINTMENT: Registers Once A Month

REGISTRATION   VISITATION
DAYS: By Appt   TIMES: By Appt.   DAYS: No   TIMES: No

EXTRAS
UNION: Yes   NON-UNION: Yes   STAND-IN: Yes PHOTO-DOUBLE: Yes
FULL SERVICE: Yes   FILM: Yes   TELEVISION: Yes
COMMERCIALS: Yes   VIDEO: Yes   PRINT: Yes
ADULT: Yes   YOUTH/CHILDREN: No

PRINCIPALS
UNION: Yes   NON-UNION: Yes   PHOTO-DOUBLE: Yes   STUNTS: No
FULL SERVICE: Yes   FILM: Yes   TELEVISION: Yes
COMMERCIALS: Yes   VIDEO: Yes   PRINT: Yes
ADULTS: Yes   YOUTH/CHILDREN: No

NOTES/COMMENTS: PHOTO MUST BE SUBMITTED FIRST. CALL 10A-10:30A M-F FOR
DATE & TIME. REGISTERS TWICE A MONTH. CONTACT: TRISH OR CHARLIE

RATING: ☆ ☆ ☆ ☆ ☆

□NATIVE AMERICAN CASTING

5805 Buchanan Street	**THOMAS BROS GUIDE: PG:** **CO-ORD:**
Los Angeles, CA 90042	**1996 EDITION: PG:** **CO-ORD:**

TELEPHONES

INFO: 213 255-6880
WORK LINES: (Men): **(Women):**
HOT LINE: 213 257-4768 **PAYROLL:**

FEES

REGISTRATION: $0.00   **PHOTO:** $0.00   **MONTHLY:** 0%

METHOD OF REGISTRATION

PHONE: Yes **MAIL PHOTO/RESUMÉ:** Yes
PHOTO SIZE & QUANTITY: 3"X5": 2 **4"X6":** 0 **8"X10":** 1
WALK-IN: No **APPOINTMENT:** Only

REGISTRATION   VISITATION

DAYS: By Appt   **TIMES:** By Appt   **DAYS:** No   **TIMES:** No

EXTRAS

UNION: Yes   **NON-UNION:** Yes   **STAND-IN:** Yes **PHOTO-DOUBLE:** Yes
FULL SERVICE: Yes   **FILM:** Yes   **TELEVISION:** Yes
COMMERCIALS: Yes   **VIDEO:** Yes   **PRINT:** Yes
ADULT: Yes   **YOUTH/CHILDREN:** Yes

PRINCIPALS

UNION: Yes   **NON-UNION:** Yes   **PHOTO-DOUBLE:** Yes   **STUNTS:** Yes
FULL SERVICE: Yes   **FILM:** Yes   **TELEVISION:** Yes
COMMERCIALS: Yes   **VIDEO:** Yes   **PRINT:** Yes
ADULTS: Yes   **YOUTH/CHILDREN:** Yes

NOTES/COMMENTS: THEY SPECIALIZE IN NATIVE AMERICAN, AND ETHNIC
GOOD TAFT-HARTLEY POTENTIAL. Contact: Bonnie Paradise

RATING: ☆ ☆ ☆

□NAT JOHNSON CASTING

5042 Wilshire Blvd. Suite 467	**THOMAS BROS GUIDE: PG:** **CO-ORD:**
Los Angeles CA 90036	**1996 EDITION: PG:** **CO-ORD:**

TELEPHONES

INFO: 310 418-2019
WORK LINES: (Men): **(Women):**
HOT LINE: 310 518 9792 **PAYROLL:**

FEES

REGISTRATION: $00.00   **PHOTO:** $0.00   **MONTHLY:** 0%

METHOD OF REGISTRATION

PHONE: No **MAIL PHOTO/RESUMÉ:** Yes
PHOTO SIZE & QUANTITY: 3"X5": 1 **4"X6":** 0 **8"X10":** 0
WALK-IN: No **APPOINTMENT:** Yes

REGISTRATION   VISITATION

DAYS: APPT ONLY **TIMES:** APPT ONLY **DAYS:** APPT ONLY **TIME:** APPT ONLY

EXTRAS

UNION: Yes   **NON-UNION:** Yes   **STAND-IN:** Yes **PHOTO-DOUBLE:** Yes
FULL SERVICE: Yes   **FILM:** Yes   **TELEVISION:** Yes
COMMERCIALS: Yes   **VIDEO:** Yes   **PRINT:** Yes
ADULT: Yes   **YOUTH/CHILDREN:** Yes

PRINCIPALS

UNION: Yes   **NON-UNION:** Yes   **PHOTO-DOUBLE:** Yes   **STUNTS:** Yes
FULL SERVICE: Yes   **FILM:** Yes **TELEVISION:** Yes
COMMERCIALS: Yes   **VIDEO: Yes**   **PRINT:** Yes
ADULTS: Yes   **YOUTH/CHILDREN:** Yes

NOTES/COMMENTS: CAST ALL TYPES. RECENT PROJECTS INCLUDE MARTIN,
ROC, SOUTH CENTRAL, MAN & THE SIGN.

RATING: ☆ ☆ ☆ ☆ ☆

☐ PAGE, JEAN MANAGEMENT

5315 Oakdale Ave.
Woodland Hills CA 91364

THOMAS BROS GUIDE: PG: 13 **CO-ORD:** F1
1996 EDITION: PG: 560   **CO-ORD:** E2

TELEPHONES
INFO: 818 703-7328
WORK LINES: (Men):   **(Women):**
HOT LINE: **PAYROLL:**

FEES
REGISTRATION: $0.00   **PHOTO:** $0.00   **MONTHLY:** 0%

METHOD OF REGISTRATION
PHONE: No   **MAIL PHOTO/RESUMÉ:** Yes
PHOTO SIZE & QUANTITY: 3"X5": 1   **4"X6":** 1   **8"X10":** 1
WALK-IN: No   **APPOINTMENT:** Only

REGISTRATION		VISITATION	
DAYS: No	**TIMES:** No	**DAYS:** No	**TIMES:** No

EXTRAS
UNION: Yes   **NON-UNION:** Yes   **STAND-IN:** Yes   **PHOTO-DOUBLE:** Yes
FULL SERVICE: Yes   **FILM:** Yes   **TELEVISION:** Yes
COMMERCIALS: Yes   **VIDEO:** Yes   **PRINT:** Yes
ADULT: No   **YOUTH/CHILDREN:** Yes

PRINCIPALS
UNION: Yes   **NON-UNION:** No   **PHOTO-DOUBLE:** Yes   **STUNTS:** No
FULL SERVICE: Yes   **FILM:** Yes   **TELEVISION:** Yes
COMMERCIALS: Yes   **VIDEO:** Yes   **PRINT:** Yes
ADULTS: No   **YOUTH/CHILDREN:** Yes

NOTES/COMMENTS: CHILDREN ONLY. 2 WEEKS-17 YEARS OLD. ALL ETHNIC. SNAPSHOTS FOR UP TO 3 YEARS OF AGE. COMPOSITES 4 YEARS PLUS. CONTACT: JEAN PAGE

RATING: ☆ ☆ ☆ ☆ ☆

☐ PRIME CASTING

7060 Hollywood Blvd. 1025
Hollywood CA 90028

THOMAS BROS GUIDE: PG: 34 **CO-ORD:** B-3
1996 EDITION: PG: 593   **CO-ORD:** C-4

TELEPHONES
INFO: 213 962-0377
WORK LINES: (Men):   **(Women):**
HOT LINE: **PAYROLL:**

FEES
REGISTRATION: $30.00 INCLUDES PHOTO   **MONTHLY:** 0%

METHOD OF REGISTRATION
PHONE: NO   **MAIL PHOTO/RESUMÉ:** Yes
PHOTO SIZE & QUANTITY: 3"X5": 1   **8"X10":** 0
WALK-IN: Yes   **APPOINTMENT:** No

REGISTRATION		VISITATION	
NON-UNION DAYS: M-F	**TIMES:** 11a-4p	**DAYS:** M-F	**TIMES:** 11a-5p
UNION DAYS: THU -F	**TIMES:** 11a-4p	**DAYS:** M-F	**TIMES:** 11a-5p

EXTRAS
UNION: Yes   **NON-UNION:** Yes   **STAND-IN:** Yes   **PHOTO-DOUBLE:** Yes
FULL SERVICE: Yes   **FILM:** Yes   **TELEVISION:** Yes
COMMERCIALS: Yes   **VIDEO:** Yes   **PRINT:** Yes
ADULT: Yes   **YOUTH/CHILDREN:** Yes

PRINCIPALS
UNION: Yes   **NON-UNION:** Yes   **PHOTO-DOUBLE:** Yes   **STUNTS:** Yes
FULL SERVICE: Yes   **FILM:** Yes   **TELEVISION:** Yes
COMMERCIALS: Yes   **VIDEO:** Yes   **PRINT:** Yes
ADULTS: Yes   **YOUTH/CHILDREN:** Yes

NOTES/COMMENTS: CAST MOSTLY SAG PROJECTS. GREAT TAFT-HARTLEY POTENTIAL. RECENT PROJECTS INCLUDE BORDELLO OF BLOOD TALES OF THE CRYPT, FLIPPING. GREAT FOR ADULTS & KIDS. $10.00 DISCOUNT W/ BACK TO ONE

RATING: ☆ ☆ ☆ ☆ ☆

❑PRODUCERS CASTING

P.O. Box 1527   **THOMAS BROS GUIDE: PG:**   **CO-ORD:**
Pacific Palisades CA 90272   **1996 EDITION: PG:**   **CO-ORD:**

TELEPHONES
INFO: 310 454-5233
WORK LINES: (Men):   **(Women):**
HOT LINE: **PAYROLL:**

FEES
REGISTRATION: $0.00   **PHOTO:** *$20.00   **MONTHLY:** 0%

METHOD OF REGISTRATION
PHONE: No   **MAIL PHOTO/RESUMÉ:** Yes
PHOTO SIZE & QUANTITY: 3"X5": 6   **4"X6":** 0   **8"X10":** 0
WALK-IN: No   **APPOINTMENT:** No

REGISTRATION		VISITATION	
DAYS: No	**TIMES:** No	**DAYS:** No	**TIMES:** No

EXTRAS
UNION: Yes   **NON-UNION:** No   **STAND-IN:** Yes   **PHOTO-DOUBLE:** Yes
FULL SERVICE: No   **FILM:** No   **TELEVISION:** No
COMMERCIALS: Yes   **VIDEO:** No   **PRINT:** Yes
ADULT: Yes   **YOUTH/CHILDREN:** No

PRINCIPALS
UNION: No   **NON-UNION:** No   **PHOTO-DOUBLE:** No   **STUNTS:** No
FULL SERVICE: No   **FILM:** No   **TELEVISION:** No
COMMERCIALS: No   **VIDEO:** No   **PRINT:** No
ADULTS: No   **YOUTH/CHILDREN:** No

NOTES/COMMENTS: CAST UNION COMMERCIALS ONLY, AFFILIATED W/ SUNSET CASTING. *CONTACT RICH HOGAN FOR PHOTOS AT 213 467-2628

RATING: ☆☆☆☆☆

❑RAINBOW CASTING

12501 Chandler Blvd. Suite 206   **THOMAS BROS GUIDE: PG:** 23   **CO-ORD:** B-2
NORTH HOLLYWOOD, CA 91607   **1996 EDITION: PG:** 562   **CO-ORD:** F-2

TELEPHONES
INFO: 818 752-CAST
WORK LINES: (Men): 818 753-8393   **(Women):** 818 753-8393
HOT LINE: 818 752-CAST   **PAYROLL:**

FEES
N-U REGISTRATION: $17.00   **N-U PHOTO:** $3.00
SA G Computer Imaging Fee : $15.00

METHOD OF REGISTRATION
PHONE: No   **MAIL PHOTO/RESUMÉ:** No
PHOTO SIZE & QUANTITY: 3"X5": 1   **4"X6":** 0   **8"X10":** 1
WALK-IN: Yes   **APPOINTMENT:** Yes

REGISTRATION		VISITATION	
DAYS: M-TH	**TIMES:** 11a-2p	**DAYS:** M-Th	**TIMES:** 11a-2p

EXTRAS
UNION: Yes   **NON-UNION:** Yes   **STAND-IN:** Yes   **PHOTO-DOUBLE:** Yes
FULL SERVICE: Yes   **FILM:** Yes   **TELEVISION:** Yes
COMMERCIALS: Yes   **VIDEO:** Yes   **PRINT:** Yes
ADULT: Yes   **YOUTH/CHILDREN:** Yes

PRINCIPALS
UNION: Yes   **NON-UNION:** Yes   **PHOTO-DOUBLE:** Yes   **STUNTS:** Yes
FULL SERVICE: Yes   **FILM:** Yes   **TELEVISION:** Yes
COMMERCIALS: Yes   **VIDEO:** Yes   **PRINT:** Yes
ADULTS: Yes   **YOUTH/CHILDREN:** Yes

NOTES/COMMENTS: REGISTRATION FOR CHILDREN IS WED & THUR 3:30 4:30. RECENT PROJECTS: MOTHER, PULP FICTION, DOUBLE DRAGON, SAFE PASSAGE, MY SO CALLED LIFE. SAG MEMBERS NO CHARGE

RATING: ☆☆☆☆☆

☐RON SMITH'S CELEBRITY LOOK-ALIKES

7060 Hollywood Blvd. 1215
Hollywood CA 90028

THOMAS BROS GUIDE: PG: 34 **CO-ORD:** B-3
1996 EDITION: PG: 593   **CO-ORD:** C-4

TELEPHONES
INFO: 213 467-3030
WORK LINES: (Men):   **(Women):**
HOT LINE: **PAYROLL:**

FEES
REGISTRATION: $0.00   **PHOTO:** $0.00   **MONTHLY:** 0%

METHOD OF REGISTRATION
PHONE: Yes   **MAIL PHOTO/RESUMÉ:** Yes
PHOTO SIZE & QUANTITY: 3"X5": 2   **4"X6":** 2   **8"X10":** 2
WALK-IN: Yes   **APPOINTMENT:** No

REGISTRATION		VISITATION	
DAYS: M,W	**TIMES:** 5p-6p	**DAYS:** M,W	**TIMES:** 5p-6p

EXTRAS
UNION: Yes   **NON-UNION:** Yes   **STAND-IN:** Yes   **PHOTO-DOUBLE:** Yes
FULL SERVICE: Yes   **FILM:** Yes   **TELEVISION:** Yes
COMMERCIALS: Yes   **VIDEO:** Yes   **PRINT:** Yes
ADULT: Yes   **YOUTH/CHILDREN:** Yes

PRINCIPALS
UNION: Yes   **NON-UNION:** Yes   **PHOTO-DOUBLE:** Yes   **STUNTS:** Yes
FULL SERVICE: Yes   **FILM:** Yes   **TELEVISION:** Yes
COMMERCIALS: Yes   **VIDEO:** Yes   **PRINT:** Yes
ADULTS: Yes   **YOUTH/CHILDREN:** Yes

NOTES/COMMENTS: CAST PEOPLE WHO LOOK LIKE CELEBRITIES OR FAMOUS PEOPLE. VERY GOOD PAY AND GREAT EXPOSURE. CONTACT: RON SMITH.

RATING: ☆ ☆ ☆ ☆

☐SCREEN CHILDREN AGENCY

12444 Ventura Blvd. 103
Studio City CA 91604

THOMAS BROS GUIDE: PG: 23 **CO-ORD:** D-4
1996 EDITION: PG: 562   **CO-ORD:** F-6

TELEPHONES
INFO: 818 846-4300
WORK LINES: (Men):   **(Women):**
HOT LINE: **PAYROLL:**

FEES
REGISTRATION: $0.00   **PHOTO:** $0.00   **MONTHLY:** 0%

METHOD OF REGISTRATION
PHONE: No   **MAIL PHOTO/RESUMÉ:** Yes
PHOTO SIZE & QUANTITY: 3"X5": 3   **4"X6":** 3   **8"X10":** 3
WALK-IN: No   **APPOINTMENT:** No

REGISTRATION		VISITATION	
DAYS: No	**TIMES:** No	**DAYS:** No	**TIMES:** No

EXTRAS
UNION: Yes   **NON-UNION:** Yes   **STAND-IN:** Yes   **PHOTO-DOUBLE:** Yes
FULL SERVICE: Yes   **FILM:** Yes   **TELEVISION:** Yes
COMMERCIALS: Yes   **VIDEO:** Yes   **PRINT:** No
ADULT: No   **YOUTH/CHILDREN:** Yes

PRINCIPALS
UNION: Yes   **NON-UNION:** Yes   **PHOTO-DOUBLE:** Yes   **STUNTS:** No
FULL SERVICE: Yes   **FILM:** Yes   **TELEVISION:** Yes
COMMERCIALS: Yes   **VIDEO:** Yes   **PRINT:** Yes
ADULTS: No   **YOUTH/CHILDREN:** Yes

NOTES/COMMENTS: GREAT CHILDREN EXTRA CASTING AGENCY. CONTACT: IRENE GALLAGHER.

RATING: ☆ ☆ ☆ ☆ ☆

❏ STAR CASTING

	THOMAS BROS GUIDE: PG:	CO-ORD:
	1996 EDITION: PG:	CO-ORD:

TELEPHONES
INFO:213 936-6543
WORK LINES: (Men):   (Women):
HOT LINE: PAYROLL:

FEES
REGISTRATION:$20.00   PHOTO:$0.00   MONTHLY: 0%

METHOD OF REGISTRATION
PHONE: Call For Info   MAIL PHOTO/RESUMÉ: No
PHOTO SIZE & QUANTITY: 3"X5": 0   4"X6": 0 8"X10":
WALK-IN: No   APPOINTMENT: CALL FOR REG INFO.

REGISTRATION   VISITATION
DAYS: No   TIMES: No   DAYS: No   TIMES: No

EXTRAS
UNION:Yes   NON-UNION:Yes STAND-IN: Yes PHOTO-DOUBLE:Yes
FULL SERVICE: No   FILM:Yes   TELEVISION:Yes
COMMERCIALS:Yes   VIDEO:Yes   PRINT:Yes
ADULT:Yes   YOUTH/CHILDREN:Yes

PRINCIPALS
UNION: Yes   NON-UNION: Yes   PHOTO-DOUBLE: Yes   STUNTS: Yes
FULL SERVICE: Yes   FILM:Yes   TELEVISION:Yes
COMMERCIALS:Yes   VIDEO:Yes   PRINT:Yes
ADULTS:Yes   YOUTH/CHILDREN:Yes

NOTES/COMMENTS: LOTS OF PROJECTS INCLUDING MUSIC VIDEO. VERY ESTABLISHED COMPANY. RECENT PROJECT INCLUDING: LAWNMOWER MAN II , THE PHOPHECY, WHITE CARGO. NOMO DODGER COMMERCIAL.

RATING: ☆ ☆ ☆ ☆ ☆

❏ SUNSET CASTING

P.O. BOX 1449	THOMAS BROS GUIDE: PG:	CO-ORD:
PACIFIC PALISADES, CA 90272	1996 EDITION: PG:	CO-ORD:

TELEPHONES
INFO:310 478-2664
WORK LINES: (Men):   (Women):
HOT LINE:9   PAYROLL:

FEES
REGISTRATION:$0.00   PHOTO:$20.00   MONTHLY: 0%

METHOD OF REGISTRATION
PHONE: No   MAIL PHOTO/RESUMÉ: No
PHOTO SIZE & QUANTITY: 3"X5": 6   4"X6": 0 8"X10": 0
WALK-IN: No   APPOINTMENT:ONLY

REGISTRATION   VISITATION
DAYS:APPT ONLY TIMES: DAYS: NO   TIMES:

EXTRAS
UNION: No   NON-UNION:Yes   STAND-IN:Yes PHOTO-DOUBLE: Yes
FULL SERVICE: No   FILM: No   TELEVISION: No
COMMERCIALS:Yes   VIDEO: No   PRINT: No
ADULT:Yes   YOUTH/CHILDREN: No

PRINCIPALS
UNION: No   NON-UNION: No   PHOTO-DOUBLE: No   STUNTS: No
FULL SERVICE: No   FILM: No   TELEVISION:Yes
COMMERCIALS: No   VIDEO: No   PRINT: No
ADULTS: No   YOUTH/CHILDREN: No

NOTES/COMMENTS: ESTABLISHED COMPANY W/ VERY EXPERIENCED CASTING DIRECTORS. GREAT NON-UNION COMMERCIAL WORK POTENTIAL.

RATING: ☆ ☆ ☆ ☆ ☆

☐**T.B.S. CASTING**

8831 Sunset Blvd., Suite 310
West Hollywood CA 90069

THOMAS BROS GUIDE: PG: 33 **CO-ORD:** F-4
1996 EDITION: PG: 593   **CO-ORD:** A-4

TELEPHONES

INFO: 310 854-1955
WORK LINES: (Men):   **(Women):**
HOT LINE: **PAYROLL:**

FEES

REGISTRATION: $20.00 cash **PHOTO:** $5.00 cash **MONTHLY:** 0%

METHOD OF REGISTRATION

PHONE: Yes   **MAIL PHOTO/RESUMÉ:** Yes
PHOTO SIZE & QUANTITY: 3"X5": 1   **4"X6":** 0   **8"X10":** 1
WALK-IN: Yes   **APPOINTMENT:** NO

REGISTRATION	VISITATION
DAYS: Tu & Th **TIMES:** 12p-3pm	**DAYS:** Tu & Th **TIMES:** 12p-3p

EXTRAS

UNION: No	**NON-UNION:** Yes	**STAND-IN:** Yes	**PHOTO-DOUBLE:** Yes
FULL SERVICE: Yes	**FILM:** Yes	**TELEVISION:** Yes	
COMMERCIALS: Yes	**VIDEO:** Yes	**PRINT:** Yes	
ADULT: Yes	**YOUTH/CHILDREN:** No		

PRINCIPALS

UNION: No	**NON-UNION:** No	**PHOTO-DOUBLE:** No	**STUNTS:** no
FULL SERVICE: No	**FILM:**	**TELEVISION:** Y	
COMMERCIALS: No	**VIDEO:** No	**PRINT:** No	
ADULTS: Yes	**YOUTH/CHILDREN:** No		

NOTES/COMMENTS: GREAT TAFT-HARTLEY POTENTIAL. PAST PROJECTS INCLUDE: EMPTY NEST, PSYCHIC FRIENDS INFOMERCIALS "EQUAL JUSTICE", "THE HAND IN THE GLOVE", "LOCKWELL", "BALTIMORE", AND "HOLLYWOOD PARK RACEWAY" ROC, LARRY SANDERS SHOW- 3 SEASONS. SAG NO FEE.

RATING: ☆ ☆ ☆ ☆ ☆

☐**terrence/atmosphere casting**

7095 Hollywood Blvd. 814
Hollywood CA 90028

THOMAS BROS GUIDE: PG: 34 **CO-ORD:** B-3
1996 EDITION: PG: 593   **CO-ORD:** C4

TELEPHONES

INFO: MAIL ONLY
WORK LINES: (Men):   **(Women):**
HOT LINE: **PAYROLL:**

FEES

REGISTRATION: $0.00   **PHOTO:** $0.00   **MONTHLY:** 0%

METHOD OF REGISTRATION

PHONE: No   **MAIL PHOTO/RESUMÉ:** Yes
PHOTO SIZE & QUANTITY: 3"X5": 2   **4"X6":** 0   **8"X10":** 2
WALK-IN: No   **APPOINTMENT:** No

REGISTRATION	VISITATION
DAYS: No **TIMES:** No	**DAYS:** No **TIMES:** No

EXTRAS

UNION: Yes	**NON-UNION:** Yes	**STAND-IN:** Yes	**PHOTO-DOUBLE:** Yes
FULL SERVICE: No	**FILM:** No	**TELEVISION:** No	
COMMERCIALS: Yes	**VIDEO:** Yes	**PRINT:** Yes	
ADULT: Yes	**YOUTH/CHILDREN:** No		

PRINCIPALS

UNION: No	**NON-UNION:** Yes	**PHOTO-DOUBLE:** Yes	**STUNTS:** No
FULL SERVICE: No	**FILM:** No	**TELEVISION:** No	
COMMERCIALS: Yes	**VIDEO:** Yes	**PRINT:** Yes	
ADULTS: Yes	**YOUTH/CHILDREN:** No		

NOTES/COMMENTS: SEND ALL SUBMISSIONS C/O TERRENCE HARRIS. GOOD COMPANY

RATING: ☆ ☆ ☆ ☆

☐TIN LIZZY AUTO CASTING

9770 E. Beach St. Ste 8   **THOMAS BROS GUIDE: PG:** 24 **CO-ORD:** A-6
Bellflower, CA 90076   **1996 EDITION: PG:**   **CO-ORD:**

TELEPHONES
INFO: 310 920-1215
WORK LINES: (Men):   **(Women):**
HOT LINE: **PAYROLL:**

FEES
REGISTRATION: $0.00   **PHOTO:** $0.00   **MONTHLY:** 0%

METHOD OF REGISTRATION
PHONE: NO   **MAIL PHOTO/RESUMÉ:** MAIL ONLY
PHOTO SIZE & QUANTITY: 3"X5": 8   **4"X6":** 0 **8"X10":** 0
WALK-IN: No   **APPOINTMENT:** No

REGISTRATION		VISITATION	
DAYS: CALL	**TIMES:** CALL	**DAYS:** No	**TIMES:** No

EXTRAS
UNION: No   **NON-UNION:** No   **STAND-IN:** No   **PHOTO-DOUBLE:** No
FULL SERVICE: No   **FILM:** No   **TELEVISION:** No
COMMERCIALS: No   **VIDEO:** No   **PRINT:** No
ADULT: No   **YOUTH/CHILDREN:** No

PRINCIPALS
UNION: No   **NON-UNION:** No   **PHOTO-DOUBLE:** No   **STUNTS:** No
FULL SERVICE: No   **FILM:** No   **TELEVISION:** No
COMMERCIALS: No   **VIDEO:** No   **PRINT:** No
ADULTS: No   **YOUTH/CHILDREN:** No

NOTES/COMMENTS: CAST CARS & VEHICLES IN MOVIES. ANY MAKE, MODEL OR CONDITION BUT MUST RUN. PHOTOS MUST BE (4) FRONT 3/4 ANGLE SHOTS & (4) REAR 3/4 ANGLE SHOTS - 3X5. THEY PAY VERY GOOD.

RATING: ☆ ☆ ☆ ☆ ☆

☐WEBSTER - KOLICH CASTING

859 N. Hollywood Way, Box 217   **THOMAS BROS GUIDE: PG:** 24 **CO-ORD:** A2
Burbank CA 91505   **1993 EDITION: PG:** 563 **CO-ORD:** C2

TELEPHONES
INFO: 818 567-0524
WORK LINES: (Men):   **(Women):**
HOT LINE: **PAYROLL:**

FEES
REGISTRATION: $0.00   **PHOTO:** $0.00   **MONTHLY:** 0%

METHOD OF REGISTRATION
PHONE: No   **MAIL PHOTO/RESUMÉ:** Yes
PHOTO SIZE & QUANTITY: 3"X5": 2   **4"X6":** 2 **8"X10":** 2
WALK-IN: No   **APPOINTMENT:** Only

REGISTRATION		VISITATION	
DAYS: By Appt	**TIMES:** By Appt	**DAYS:** By Appt	**TIMES:** By Appt

EXTRAS
UNION: Yes   **NON-UNION:** Yes   **STAND-IN:** Yes   **PHOTO-DOUBLE:** Yes
FULL SERVICE: Yes   **FILM:** Yes   **TELEVISION:** Yes
COMMERCIALS: Yes   **VIDEO:** Yes   **PRINT:** Yes
ADULT: Yes   **YOUTH/CHILDREN:** Yes

PRINCIPALS
UNION: No   **NON-UNION:** No   **PHOTO-DOUBLE:** No   **STUNTS:** No
FULL SERVICE: No   **FILM:** No   **TELEVISION:** No
COMMERCIALS: No   **VIDEO:** No   **PRINT:** No
ADULTS: No   **YOUTH/CHILDREN:** No

NOTES/COMMENTS:

RATING: ☆ ☆ ☆ ☆ ☆

☐WILD BUNCH, The

5854 Jamieson Avenue
Encino CA 90069

THOMAS BROS GUIDE: PG: CO-ORD:
1996 EDITION: PG: CO-ORD:

TELEPHONES
INFO: 818 342-8282
WORK LINES: (Men):   (Women):
HOT LINE: PAYROLL:

FEES
REGISTRATION: $15.00 initial PHOTO: $5.00 cash QUARTERLY: $15.00

METHOD OF REGISTRATION
PHONE: Yes   MAIL PHOTO/RESUMÉ: Yes
PHOTO SIZE & QUANTITY: 3"X5": 4   4"X6": 0 8"X10": 4
WALK-IN: No   APPOINTMENT: Yes

REGISTRATION   VISITATION
DAYS: CALL FOR INFO   TIMES: CALL FOR INFO   DAYS:
TIMES:

EXTRAS
UNION: Yes	NON-UNION: Yes	STAND-IN: Yes	PHOTO-DOUBLE: Yes
FULL SERVICE: Yes	FILM: Yes	TELEVISION: Yes	
COMMERCIALS: Yes	VIDEO: Yes	PRINT: Yes	
ADULT: Yes	YOUTH/CHILDREN: No		

PRINCIPALS
UNION: Yes	NON-UNION: Yes	PHOTO-DOUBLE: Yes	STUNTS: Yes
FULL SERVICE: Yes	FILM: Yes	TELEVISION: Yes	
COMMERCIALS: Yes	VIDEO: Yes	PRINT: Yes	
ADULTS: Yes	YOUTH/CHILDREN: No		

NOTES/COMMENTS: GREAT TAFT-HARTLEY POTENTIAL. THE MOST UNIQUE &
UNUSUAL CHARACTERS ANY PRODUCERS CAN REQUEST. TERRIFIC PEOPLE TO
WORK FOR. ALSO HAS GREAT BAR-B-QUES. SOMETIMES HIGHER PAY.

RATING: ☆ ☆ ☆ ☆ ☆

☐XTRAS CASTING

P.O. BOX 4145
Valley Village CA 91617

THOMAS BROS GUIDE: PG: CO-ORD:
1996 EDITION: PG: CO-ORD:

TELEPHONES
INFO: MAIL ONLY
WORK LINES: (Men):   (Women):
HOT LINE: PAYROLL:

FEES
REGISTRATION: $0.00   PHOTO: $0.00   MONTHLY: 0%

METHOD OF REGISTRATION
PHONE: No   MAIL PHOTO/RESUMÉ: Yes
PHOTO SIZE & QUANTITY: 3"X5": 2   4"X6": 0 8"X10": 2
WALK-IN: No   APPOINTMENT: No

REGISTRATION   VISITATION
DAYS: No   TIMES: No   DAYS: No   TIMES: No

EXTRAS
UNION: Yes	NON-UNION: Yes	STAND-IN: Yes	PHOTO-DOUBLE: Yes
FULL SERVICE: Yes	FILM: Yes	TELEVISION: Yes	
COMMERCIALS: Yes	VIDEO: Yes	PRINT: Yes	
ADULT: Yes	YOUTH/CHILDREN: No		

PRINCIPALS
UNION: No	NON-UNION: No	PHOTO-DOUBLE: No	STUNTS: No
FULL SERVICE: No	FILM: No	TELEVISION: No	
COMMERCIALS: No	VIDEO: No	PRINT: No	
ADULTS: No	YOUTH/CHILDREN: No		

NOTES/COMMENTS: SEND ALL SUBMISSIONS TO THOMAS THACKER. GOOD
REPUTABLE HARDWORKING COMPANY. **Recent projects include Pacific Blue,
Innocent Victim, Honey We Shrunk Ourselves,. Also Commercial and print work**

RATING: ☆ ☆ ☆ ☆

Last Minute HOLLYWOOD Extra Casting Agencies UPDATES

Please call for complete registration details

☐ A.I.M. Casting	(213) 467-9155
☐ Body Double & Parts	(310) 276-9836
☐ DMD Management	(213) 368-6156
☐ Film Casting Associates	(310) 657-8457
☐ Talent Casting	(310) 271-5995

Non-Rated Casting Agents

I **DO NOT RECOMMEND** YOU REGISTERING WITH THE FOLLOWING AGENCIES AT THIS TIME, BECAUSE OF VARIOUS CRITERIA, E.G ...*LACK OF TRUE BACKGROUND ACTING OPPORTUNITIES, PAST RECORD PERFORMANCES, LESS THAN PROFESSIONAL BUSINESS PRACTICES, INCLUDING BUT NOT LIMITED TO NON-PAYMENT & EXORBITANTLY LATE PAYMENT FOR JOBS WORKED, "THE OLD CHECK IS IN THE MAIL ROUTINE" (I BELIEVE THE SAYING STARTED IN HOLLYWOOD), THE SELLING OF JOBS, BEING REQUIRED TO TAKE EXPENSIVE ACTING CLASSES & PHOTOS, MANAGEMENT FEES AND SUCH, FAVORITISM IN HIRING PRACTICES, LACK OF OR DEBATABLE CASTING EXPERIENCES OR DEBATABLE MANAGEMENT ETHICS. ALL IN ALL I CAN NOT SEE YOU THROWING AWAY YOUR HARD EARNED MONEY OR WASTING YOUR VALUABLE TIME WITH THE FOLLOWING AGENCIES WHEN THERE ARE SO MANY GREAT PROFESSIONAL, HONEST, DEDICATED AND ETHICAL CASTING AGENCIES TO WORK WITH IN THE PREVIOUS PAGES. YOU HAVE BEEN WARNED, AN UNINFORMED PERSON AND HIS MONEY ARE SOON PARTED. BE SMART. USE YOUR OWN JUDGEMENT IF YOU DECIDE TO CONSIDER REGISTERING WITH ANY OF THE AGENCIES LISTED ON THE NEXT PAGE. THEY DO GET JOBS FROM TIME TO TIME, THAT IS HOW THEY GET YOU TO FEEL THAT THEY WILL WORK YOU A LOT. HOWEVER **DON'T BELIEVE THE HYPE.** ALSO BE AWARE OF THE ADS LISTED IN ANY FREE OR THROWAWAY PUBLICATIONS, THE PAPERS DON'T CHECK OUT THE COMPANIES OR THE INDIVIDUALS, THEY JUST TAKE THE MONEY.*

A GOOD RULE OF THUMBS IS: **NEVER PAY MORE THAN $20.00*** TO REGISTER UNLESS YOU HAVE FOUND THE AGENCIES LISTED IN **"BACK TO ONE"** WITH A "WORTHWHILE" RATING. *SEE NOTES/RATING SECTION IN THE PREVIOUS LISTINGS, THERE WILL ALWAYS BE EXCEPTION TO THIS RULE. (*NON-UNION PEOPLE ESPECIALLY. HOWEVER CASTING AGENCIES ARE NOT ALLOWED BY CONTRACT TO CHARGE **SAG** MEMBERS A FEE, ALTHOUGH MOST GET AWAY WITH CHARGING BY CALLING IT SOME TYPE OF "PROCESSING FEE" AND/OR "PHOTO FEE", WHICH THE UNION ALLOWS. SOMETIMES THIS IS NECESSARY. CALL YOUR UNION TO VOICE YOUR CONCERN REGARDING THIS ISSUE)AGAIN,* BE SMART *AND WE'LL SEE* **YOU** IN *THE MOVIES!*

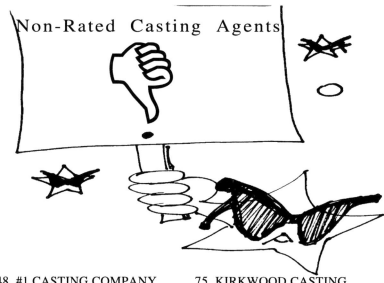

Non-Rated Casting Agents

48. #1 CASTING COMPANY
49. ACT NOW CASTING
50. ACTORS UNLIMITED
51. ALLEN CUMMINGS CASTING
52. ANGEL'S CASTING
53. AROCHA'S CASTING
54. AVA SHEVITT CASTING
55. BEVERLY -HILLS CASTING
56. BLUE MOON CASTING
57. CELEBRITY IMAGES CAST.
58. CHARLES MATTHEWS CAST.
59. CHARLES SPELLMAN CAST.
60. CHARISMA CASTING
61. CLASSIC CASTING
62. COMPLETE CASTING
63. CREATIVE CASTING
64. ELIZABETH BROOKS CAST
65. ENTERTAINMENT EXPRESS
66. ETC CASTING
67. FANTASY CASTING
68.
69. FOTO-CASTING
70. FIVE STAR CASTING
71. GILSONS CASTING
72. HOOD CASTING
73. INTRA-WORLD CASTING
74. J.D. RIPLEY CASTING

75. KIRKWOOD CASTING
76. M.A.D.S. TALENT
77. MANNEQUINS CASTING
78.
79. NEW TALENT CASTING
80. P.A.S. CASTING
81. PLATINUM CASTING
82. PRODUCTION CONNECTION
83. FIRST TAKE CASTING
84.
85. MODELS GUILD
86. MORENO CASTING
87. OUTLAW CASTING
88. PATTI KIRKPATRICK CAST.
89. R & R MANAGEMENT
90. ROGANI CASTING
91. TAURUS CASTING
92. TAYLOR CASTING
93. THE CASTING TREE
94. TOP HAT CASTING
95. 21th CENTURY CASTING
96. UNIVERSAL CASTING
97. VANITY CASTING
98. VICTOR KUBICHEK
99. WEST COAST CASTING
100. W.R.E.N. CASTING

Companies Out of Business ?

According to our research, the following companies are out of business. Their telephone numbers were disconnected and no new numbers were available, mail to their last known address was returned, they did not respond to our request for information, and they could not be contacted through our vast network of contacts or our extensive research:

0. A.C.I. CASTING
1. ATMOSPHERE ACTION
2. ANOTHER CASTING COMPANY
3. BEN'S CASTING
4. BENNY RIVERIA CASTING
5. BRITNEY LYNNE & COMPANY
6. C.D.I. CASTING
7. CASTAWAY CASTING
8. CASTBUSTERS
9. CASTING PLUS
10. CINEMA ONE CASTING
11. COACHELLA VALLEY CASTING
12. CREATIVE CONCEPTS
13. DARLA CRIST CASTING
14. DIAMOND CASTING
15. D.I.S.C. CASTING
16. D.M.C. CASTING
17. DOLPHIN CASTING
18. E.H. CASTING
19. ENCORE TALENT INC.
20. ENTERPRISE CASTING
21. ENTERTAINMENT CASTING
22. EXTRAS FOR TV COMMERCIALS
23. EXTRA SPECIAL PEOPLE
24. EXTRAS UNLIMITED
25. FILMTRAIN CASTING
26. FIVE STAR CASTING
27. FOCUS MANAGEMENT
28. GREY IMAGES CASTING
29. H.J.M.
31. INTERCONTINENTAL CASTING
32. INTERNATIONAL CASTING
33. INTERNATIONAL ENTERT.
34. J.S.D. ASSOCIATES
35. KIDS HOLLYWOOD CONNECTION
36. L'IMAGE CASTING
37. KIDS KASTING
38. M.A.D.S. CASTING
39. MANNEQUINS CASTING
40. McROBERTS & ASSOCIATES
41. METRO CASTING
42. NANCY MOTT CASTING
43. NATIONWIDE CASTING
44. NATIONAL CASTING
45. NEW FACES CASTING
46. NEW MEDIA CASTING
47. NEW STAR CASTING
48. O'BRIEN CASTING
49. PAMELA HOWARD CASTING
50. PATTERSON CASTING
51. PAULA SMITH CASTING
52. PEGASEUS CASTING
53. PHOTO CASTING PRODUCTION
54. PIX CASTING
55. PRE-PRODUCTION CASTING
56. PRESTIGE ENTERTAINMENT
57. PRODUCTION NETWORK
58. QUANTUM CASTING
59. RENT-A-GANG
60. ROX-LIN TALENT
61. SALLY PERLE CASTING
62. SHARP PRODUCTIONS
63. S.L.T. CASTING
64. STUDIO CASTING
65. SUPERIOR CASTING
66. TAKE ONE STUDIOS
67. TALENT AMERICA
68. TEAM CASTING
69. TELE-CAST INTERNATIONAL
70. THE CASTING GROUP
71. TOUCH OF TALENT CASTING
72. TOP NOTCH CASTING
73. UNIQUE CASTING GROUP
74. UNITED CASTING
75. VANDELL CASTING
76. VANITY TALENT CASTING
77. VISION CASTING
78. WAYNE KING CASTING
79. WEST COAST CASTING.

EXTRA NOTE

EXTRA NOTE

☎ Extra Calling-In Services ☎

☆ **BONUS:** Receive a **$5.00** discount off your first month's service if you tell the service that you were referred by **BACK TO ONE PUBLICATIONS.** To qualify you must send/take a copy of the cover of **"BACK TO ONE"** along with your submission.
Note: Initial set up fees include first month's service.

☎ DIRECT LINE

CALL-IN SERVICE
PARKWAY PLAZA.
23945 CALABASAS RD., STE 113A
CALABASAS, CA 91302
1996 THOMAS GUIDE PG 559 Coord E-4
(818) 753-8064
Contact - CHARLES ALESSI
Initial set-up $75.00
Fee monthly $45.00
Photos if needed $10.00
Calls for union and non-union EXTRAS.

☎ EXTRA EFFORT

14431 VENTURA BLD., STE. 277,
SHERMAN OAKS, CA 91423
✍ MAIL ADDRESS ONLY ✍
(818) 981-1144
Contact: SANDRA REITH
Initial set-up $75.00
Fee monthly $50.00
Calls for union, non-union EXTRAS
& union, non-union principals.

☎ EXTRA PHONE

1723 W. Burbank Blvd.
Burbank, CA. 91506
1996 THOMAS GUIDE PG 533 Coord H-7
(818) 972-9474
Contact: KRISHA, LAURA,
EDEN, JENNIFER
Initial set-up $90.00
Fee monthly $45.00
Photos if needed $4.00
Calls for union, non-union EXTRAS
& union, non-union principals.

☎ RAPID CASTING

224 E. Olive Ave. # 217,
Burbank, CA 91502
1996 THOMAS GUIDE PG 533 Coord E-7
(818) 558-6270
Contact: GEORGE or MICAH
$85.00 1-time Processing Fee.
10% per booking.
They place calls for union, non-union EXTRAS.
Specialize in 18-25 yr. look younger.

☎ STARTING POINT CALLING SERVICE

1827 12th Ave,
LOS ANGELES, CA 90019
1996 THOMAS GUIDE PG 633 Coord F-5
(213) 730-8509
Contact: GIL JARMOND
Initial set-up $40.00
Fee monthly $40.00
Calls for union, non-union EXTRAS
& union, non-union principals.

☎ T.C.A.

(818) 769-3350   Contact:
TERRI CRANEY -By Appt only
Initial set-up $45.00 cash
Fee monthly $45.00
Calls for union, non-union EXTRAS
& union, non-union principals.

☎ VCM TALENT MGMT

1607 N. El Centro. # 15,
Hollywood, CA 90028
1996 THOMAS GUIDE PG 533 Coord H-7
(818) 558-6270
Contact: VALENTINA
$139.00 yr. plus 10% per booking
Calls for union, non-union EXTRAS.
Special Dept for 18-25 yr. who look younger.

UNIONS -- How To Join Them

A.F.T.R.A.

REPRESENTING: TELEVISION, RADIO, COMMERCIAL
6922 HOLLYWOOD BLVD.
8TH FLOOR
P.O. BOX 4070
HOLLYWOOD, CA 90078
THOMAS BROS. GUIDE PAGE: 593 Co-Ord: D-4
TELEPHONE: (213) 461-8111
RECORDS, INDUSTRIAL
FEE: $800.00 DUES: $42.50
HOW TO JOIN: (213) 461-8111 ext. 506

ACTOR'S EQUITY

REPRESENTING: LEGITIMATE THEATRE ACTORS
6430 SUNSET BLVD.
SUITE 1002
HOLLYWOOD, CA 90028
THOMAS BROS. GUIDE PAGE: 593 Co-Ord: F-4
TELEPHONE: (213) 462-2334
FEE: $800.00 DUES: $35.00
HOW TO JOIN: No info over telephone. Send S.A.S.E.
ask for joining info, eligibility, and membership.

SCREEN ACTORS GUILD

REPRESENTING: THEATRICAL, TV, COMMERCIAL
5757 WILSHIRE BOULEVARD
LOS ANGELES, CA 90036-3600
THOMAS BROS. GUIDE PAGE: 633 Co-Ord: C-2
TELEPHONE: (213) 954-1600
FEE: $1044.00 DUES: $42.50
HOW TO JOIN: (213) 549-6772 (recorded information)
Membership Services Dept. : (213) 549-6778

The Association of Film Commissioners International

is a non-profit educational organization founded in 1975 to serve the growing needs of on-location film and television production.

Their __primary__ responsibility is to attract film and video production to their area in order to accrue locally-realized benefits from **hiring local crews and talent,** *renting local equipment, using hotel rooms, rental cars, catering services or any number of goods and services supplied on location.*

Originally, the AFCI was formed by a small group of film commissioners who wanted to share information and learn from one another's experiences. Since then, the AFCI has expanded into a worldwide network of more than 240 commissions from 19 countries. All are devoted to the business of facilitating on-location film and television production activity which generates billions of dollars annually.

Film commissions, set up by cities, counties, states, provinces or federal governments, are generally operated and funded by various agencies of government, such as the governor's office, the mayor's office, the county board of supervisors, chambers of commerce, convention and visitors bureaus, travel commissions, and business and economic development departments.

The first commission was formed in the USA during the late 1940s in response to the need for film companies to have a local government liaison who could coordinate local services such as police, state troopers and highway patrols, road and highway departments, fire departments, park rangers and all of the other essential municipal and government services for shooting a production on location.

As more production companies began to look beyond the limits of a regular production center for realistic and varied locations, more cities and states began to see the need for production coordination liaisons. They were also keenly aware of the economic benefits brought by film and video production companies to their areas.

The services provided by film commissions have expanded in response to the growth of on-location filming itself. For producers of film, episodic television and commercials, film commissions today provide a range of free services, from scouting locations within their area to troubleshooting with local officials to helping cut through paperwork and bureaucratic red tape. Some provide hard economic incentives, such as tax rebates and hotel discounts for location scouts. Others offer a variety of essential free services like research for screenwriters or liaison work with local government agencies.

Although the membership of AFCI is uniquely diverse, all the commissions have one common goal: to attract filmmakers and videographers to their respective regions by providing services that an out-of-town producer would be hard-pressed to acquire without their assistance.

As the 21st century approaches and on-location production expands worldwide, the benefits of working with film commissions are sure to increase to meet these global production demands.

Contact the film commission in your area or wherever you want to go obtain background acting jobs and express your interest in acquiring the names of production companies set to film in that areas.

Contact those productions companies and inquire about who is responsible for casting the extras for the project and follow up on the information you receive. You may need to call the production companies several times until you contact someone who has the information you seek. Remember you are a part of the talent pool in the area would like the information so you may obtain work in your local area. Call regularly. Always be polite and professional! Go for it!

Association of Film Commission Intl.
AFCI MEMBER DIRECTORY

AUSTRALIA
New South Wales Film & Television Office
John Meredith
Level 6, 1 Francis St.
Sydney, NSW 2010
AUSTRALIA
61-2-380-5599
FAX: 61-2-360-1090

Queensland Pacific Film & TV Comm.
Robin James
111 George St., 16th Fl.
Brisbane, Queensland
4000 AUSTRALIA
61-7-224-4114
FAX: 61-7-224-4077

AUSTRIA
Cineaustria
Peter Katz
11601 Wilshire Blv.,
Ste: 2480
Los Angeles, CA 90025
USA
310-477-3332
FAX: 310-477-5141

BAHAMAS
Bahamas Film and Television Commission
Darlene Davis
3450 Wilshire Blv., Ste: 208
Los Angeles, CA 90010
USA
213-385-0033
FAX: 213-383-3966

BRITISH V.I.
British Virgin Islands Film Commission
Russell Harrigan
Chief Minister's Office
Rd. Town - P.O. Box 134
Tortola, BRITISH V.I.
809-494-4119,x221
FAX: 809-494-6413

CANADA
Alberta Economic Development & Tourism
Lindsay Cherney
10155 102 St., 12th Fl.
Edmonton, AB T5J-4L6
CANADA
403-427-2005
FAX: 403-427-5924

Calgary Film Services
P.O Box 2100, Station
M (#6)
Calgary, AB T2P 2M5
CANADA
403-268-1483
FAX: 403-268-1946

Edmonton Motion Picture & TV Bureau
Doug Clement
9797 Jasper Ave.
Edmonton, AB T5J 1N9
CANADA
403-424-7870
800-661-6965
FAX: 403-426-0535

British Columbia Film Commission
Mark DesRochers
601 West Cordova St.
Vancouver, BC V6B 1G1
CANADA
604-660-2732

FAX: 604-660-4790

Burnaby Film Office
Phil Sanderson
4949 Canada Way
Burnaby, BC V5G 1M2
CANADA
604-294-7231
FAX: 604-294-7220

Okanagan-Similkameen Film Commission
Milton H. Cook
27-9015 Westside Road
Kelowna, BC V1Y 8B2
CANADA
604-769-1834
FAX: 604-769-1864

Thompson-Nicola Film Commission
Rino Elverhoy
2079 Falcon Road
Kamloops, BC V2C 4J2
CANADA
604-372-9336
FAX: 604-372-5048

Victoria/Vancouver Island Film Comm.
David B. Mills
525 Fort St.
Victoria, BC V8W 1E8
CANADA
604-386-3976
FAX: 604-385-3552

CIDO/Location Manitoba
Carole Vivier
Ste. 333-93 Lombard
Ave.

Winnipeg, MB R3B 3B1
CANADA
204-947-2040
FAX: 204-956-5261

**New Brunswick Film/
Video Commission**
Ted Bringloe
P.O. Box 6000
Fredericton, NB E3B
5H1 CANADA
506-453-2553
FAX: 506-453-2416

**Service Industries
Division, DITT**
John King
P.O. Box 8700
St. John's, Newfound-
land A1B 4J6 CANADA
709-729-5632
800-563-2299
FAX: 709-729-5936

**Yellowknife Economic
Dev. Authority**
Archie Gillies
Box 1688
Yellowknife, NT X1A
2P3 CANADA
403-873-5772
FAX: 403-920-5649

**Nova Scotia Film Dev.
Corp./Location Svc**
Helen Wickwire Foster
1724 Granville St.
Halifax, NS B3J 1X5
CANADA
902-424-7185
FAX: 902-424-0563

**Ontario Film Develop-
ment Corporation**
Gail Thomson
175 Bloor St. E., Ste:
300, North Tower
Toronto, ONT M4W
3R8 CANADA
416-314-6858
FAX: 416-314-6876
213-960-4787
FAX: 213-960-4786

**Toronto Film and
Television Office**
David Plant
2nd Fl W, City Hall
Toronto, ONT M5H 2N2
CANADA
416-392-7570
FAX: 416-392-0675

**Prince Edward Island
Film Office**
Berni Wood
West Royalty Industrial
Park
Charlottetown, PEI C1E
1B0 CANADA
902-368-6329
FAX: 902-368-6301

**Province of Quebec
Film Office**
France V. Nadeau
1755, Rene-Levesque
Blvd East, Ste: 200
Montreal, QB H2K 4P6
CANADA
514-873-7768
514-873-5027

FAX: 514-873-4388

**Montreal Film &
Television
Commmission**
Andre Lafonde
5650 D'Iberville, 4th Fl.
Montreal, QB H2G 3E4
CANADA
514-872-2883
FAX: 514-872-1153

**Quebec City Film
Bureau**
Liliane Tremblay
171 St.-Paul St., # 100
Quebec City, QB G1K
3W2 CANADA
418-692-5338
FAX: 418-692-5602

**Locations
Saskatchewan**
Mark Prasuhn
2445 -13th Ave., Ste: 340
Regina, Saskatchewan
S4P OW1 CANADA
306-347-3456
213-848-7223
FAX: 306-359-7768

City of Regina
Mark Gregory
P.O. BOX 1790
Regina, SASK S4P 3C8
CANADA
306-777-7486
FAX: 306-777-6803

Yukon Film Com.
Patti Howlett

P.O. Box 2703
Whitehorse, YT Y1A
2C6 CANADA
403-667-5400
FAX: 403-667-2634

FRANCE
Rhone-Alpes Film Commission
Serge Tachon
7 Place Antonin Poncet
Lyon, Rhone-Alpes
69002 FRANCE
33-78-37-4348
FAX: 33-78-37-5041

South of France Film Commission
Dana Theveneau
Rue Emile Miramont
Entrecasteaux, Var
83570 FRANCE
33-94-04-4070
FAX: 33-94-04-4998

GERMANY
Munich Film Information Office
Eberhard Hauff
Kaiserstrasse 39
Muenchen, D-80801
GERMANY
49-89-38 19 04-32
49-89-38 19 04-0
FAX: 49-89-38 19 04-38

HONG KONG
Hong Kong Film Liaison
Barbara Bryant
10940 Wilshire Blv.,

Ste: 1220
Los Angeles, CA 90024
USA
310-208-2678
FAX: 310-208-1869

ISRAEL
Israel Film Centre
Shlomo Sternfeld
30 Agron St.
Jerusalem, 94190
ISRAEL
972-2-220608
213-658-7924
FAX: 972-2-236303

JAMAICA
JAMPRO/Jamaica Film & Ent. Office
acqueline A. Neath
35 Trafalgar Rd, 3rd Fl
Kingston, 10
JAMAICA
809-929-9450
809-926-4613
FAX: 809-924-9650

MEXICO
Instituto Mexicano de Cinematografia
Francisco Osornio
Tepic #40, P.B. Colonia
Roma Sur
Mexico City, C.P. 06760
MEXICO
525-584-72-83
525-564-41-87
FAX: 525-574-07-12

SRI LANKA
Sri Lanka Film

Commission
Chandran Rutnam
4269 Via Marina #9
Marina del Rey, CA
90292-5013 USA
310-301-8173
FAX: 310-823-0862

THAILAND
Thailand Film Promotion Center
Eddie Chaturachinda
599 Bumrung Muang
Road
Bangkok, 10100
THAILAND
66-2-223-4690
66-2-223-4474
FAX: 66-2-223-2586

ENGLAND
British Film Com.
Sydney Samuelson /
Andrew Patrick
70 Baker St.
London, W1M 1DJ
ENGLAND
44-171-224-5000
FAX: 44-171-224-1013

Bath Film Office
Richard Angell
The Pump Room, Stall St.
Bath, Avon BA1 1LZ
UNITED KINGDOM
44-1225-477-711
FAX: 44-1225-477-221

Isle of Man Film Commission

Hilary Dugdale
Sea Terminal Buildings
Douglas, Isle of Man
Great Britain
44-1624-686841
FAX: 44-1624-686800

**The City of Liverpool
Film Office**
Helen Bingham / Lynn
Saunders
William Brown St.,
Central Libraries
Liverpool, L3 8EW
ENGLAND
44-151-225-5446
FAX: 44-151-207-1342

**Northern Screen
Commission**
Dr. Paul Mingard
Studio 15 - Design
Works - William St.
Felling, Gateshead, Tyne
& Wear NE10 OJP
ENGLAND
44-191-469-1000
FAX: 44-191-469-7000

**Yorkshire Screen
Commission**
Sue Lathan
The Workstation, 15
Paternoster Row
Sheffield, Yorkshire S1
2BX
UNITED KINGDOM
44-1142-799-115
44-1142-796-811
FAX: 44-1142-798-593
FAX: 44-1142-796-522

SCOTLAND/WALES
**Scottish Screen
Locations**
Celia Stevenson
Filmhouse, 88 Lothian
Road
Edinburgh, EH3 9BZ
SCOTLAND
44-131-229-1213
FAX: 44-131-229-1070

**Edinburgh & Lothian
Screen Industries**
George Carlaw
Filmhouse, 88 Lothian
Road
Edinburgh, EH3 9BZ
SCOTLAND
44-131-228-5960
FAX: 44-131-228-5967

**Gwynedd Film Office/
Marketing & Tourism**
Hugh Edwin Jones
Gwynedd County
Council 2
Bangor, Gwynedd LL57
4BN WALES
44-1248-670007
FAX: 44-1248-670112

UNITES STATES
ALABAMA
Alabama Film Office
Michael Boyer
401 Adams Ave.
Montgomery, AL 36130
800-633-5898

FAX: 205-242-2077

ALASKA
Alaska Film Office
3601 C St., Ste. 700
Anchorage, AK 99503
907-562-4163
FAX: 907-563-3575

ARIZONA
Arizona Film Com.
Linda Peterson Warren
3800 N. Central Ave.,
Building D
Phoenix, AZ 85012
602-280-1380
800-523-6695
FAX: 602-280-1384

**Apache Junction
Chamber of Commerce**
Carolyn A. Doty
P.O. Box 1747
Apache Junction, AZ
85217-1747
602-982-3141
FAX: 602-983-3234

**Cochise County Film
Commission**
Linda M. Small
1415 W. Melody Lane,
Building B
Bisbee, AZ 85603
602-432-9454
602-432-9200
FAX: 602-432-5016

**Greater Flagstaff
Economic Council**
David L. Spaur

1300 S. Milton, Ste:125
Flagstaff, AZ 86001
602-779-7658
800-575-7658
FAX: 602-556-0940

Globe Miami Film Commission
Sheldon Miller
1360 North Broad St.,
U.S. 60
P.O. Box 2539
Globe, AZ 85502
602-425-4495
800-804-5623
FAX: 602-425-3410

Holbrook Film Commission
William A. Kelly
465 North First Ave.
P.O. Box 70
Holbrook, AZ 86025
602-524-6225
FAX: 602-524-2159

Navajo Nation Film Office
Mary Whitehair Long
P.O. Box 2310
Window Rock, AZ
86515
602-871-6656
602-871-6655
FAX: 602-871-7355

Page/Lake Powell Film Commission
Joan Nevills-Staveley
106 S. Lake Powell Bl.
P.O. Box 727

Page, AZ 86040
602-645-2741
FAX: 602-645-3181

City of Phoenix Motion Picture Office
Luci Marshall
200 West Washington,
10th Fl.
Phoenix, AZ 85003-1611 USA
602-262-4850
FAX: 602-534-2295

City of Prescott
Daiton Rutkowski
P.O. Box 2059
Prescott, AZ 86302
602-445-3500
FAX: 602-776-6255

Scottsdale Film Office
Jan Horne
3939 Civic Center Blvd
Scottsdale, AZ 85251
602-994-2636
FAX: 602-994-7780

Sedona Film Com.
Frank Miller
P.O. Box 2489
Sedona, AZ 86339
520-204-1123
FAX: 520-204-1064

Tucson Film Office
Tom Hilderbrand
32 North Stone Ave.,
Ste: 100
Tucson, AZ 85701
602-791-4000

602-429-1000
FAX: 602-791-4963

Wickenburg Film Commission
Julie Brooks
216 North Frontier St.
P.O. Drawer CC
Wickenburg, AZ 85358
602-684-5479
FAX: 602-684-5470

Yuma Film Com
Yvonne Taylor
P.O. Box 230
Yuma, AZ 85366
602-341-1616
602-782-2567
FAX: 602-343-0038

ARKANSAS
Arkansas Motion Picture Dev. Office
Suzy Lilly
1 State Capital Mall,
Room 2C-200
Little Rock, AR 72201
501-682-7676
FAX: 501-682-FILM

Eureka Springs Chamber of Commerce
Bob Purvis
P.O. Box 551
Eureka Springs, AR
72632
501-253-8737

CALIFORNIA
California Film Commission

Patti Stolkin Archuletta
6922 Hollywood Blv.,
Ste: 600
Hollywood, CA 90028-6126
213-736-2465
800-858-4PIX
FAX: 213-736-2522

**City of Big Bear Lake
Film Office**
Romy David
39707 Big Bear
P.O. Box 10000
Big Bear Lake, CA 92315
909-878-3040
FAX: 909-866-6766

**Chico Chamber of
Commerce**
Susan Peterson
500 Main St.
P.O. Box 3038
Chico, CA 95927
916-891-5556 x 326
FAX: 916-891-3613

**Catalina Island Film
Commission**
Shirley Davy
P.O. Box 217
Avalon, CA 90704
310-510-7646
FAX: 310-510-1646

**El Dorado/Tahoe Film
Commission**
Kathleen Dodge
542 Main St.
Placerville, CA 95667

916-626-4400
800-457-6279
FAX: 916-642-1624

**Eureka-Humboldt
County CVB**
Kathleen Gordon-Burke
1034 Second St.
Eureka, CA 95501-0541
707-443-5097
800-338-7352 in CA
800-346-3482
FAX: 707-443-5115

**City of Fillmore Film
Commission**
Noreen Withers
524 Sespe Ave.
P.O. Box 487
Fillmore, CA 93016
805-524-3701
FAX: 805-524-5707

**Kern County Board of
Trade**
Ann Gutcher
2101 Oak St.
P. O. Bin 1312
Bakersfield, CA 93302
805-861-2367
FAX: 805-861-2017

**Long Beach Office of
Special Events**
Jo Ann Burns
One World Trade Center,
Ste: 300
Long Beach, CA 90831-0300
310-436-7703
310-613-6256 Mobile

FAX: 310-435-5653

**Motion Picture and
Television Division**
Jonathan Roberts
6922 Hollywood Blv.,
Ste: #614
Los Angeles, CA 90028
213-461-8614
FAX: 213-847-5009

**Monterey County Film
Commission**
Julie Armstrong
801 Lighthouse Ave.
P.O. Box 111
Monterey, CA 93942-0111
408-646-0910
FAX: 408-655-9244

**Orange County Film
Office**
Cristi J. Silverberg
One City Blv. W, Ste: 401
Orange, CA 92668
714-634-2900
FAX: 714-978-0742

**Palm Springs Desert
Resourts CVB**
Kim McNulty
69-930 Highway 111,
Suite 201
Rancho Mirage, CA 92270
619-770-9000
800-96-RESORTS
FAX: 619-770-9001

City of Pasadena

Ariel Penn
100 N. Garfield Ave. #103
Pasadena, CA 91109
818-405-4152
FAX: 818-405-4785

Placer County Film Office
Jennifer Jasper
13460 Lincoln Way, #A
Auburn, CA 95603
916-887-2111
FAX: 916-887-2134

Redding Convention & Visitors Bureau
Sherry Ferguson
777 Auditorium Drive
Redding, CA 96001
916-225-4100
800-874-7562
FAX: 916-225-4354

Ridgecrest Film Commission
Ray Arthur
100 W. California Ave.
Ridgecrest, CA 93555
619-375-8202
800-847-4830
FAX: 619-371-1654

Inland Empire Film Commission
Sheri Davis
3281 East Guasti Road,
Ste: 100
Ontario, CA 91761
909-390-8080 ext 231
FAX: 909-390-8077

Sacramento Area Film Commission
Jan Decker
1421 K St.
Sacramento, CA 95814
916-264-7777
FAX: 916-264-7788

San Diego Film Commission
Wally Schlotter
402 West. Broadway,
Ste. 1000
San Diego, CA
92101-3585
619-234-3456
FAX: 619-234-0571

San Francisco Film & Video Arts Comm.
Lorrae Rominger
Mayor's Office - 401
Van Ness Ave., #417
San Francisco, CA
94102
415-554-6244
FAX: 415-554-6503

San Jose Film & Video Commission
Joe O'Kane
333 West San Carlos,
Ste. #1000
San Jose, CA 95110
408-295-9600
800-726-5673
FAX: 408-295-3937

San Luis Obispo County Film Com.
Jonni Eylar

1041 Chorro St., Ste. E
San Luis Obispo, CA
93401
805-541-8000
FAX: 805-543-9498

Santa Barbara County Film Council
Robert J. Weirick
5390 Overpass Rd., Ste. F
P.O. Box 92111
Santa Barbara, CA
93190-2111
805-962-6668
FAX: 805-969-5960

Santa Clarita SCV Film Liaison Office
Cheryl Adams
23920 Valencia Blv.,
Ste: 125
Santa Clarita, CA
91355-2175
800-4FILMSC
805-259-4787
FAX: 805-259-8628

Santa Cruz County Conf. & Vis. Council
701 Front St.
Santa Cruz, CA 95060
408-425-1234
FAX: 408-425-1260

Santa Monica Mountains NRA
Alice Allen
30401 Agoura Road,
Ste: 100
Agoura Hills, CA 91301
818-597-1036 ext 212

FAX: 818-597-8537

Sonoma County Film Liaison Office
Sheree Green
5000 Roberts Lake Road, Ste: A
Rohnert Park, CA 94928
707-586-8100
707-586-8110
FAX: 707-586-8111

Temecula Valley Film Council
Jo Moulton
43174 Business Park Dr.
Temecula, CA 92590
909-699-6267
FAX: 909-694-1999

COLORADO
Colorado Motion Picture & TV Com.
Michael Klein
1625 Broadway, Ste: #1700
Denver, CO 80202
303-620-4500
FAX: 303-620-4545

Boulder County Film Commission
Shelly Helmerick
P.O. Box 73
Boulder, CO 80306
303-442-1044
800-444-0447
FAX: 303-938-8837

Fremont/Custer County Film Com.
Greg Tabuteau
P.O. Box 8
Canon City, CO 81215
719-275-5149

Colorado Springs Film Commission
Paula Vickerman
30 South Nevada Ave., Ste: #405
Colorado Springs, CO 80903
719-578-6943
FAX: 719-578-6394

Mayor's Office of Art, Culture & Film
Ronald F. Pinkard
280 14th St.
Denver, CO 80202
303-640-2686
FAX: 303-640-2737

Fort Morgan Area Film Commission
Sandy Schneider
710 East Railroad Ave.
P.O. Box 100
Fort Morgan, CO 80701
303-867-3001
FAX: 303-867-3039

Greeley/Weld County Film Commission
Leeann Sterling
1407 8th Ave.
Greeley, CO 80631
303-352-3566
FAX: 303-352-3572

Yampa Valley Film

Board, Inc
Stacey Kramer
Box 772305
Steamboat Springs, CO 80477
303-879-0882
FAX: 303-879-2543

Trinidad Film Com.
Jean Corley
136 West Main St.
Trinidad, CO 81082
719-846-9412
800-748-1970
FAX: 719-846-4550

CONNECTICUT
Connecticut Film, Video & Media Office
Bert Brown
865 Brook St.
Rocky Hill, CT 06067-3405
203-258-4339
203-258-4399
203-258-4301
FAX: 203-258-4275

Danbury Film Office
Margaret Gagnon
72 West St.
P.O. Box 406
Danbury, CT 06813
203-743-0546
800-841-4488
FAX: 203-794-1439

Delaware Film Office
Carol Myers
99 Kings Highway
P.O. Box 1401

Dover, DE 19903
302-739-4271
800-441-8846
FAX: 302-739-5749

WASHINGTON, D.C.
**Mayor's Office of
Motion Picture & TV**
Crystal Palmer
717 14th St., NW, 12th Fl.
Washington, D.C. 20005
202-727-6600
FAX: 202-727-3787

FLORIDA
**Florida Entertainment
Commission**
John Reitzammer
505 17th St.
Miami Beach, FL 33139
305-673-7468
FAX: 305-673-7168

**Space Coast Film
Commission**
Bonnie King
c/o Brevard Cty Gvt Ctr,
2725 St. Johns
Melbourne, FL 32940
407-633-2110
800-93-OCEAN
FAX: 407-633-2112

**Film & Television
Office**
Elizabeth Wentworth
200 East Las Olas Blv.,
Ste #1850
Fort Lauderdale, FL
33301
305-524-3113

FAX: 305-524-3167

**Lee County Film
Office**
Beverly Fox
2180 W. 1st St., Ste: 306
Fort Myers, FL
33901-3219
800-330-3161
941-338-3189
FAX: 941-338-3227

**Jacksonville Film & TV
Office**
Todd Roobin
128 E. Forsythe St.,
Ste: 505
Jacksonville, FL 32202
904-630-2522
FAX: 904-630-1485

**Florida Keys & Key
West Film Commission**
Virginia Panico
402 Wall St.
P.O. Box 984
Key West, FL 33040
305-294-5988
800-527-8539
FAX: 305-294-7806

**Miami/Dade Office of
Film, TV, & Print**
Jeff Peel
111 Northwest 1st St.,
Ste: 2510
Miami, FL 33128
305-375-3288
FAX: 305-375-3266

Northwest Florida/

Okaloosa Film Comm.
Christine Pincince
1170 Martin Luther
King, Jr. Blvd.#717
P.O. Box 4097
Ft. Walton Beach, FL
32547-4097
904-651-7374
FAX: 904-651-7378

**Ocala/Marion County
Film Commission**
Sue Sargent-Latham
110 E. Silver Springs Bl.
Ocala, FL 34470
904-629-2757
FAX: 904-629-1581

**Metro Orlando Film &
Television Office**
Katherine Ramsberger
200 East Robinson St.,
Ste: #600
Orlando, FL 32801
407-422-7159
FAX: 407-843-9514

**Palm Beach County
Film Liaison Office**
Chuck Elderd
1555 Palm Beach Lakes
Blvd., Ste: 204
West Palm Beach, FL
33401
407-233-1000
FAX: 407-683-6957

**Central Florida
Development Council**
Carolyn G. Simpson
600 No. Broadway, #300

P.O. Box 1839
Bartow, FL 33830
813-534-4371
FAX: 813-533-1247

City of Tampa Motion Picture & TV Dev
Pat Hoyt
306 East Jackson
Tampa, FL 33602
813-274-8419
813-274-7501
FAX: 813-274-7176

Volusia County Film Office
Dan Ryan
123 E. Orange Ave.
P.O. Box 910
Daytona Beach, FL 32114
904-255-0415
800-544-0415
FAX: 904-255-5478

GEORGIA
Georgia Film & Videotape Office
Norman Bielowicz
285 Peachtree Center Ave., Ste 1000
Atlanta, GA 30303
404-656-3591
FAX: 404-651-9063

Savannah Film Commission
Jay M. Self
c/o City Manager's Office
P.O. Box 1027

Savannah, GA 31402
912-651-3696
FAX: 912-238-0872

HAWAII
Hawaii Film Office
Georgette Deemer
P.O. Box 2359
Honolulu, HI 96804
808-586-2570
FAX: 808-586-2572

Big Island Film Office
Marilyn Killeri
25 Aupuni St., Rm 219
Hilo, HI 96720
808-961-8366
FAX: 808-935-1205

Kauai Film Com.
Judy Drosd
4280-B Rice St.
Lihue, HI 96766
808-241-6390
FAX: 808-241-6399

Maui Film Office
Georja Skinner
200 South High St.
Wailuku, Maui, HI 96793
808-243-7710
808-243-7415
FAX: 808-243-7995

Oahu Film Office
Walea L. Constantinau
530 South King St., Room 306
Honolulu, HI 96813
808-527-6108

FAX: 808-523-4666

IDAHO
Idaho Film Bureau
Peg Owens Crist
700 W. State St., 2nd Fl.
Box 83720
Boise, ID 83720-0093
208-334-2470
800-942-8338
FAX: 208-334-2631

ILLINOIS
Illinois Film Office
Suzy Kellett
100 West Randolph, Ste: 3-400
Chicago, IL 60601
312-814-3600
FAX: 312-814-6175

Chicago Film Office
Charles Geocaris
1 North LaSalle, Ste: 2165
Chicago, IL 60602
312-744-6415
FAX: 312-744-1378

Quad Cities Dev. Group/Film Coalition
John C. Gardner
1830 2nd Ave., Ste: 200
Rock Island, IL 61201
309-326-1005
FAX: 309-788-4964

INDIANA
Indiana Film Com.
Jane Rulon
1 North Capitol, #700
Indianapolis, IN

46204-2288
317-232-8829
FAX: 317-233-6887

IOWA
Iowa Film Office
Wendol M. Jarvis
200 East Grand Ave.
Des Moines, IA 50309
515-242-4726
800-779-3456
FAX: 515-242-4859

Cedar Rapids Area Film Commission
Alice Anderson
119 First Ave. SE
P.O. Box 5339
Cedar Rapids, IA
52406-5339
319-398-5009
800-735-5557
FAX: 319-398-5089

Greater Des Moines Film Commission
Annette Hacker
601 Locust St., Ste: 222
Des Moines, IA 50309
515-286-4960
800-451-2625
FAX: 515-244-9757

KANSAS
Kansas Film Com.
Vicky Henley
700 SW Harrison St.,
Ste: 1300
Topeka, KS 66603
913-296-4927
FAX: 913-296-6988

Kansas III Film Com./ Lawrence CVB
Judy Billings
734 Vermont
Lawrence, KS 66044
913-865-4411
FAX: 913-865-4400

Manhattan Film Commission
Becky Blake
555 Poyntz, Ste: 290
Manhattan, KS 66502
913-776-8829

Wichita Convention & Visitors Bureau
Gene Countryman
100 So. Main, Ste: 100
Wichita, KS 67202
316-265-2800
FAX: 316-265-0162

KENTUCKY
Kentucky Film Commission
Russ Slone
500 Mero St., 2200
Capitol Plz Tower
Frankfort, KY 40601
502-564-3456
800-345-6591
FAX: 502-564-7588

LOUISIANA
Louisiana Film Commission
David Jones
P.O. Box 44320
Baton Rouge, LA
70804-4320

504-342-8150
FAX: 504-342-7988

Jeff Davis Parish Film Commission
Tesa Laviolette
P.O. Box 1207
Jennings, LA
70546-1207
318-821-5534
FAX: 318-821-5536

New Orleans Film And Video Commission
Kimberly Carbo
1515 Poydras St., Ste: 1200
New Orleans, LA 70112
504-565-8104
FAX: 504-565-8108

Shreveport-Bossier Film Commission
Betty Jo Lebrun
P.O. Box 1761
Shreveport, LA 71166
318-222-9391
800-551-8682
FAX: 318-222-0056

MAINE
Maine Film Office
D. Lea Girardin
State House Station 59
Augusta, ME 04333
207-287-5707
FAX: 207-287-5701

MARYLAND
Maryland Film Com.
Michael B. Styer

601 North Howard St.
Baltimore, MD
21201-4582
410-333-6633
800-333-6632
FAX: 410-333-0044

MASSACHUSETTS
Massachusetts Film Office
Robin Dawson
10 Park Plaza, Ste: 2310
Boston, MA 02116
617-973-8800
FAX: 617-973-8810

Boston Film Bureau
Peggy Ings
Room 716,
Boston City Hall
Boston, MA 02201
617-635-3245
FAX: 617-635-3031

MICHIGAN
Michigan Film Office
Janet Lockwood
525 West Ottawa
P.O. Box 30004
Lansing, MI 48933
517-373-0638
800-477-3456
FAX: 517-373-3872

Mayor's Office for Film & Television
Paul J. Piper
1126 City-County Building
Detroit, MI 48226
313-224-3430

FAX: 313-224-4128

MINNESOTA
Minnesota Film Board
Randy Adamsick / Kelly Pratt
401 No. 3rd St., Ste: 460
Minneapolis, MN 55401
612-332-6493
FAX: 612-332-3735

MISSISSIPPI
Mississippi Film Office
Ward Emling
Box 849
Jackson, MS 39205
601-359-3297
FAX: 601-359-5757

Columbus Film Commission
Carolyn Denton
P.O. Box 789
Columbus, MS 39703
601-329-1191
800-327-2686
FAX: 601-329-8969

Mississippi Gulf Coast Film Office
Jennifer White
P.O. Box 569
Gulfport, MS 39502
601-863-3807
FAX: 601-863-4555

Natchez Film Com.
P.O. Box 1485
Natchez, MS 39121
601-446-6345
800-647-6724

FAX: 601-442-0814

Oxford Film Com.
P.O. Box 965
Oxford, MS 38655
601-234-4680
FAX: 601-234-4655

Tupelo Film Com.
Jim Palmer
P.O. Box 1485
Tupelo, MS 38802-1485
601-841-6454
800-533-0611
FAX: 601-841-6558

Vicksburg Film Commission
Al Elmore
P.O. Box 110
Vicksburg, MS 39180
601-636-9421
800-221-3536
FAX: 601-636-9475

MISSOURI
Missouri Film Office
Kate Arnold-Schuck
301 West High, Rm. 630
P.O. Box 118
Jefferson City, MO 65102
314-751-9050
FAX: 314-751-7384

Kansas City, Missouri Film Office
Patti Watkins
10 Petticoat Lane, Ste: 250
Kansas City, MO 64106
816-221-0636

FAX: 816-221-0189

Saint Louis Film Office
Audrey Hutti
330 North 15th St.
Saint Louis, MO 63103
314-622-3400 x409
FAX: 314-421-2489

MONTANA
Montana Film Office
Lonie Stimac
1424 9th Ave.
Helena, MT 59620
406-444-2654
800-553-4563
FAX: 406-444-1800

Great Falls Reg. Film Liaison
Peggy Gentry
815 2nd St. South
P.O. Box 2127
Great Falls, MT 59403
800-735-8535
FAX: 406-761-6129

NEBRASKA
Nebraska Film Office
Mary Ethel Emanuel
P.O. Box 94666
Lincoln, NE 68509-4666
402-471-3797
800-228-4307
FAX: 402-471-3026

Omaha Film Com,
Julie Ginsberg /Kathy Sheppard
6800 Mercy Rd, Ste: 202
Omaha, NE 68106-2627

402-444-7736
402-444-7737
FAX: 402-444-4511

NEVEDA
Motion Picture Division/C.E.D.
Robert Hirsch
555 East Washington, Ste: 5400
Las Vegas, NV 89101
702-486-2711
FAX: 702-486-2712

NEW HAMPSHIRE
New Hampshire Film & TV Bureau
Ann Kennard
172 Pembroke Road
P.O. Box 1856
Concord, NH 03302-1856
603-271-2598
FAX: 603-271-2629

NEW JERSEY
New Jersey Motion Picture/TV Com.
Joseph Friedman
153 Halsey St.
P.O. Box 47023
Newark, NJ 07101
201-648-6279
FAX: 201-648-7350

NEW MEXICO
New Mexico Film Office
Linda Taylor Hutchison
1050 Old Pecos Trail
Santa Fe, NM 87503

505-827-7365
800-545-9871
FAX: 505-827-7369

Albuquerque TV & Film Commission
Victoria Dye
P.O. Box 26866
Albuquerque, NM 87125-6866
505-842-9918
FAX: 505-247-9101

Las Cruces Film Commission
Ted Scanlon
311 No. Downtown Mall
Las Cruces, NM 88001
505-524-8521
800-FIESTAS
505-525-2112 (prvt)
FAX: 505-524-8191

Los Alamos County Film Office
Janet Rose
P.O. Box 460
Los Alamos, NM 87544-0460
505-662-8105
FAX: 505-662-8399

NEW YORK
NewYorkSt.Gov's Off. /MP-TV Dev.
Pat Kaufman
Pier 62 W 23rd St at Hudson River #307
New York, NY 10011
212-929-0240
FAX: 212-929-0506

Greater Buffalo Conv. & Vis. Bureau
Mary E. Summers
107 Delaware Ave.
Buffalo, NY
14202-2801
716-852-0511 x 267
800-283-3256
FAX: 716-852-0131

Hudson Valley Film & Video Office, Inc.
Diane Witmer
40 Garden St., 2nd Fl.
Poughkeepsie, NY
12601
914-473-0318
FAX: 914-473-0082

Mayor's Off. Film, Theatre & Broadcastng
Patricia Reed Scott
1697 Broadway, 6th Fl.
New York, NY 10019
212-489-6710
FAX: 212-307-6237

Rochester/Finger Lakes Film/Video Off.
Jerry Stoeffhaas
126 Andrews St.
Rochester, NY
14604-1102
716-546-5490
FAX: 716-232-4822

NORTH CAROLINA
No. Carolina Film Office
William Arnold
430 North Salisbury St.
Raleigh, NC 27611

919-733-9900
800-232-9227
FAX: 919-715-0151

Western North Carolina Film Com.
Mary Nell Webb
P.O. Box 1258
Arden, NC 28704
704-687-7234
FAX: 704-687-7552

Durham Convention & Visitors Bureau
Donna Bailey-Taylor
101 East Morgan St.
Durham, NC 27701
919-687-0288
800-446-8604
FAX: 919-683-9555

Greater Wilmington Film Office
Mark Stricklin
#1 Estell Lee Place
P.O. Box 330
Wilmington, NC 28401
910-762-2611
FAX: 910-762-9765

Winston-Salem Piedmont Triad Film Comm.
Christy Johnson
601 West 4th St.
Winston-Salem, NC
27101
910-777-3787
FAX: 910-761-2209

NORTH DAKOTA

North Dakota Film Commission
Jeff Eslinger
604 East Blv., 2nd Fl.
Bismarck, ND 58505
800-328-2871
701-328-2874
701-328-2525
FAX: 701-328-4878

OHIO
Ohio Film Commission
Eve Lapolla
77 So. High St., 29th Fl.
P.O. Box 1001
Columbus, OH
43266-0413
614-466-2284
800-848-1300
FAX: 614-466-6744

Greater Cincinnati Film Commission
Lori Holladay
632 Vine St., #1010
Cincinnati, OH 45202
513-784-1744
FAX: 513-768-8963

Greater Dayton Film Commission
Ann Fensel
448 Red Haw Road
Dayton, OH 65405
513-277-8090
FAX: 513-277-8090

OKLAHOMA
Oklahoma Film Office
Mary Nell Clark
440 So Houston, Ste: 304

Tulsa, OK 74127-8945
918-581-2660
800-766-3456
FAX: 918-581-2244

OREGON
Oregon Film & Video Office
David Woolson
121 SW Salmon St.,
Ste: 300
Portland, OR 97204
503-229-5832
FAX: 503-229-6869

PENNSYLVANIA
Pennsylvania Film Bureau
Ted Hanson
Forum Bldg, Rm 449
Harrisburg, PA 17120
717-783-3456
FAX: 717-234-4560

Greater Philadelphia Film Office
Sharon Pinkenson
1600 Arch St., 12th Fl.
Philadelphia, PA 19103
215-686-2668
FAX: 215-686-3659

Pittsburgh Film Office
Dawn Keezer
Benedum Trees
Building, Ste: 1300
Pittsburgh, PA 15222
412-261-2744
FAX: 412-471-7317

PUERTO RICO

Puerto Rico Film Commission
Manuel A. Biascoechea
355 F.D. Roosevelt Ave/
Fomento Bldg #106
San Juan, PR 00918
809-758-4747
809-754-7110
FAX: 809-756-5706

SOUTH CAROLINA
So.Carolina Film Office
Isabel Hill
P.O. Box 7367
Columbia, SC 29202
803-737-0490
FAX: 803-737-3104

Upstate S.C. Film & Video Association
Angela Lockman
P.O. Box 10048
Greenville, SC 29603
803-239-3712
FAX: 803-282-8549

South Dakota Film Commission
Gary Keller
711 East Wells Ave.
Pierre, SD 57501-3369
800-952-3625
605-773-3301
FAX: 605-773-3256

SOTH DAKOTA
Badlands Film Commission
Mary Jane TerEick
P.O. Box 58
Kadoka, SD 57543-0058

605-837-2229
1-800-467-9217
FAX: 605-837-2161

TENNESSEE
Tennessee Film/Ent./ Music Comm.
Marsha Blackburn
320 6th Ave. No., 7th Fl.
Nashville, TN 37243
615-741-3456
800-251-8594
FAX: 615-741-5829

Memphis/Shelby County Film Com.
Linn Sitler
Beale St. Landing/245
Wagner Pl. #4
Memphis, TN 38103-3815
901-527-8300
FAX: 901-527-8326

Nashville Film Office
Darrah Meeley
161 Fourth Ave. North
Nashville, TN 37219
615-259-4777
FAX: 615-256-3074

TEXAS
Texas Film Commission
Tom Copeland
P.O. Box 13246
Austin, TX 78711
512-463-9200
FAX: 512-463-4114

Amarillo Film Office
Scott Owings

1000 South Polk St.
Amarillo, TX 79101
806-374-1497
800-692-1338
FAX: 806-373-3909

City of Austin
Gary Bond
P.O. Box 1088
Austin, TX 78767
512-499-2404
FAX: 512-499-6385

**Dallas/Fort Worth
Regional Film Comm.**
Roger Burke
P.O. Box 610246
DFW Airport, TX 75261
214-621-0400
800-234-5699
FAX: 214-929-0916

El Paso Film Com.
Susie Gaines
1 Civic Center Plaza
El Paso, TX 79901
915-534-0698
800-351-6024
FAX: 915-532-2963

Houston Film Com.
Rick Ferguson
801 Congress
Houston, TX 77002
713-227-3100
800-365-7575
FAX: 713-223-3816

**Irving Texas Film
Commission**
Ellen Sandoloski

6309 North O'Connor
Road, Ste: 222
Irving, TX 75039-3510
214-869-0303
800-2-IRVING
FAX: 214-869-4609

**San Antonio Film
Commission**
Kathy Rhoads
P.O. Box 2277
San Antonio, TX 78230
210-270-8700
800-447-3372x730/777
FAX: 210-270-8782

VIRGIN ISLANDS
**U.S. Virgin Islands
Film Promotion Off.**
Manny Centeno
P.O. Box 6400
St. Thomas, V.I. 00804
USVI
809-775-1444
809-774-8784
FAX: 809-774-4390

UTAH
Utah Film Commission
Leigh von der Esch
324 South State, Ste 500
Salt Lake City, UT
84114-7330
801-538-8740
800-453-8824
FAX: 801-538-8886

**Central Utah Film
Commission**
Marilyn Toone
51 South University

Ave., Ste: 110
Provo, UT 84601
801-370-8390
800-222-8824
FAX: 801-370-8050

**Color Country Film
Commission**
Penny Shelley
Mark Wade
906 N. 1400 West
St. George, UT 84770
801-628-4171
800-233-8824
FAX: 801-673-3540

**Kanab/Kane County
Film Commission**
Steve Puro
41 South 100 East
Kanab, UT 84741
801-644-5033
800-SEE-KANE
FAX: 801-644-5923

**Moab To Monument
Valley Film Com.**
Bette Stanton
50 East Center #1
Moab, UT 84532
801-259-6388
801-587-3235
FAX: 801-259-6399

**3 Park City Film
Commission**
Nancy Volmer
P.O. Box 1630
Park City, UT 84060
801-649-6100
800-453-1360

FAX: 801-649-4132

VIRGINIA
Virginia Film Office
Marcie Oberndorf-Kelso
901 East Byrd St., 19th
Flr. (Zip 23219)
P.O. Box 798
Richmond, VA
23206-0798
804-371-8204
FAX: 804-371-8177

Metro Richmond CVB
& Film Office
Susan Motley
550 East Marshall St.
Richmond, VA 23219
804-782-2777
800-365-7272
FAX: 804-780-2577

WASHINGTON
Washington State Film
& Video Office
2001 6th Ave., Ste: 2600
Seattle, WA 98121
206-464-7148
FAX: 206-464-7222

Tacoma-Pierce County
Film Office
Jacki Skaught
906 Broadway
P.O. Box 1754
Tacoma, WA
98401-1754
206-627-2836
FAX: 206-627-8783

WEST VIRGINIA

West Virginia Film
Office
Mark McNabb
State Capital, Building
6, Room 525
Charleston, WV
25305-0311
304-558-2234
800-982-3386
FAX: 304-558-1189

WISCONSIN
Wisconsin Film Office
Stan Solheim
123 West Washington
Ave., 6th Fl.
Madison, WI 53702-
0001
608-267-3456
FAX: 608-266-3403

City of Milwaukee
Film Liaison
Jennifer Burkel
809 North Broadway
Milwaukee, WI 53202
414-286-5700
FAX: 414-286-5904

WYOMING
Wyoming Film Office
Bill D. Lindstrom
I-25 and College Drive
Cheyenne, WY
82002-0240
307-777-7777
800-458-6657
FAX: 307-777-6904

Jackson Hole Film
Commission

Deborah Supowit
P.O. Box E
Jackson, WY 83001
307-733-3316
FAX: 307-733-5585

VENEZUELA
Venezuelan Film &
Television Office
Michael J. Cooper
Centro Profesional Santa
Paula,Torre B
Caracas, 1060
VENEZUELA
58-2-985-2348
FAX: 58-2-985-2348

SAG Franchised Talent Agents 1996

This is a complete national list of all talent agents currently franchised by SAG; if any information is incorrect, please notify your local SAG office. The Abbreviations following the agent's phone number indicate the type of representation offered by the agency:

(T) Theatrical/Television (C) Commercial (FS) Full Service (Y) Young (A) Adults

ARIZONA
1616 East Indian School Road
Phoenix, AZ 85016
(602) 265-2712

ATLANTA
Paces Ferry Road N.E., Suite #334
Atlanta, GA. 30305
(404) 239-0131

BOSTON
11 Beacon Street #512
Boston, MA. 02108
(617) 742-2688

CHICAGO*
75 E. Wacker Drive, 14th Fl.
Chicago, IL. 60601
(312) 372-8081

CLEVELAND*
1030 Euclid Ave., Suite #429
Cleveland, OH 75206
(216) 579-9305

DALLAS
6060 N. Central Expressway #302/LB 604
Dallas, TX 75206
(214) 363-8300

DENVER*
950 S. Cherry Street, #502
Denver, CO 80222
(302) 757-6226

DETROIT
28690 Southfield Road
Lathrup Village, MI 48076
(810) 559-9540

FLORIDA***
7300 N. Kendall Drive, Suite #620
Miami, FL 33156-7840
(305) 670-7677

HAWAII
949 Kapiolani Blvd., #105
Honolulu, HI 96814
(808) 596-0388

HOUSTON
2650 Fountainview # 326
Houston, TX 77057
(713) 972-1806

MINNEAPOLIS/ ST. PAUL*
708 N. 1st Street, Suite #343A
Minneapolis, MN 55401
(612) 371-9120

NASHVILLE
1108 17th Ave. South
Nashville, TN 37212
(615) 327-2944

NEW YORK
1515 Broadway, 44th Fl.
New York, N.Y. 10036
(212) 944-1030

PHILADELPHIA
230 S. Board Street 10th Fl.
Philadelphia, PA 19102
(215) 545-3150

ST. LOUIS*
909 Olive Street #400
St. Louis, MO 63101
(314) 231-8410

SAN DIEGO
7827 Convoy Court #400
San Diego, CA 92111
(619) 278-7695

SAN FRANCISCO
235 Pine Street, #11
San Francisco, Ca. 94104
(415) 391-7510

SEATTLE*
608 Valley Street, #200
Seattle, WA 98109
(206) 282-2506

WASHINGTON/BALTIMORE
4330 East West Highway, Suite #204
Bethesda, MD 20814
(310) 657-2560

* AFTRA offices which also handle SAG business for their areas.
** Denver is a regional office which also covers Nevada, New Mexico & Utah.
*** Florida is a regional office which also covers Alabama, Arkansas, Louisiana, Mississippi, No. Carolina, So. Carolina, W. Virginia, U.S. Virgin Islands, Puerto Rico and the Caribbean.

HOLLYWOOD
All agents listed below have Los Angeles addresses and (213) area codes unless otherwise noted.

BH- Beverly Hills   NH- North Hollywood

A S A, 4430 Fountain Avenue, Suite #A (90029) 662-9787 (FS)

ABOVE THE LINE AGENCY, 9200 Sunset Boulvard, Suite 401 (90069) (310)859-6115 (T-A)

ABRAMS ARTISTS & ASSOC, 9200 Sunset Blvd, Suite 625 (90069) (310)859-0625 (FS)

ABRAMS-RUBALOFF & LAWRENCE, 8075 West Third Street, Suite 303 (90048) 935-1700 (FS)

ACME TALENT & LITERARY, TALENT AGENCY, 6310 San Vicente Boulevard, Suite 520, Los Angeles, (90048) 954-2263 (FS)

AFH MANAGEMENT,TALENT AGENCY, 7819 Beverly Blvd. (90036) 932-6042 (FS)

AGENCY FOR PERFORMING ARTS, 9000 Sunset Blvd, Suite 1200 (90069) (310)273-0744 (FS-A)

AGENCY, THE, 10351 Santa Monica Blvd, Suite #211 (90025) (310)551-3000 (FS-A)

AIMEE ENTERTAINMENT, 15000 Ventura Blvd., Suite 340, Sherman Oaks (91401) (818)783-9115

ALLEN TALENT AGENCY, 11755 Wilshire Blvd., Suite 1750 (90025) (310)474-7524

ALLEN TALENT, BONNI, 260 S Beverly Drive, BH (90212) (310)247-1865

ALLIANCE TALENT INC., 8949 Sunset Boulevard, Suite 202, West Hollywood (90069) (310)858-1090 (FS)

ALVARADO AGENCY, CARLOS, 8455 Beverly Boulevard, Suite 406 (90048) 655-7978

AMBROSIO/MORTIMER, 9150 Wilshire Boulevard, Suite #175, BH (90212) (310)274-4274 (FS-A)

AMSEL, EISENSTADT & FRAZIER, 6310 San Vicente Blvd, Suite #401 (90048) 939-1188

ANGEL CITY TALENT, 1680 Vine Street, Suite 716 (90028) 463-1680

APODACA AGENCY, CHRIS, 2049 Century Park East, Suite #1200 (90067) (310)284-3484 (FS)

APODACA/MUNRO TALENT AGENCY, 13801 Ventura Blvd., Sherman Oaks (91423) (818)380-2700 (FS)

ARTHUR, IRVIN ASSOCIATES LTD, 9363 Wilshire Boulevard, Suite 212, BH (90210) (310)278-5934

ARTIST MANAGEMENT AGENCY, 4340 Campus Drive #210, Newport Beach (92660) (714)261-7557

ARTIST NETWORK, 12001 Ventura Place, Suite 331, Studio City (91604) 651-4244

ARTISTS AGENCY, 10000 Santa Monica Blvd, Suite 305 (90067) (310)277-7779 (FS)

ARTISTS GROUP, LTD, 10100 Santa Monica Blvd., Suite 2409, Los Angeles, (90067) (310)552-1100 (FS)

ATKINS AND ASSOCIATES, 303 S Crescent Heights (90048) 658-1025

B O P - LA TALENT AGENCY, 1467 N Tamarind Avenue (90028) 466-8667

BAMM TALENT AGENCY, 8609 Sherwood Drive, West Hollywood (90069) (310)652-6252 (C-A)

BADGLEY & CONNOR, 9229 Sunset Boulevard, Suite 311 (90069) (310)278-9313 (FS)

BAIER-KLEINMAN INTERNATIONAL, 3575 West Cahuenga Blvd., Suite 500 (90068) (818)761-1001 (T-A)

BALDWIN TALENT, INC, 500 Sepulveda Blvd., 4th Floor (90049) (310)472-7919 (FS)

BALL, BOBBY TALENT AGENCY, 8075 W 3rd Street, Suite #550 (90048) 964-7300 (FS)

BARR, RICKEY TALENT AGENCY, 1010 Hammond, Suite 202 (90069) (310)276-0887

BAUMAN, HILLER & ASSOCIATES, 5757 Wilshire Blvd, Penthouse 5 (90036) 857-6666

BDP & ASSOC TALENT AGENCY, 10637 Burbank Blvd, NH (91601) (818)506-7615

BENNETT AGENCY, SARA, 6404 Hollywood Blvd, Suite #327 (90028) 965-9666 (FS)

BENSON, LOIS J, 8360 Melrose Avenue, Suite #203 (90069) 653-0500

BERZON, MARIAN TALENT AGENCY, 336 East 17th Street, Costa Mesa (92627) (714)631-5936

BIGLEY AGENCY, THE, 6442 Coldwater Canyon Avenue, Suite 211, NH (91606) (818)761-9971 (FS-A)

BIKOFF AGENCY, LTD, YVETTE, 621 N Orlando, Suite #8, West Hollywood (90048) 655-6123 (FS)

BLACK, BONNIE TALENT AGENCY, 4405 Riverside Drive, Suite 305, Burbank (91505) (818)840-1299 (FS-A)

BLAKE AGENCY, THE, 415 N. Camden Drive, Suite #121, BH (90210) (310)246-0241 (T-A)

BLOOM, J MICHAEL, 9255 Sunset Boulevard, 7th Floor (90069) (310)275-6800 (FS-A)

BORDEAUX,NICOLE TALENT AGENCY, 616 N. Robertson Blvd., 2nd Floor, West Hollywood (90069) (310)289-2550 (C-A)

BORINSTEIN ORECK BOGART, 8271 Melrose Avenue, Suite 110 (90046) 658-7500 (T-A)

BRAND MODEL AND TALENT, 17941 Skypark Circle, Suite F, Irvine (92714) (714)251-0555 (FS)

BRANDON & ASSOC, PAUL, 1033 N Carol Drive, Suite #T-6 (90069) (310)273-6173 (T-A)

BRANDON'S COMMERCIALS UNLIMITED, S.W., 9601 Wilshire Boulevard, BH (90210) (310)888-8788 (FS)

BRESLER, KELLY & ASSOCIATES, 15760 Ventura Blvd, Suite 1730, Encino, (91436) (818)905-1155

BREWIS AGENCY, ALEX, 12429 Laurel Terrace Dr, Studio City (91604) (818)509-0831

BRUSTEIN COMPANY, 2644 30th Street, 1st Floor, Santa Monica (90405) (310)452-3330 (T-A)

BUCHWALD & ASSOCIATES, DON, 9229 Sunset Boulevard, West Hollywood (90069) (310)278-3600 (T)

BURKETT TALENT AGENCY, 12 Hughes, Suite D-100, Irvine (92714) (714)830-6300 (FS)

BURTON AGENCY, IRIS, 1450 Belfast Drive (90069) (310)652-0954 (FS-Y)

C LA VIE MODEL AND TALENT, 7507 Sunset Boulevard, Suite #201 (90046) 969-0541 (FS-A)

CL INC, 843 N. Sycamore Avenue (90038) 461-3971

CNA, 1801 Avenue Of The Stars, Suite #1250 (90067) (310)556-4343 (FS-A)

CACTUS TALENT AGENCY, 13601 Ventura Boulevard, Suite #112, Sherman Oaks (91423) (818)986-7432 (FS-A)

CAMDEN, 822 S Robertson Blvd, Suite 200 (90035) (310)289-2700

CAMERON & ASSOCIATES, BARBARA, 8369 Sausalito Avenue, Suite A, West Hills (91304) (818)888-6107 (FS-Y)

CAPITAL ARTISTS, 8383 Wilshire Boulevard, Suite 954, BH (90211) 658-8118 (T)

CAREER ARTISTS INTERNATIONAL, 11030 Ventura Blvd, Suite #3, Studio City (91604) (818)980-1315 (FS-A)

CARROLL AGENCY, WILLIAM, 139 N San Fernando Rd, Suite A, Burbank (91502) (818)848-9948 (FS)

CASTLE-HILL TALENT AGENCY, 1101 S Orlando Avenue (90035) 653-3535 (FS)

CAVALERI & ASSOCIATES, 849 South Broadway, Suite #750 (90014) 683-1354 (FS)

CENTURY ARTISTS, LTD, 9744 Wilshire Boulevard, Suite #308, BH (90212) (310)273-4366 (T-A)

CHASIN AGENCY, THE, 8899 Beverly Blvd., Suite #713 (90048) (310)278-7505 (T-A)

CHATEAU BILLINGS TALENT AGENCY, 5657 Wilshire Blvd., Suite 340 (90036) 965-5432 (FS)

CHUTUK & ASSOCIATES, JACK, 2121 Avenue of the Stars, Suite #700 (90067) (310)552-1773 (T-A)

CINEMA TALENT AGENCY, 2609 Wyoming Avenue, Burbank (91505) (818)845-3816 (FS)

CIRCLE TALENT ASSOCIATES, 433 N. Camden Drive, Suite #400, BH (90212) (310)285-1585 (FS)

CLARK COMPANY, W RANDOLPH, 2431 Hyperion Avenue (90027) 953-4960 (FS)

CLER MODELING, COLLEEN, 120 S Victory Boulevard, Suite #206, Burbank (91502) (818)841-7943 (FS-Y)

COAST TO COAST TALENT GROUP, INC., 4942 Vineland Ave, Suite #200, NH (91601) (818)762-6278 (FS)

COLOURS MODEL & TALENT MANAGEMENT AGENCY, 8344 1/2 West Third Street (90048) 658-7072 (FS)

CONTEMPORARY ARTISTS, LTD., 1427 Third Street Promenade, Suite #205, Santa Monica (90401) (310)395-1800 (FS)

COPPAGE COMPANY, THE, 11501 Chandler Boulevard, NH (91601) (818)980-1106 (T-A)

CORALIE JR. THEATRICAL AGENCY, 4789 Vineland Avenue, Suite #100, NH (91602) (818)766-9501 (FS)

COSDEN AGENCY, THE, 3518 West Cahuenga Blvd., Suite 216 (90068) 874-7200 (FS)

CRAIG AGENCY, THE, 8485 Melrose Place, Suite #E (90069) 655-0236 (T-A)

CREATIVE ARTISTS AGENCY, LLC, 9830 Wilshire Blvd, BH (90212) (310)288-4545 (FS-A)

CROW & ASSOCIATES, SUSAN, 1010 Hammond Street, Suite #102, West Hollywood (90069) (310)859-9784 (FS)

CUMBER ATTRACTIONS, LIL, 6363 Sunset Boulevard, Suite #807 (90028) 469-1919 (FS)

CUNNINGHAM, ESCOTT & DIPENE, 10635 Santa Monica Blvd., Suite 130 (90025) (310)475-2111 (FS-A)

DH, TALENT AGENCY, 1800 N. Highland Avenue, Suite #300 (90028) 962-6643 (FS)

DZA TALENT AGENCY, 8981 Sunset Blvd., Suite 204 (90069) (310)274-8025 (FS-A)

DADE/SCHULTZ ASSOCIATES, 11846 Ventura Blvd, Suite #201, Studio City (91604) (818)760-3100

DAVIS, MARY WEBB TALENT AGENCY, 515 N La Cienega Blvd. (90048) (310)652-6850 (FS-A)

DEVROE AGENCY, THE, 6311 Romaine Street (90038) 962-3040 (FS-A)

DURKIN ARTISTS, 12229 Ventura Blvd.,, Suite 202, Studio City (91604) (818)762-9936 (FS)

DYTMAN AND SCHWARTZ, TALENT AGENCY, 9200 Sunset Blvd., Suite 809 (90069) (310)274-8844 (T-A)

EFENDI, TALENT AGENCY, 1923 1/2 Westwood Blvd., Suite #3 (90025) 957-0006 (FS)

ELITE MODEL MANAGEMENT, 345 N. Maple Drive, Suite #397, BH (90210) (310)274-9395 (FS-A)

ELLIS TALENT GROUP, 6025 Sepulveda Boulevard, Suite #201, Van Nuys (91411) (818)997-7447 (T-A)

EPSTEIN-WYCKOFF & ASSOCIATES, 280 S. Beverly Drive, Suite #400, BH (90212) (310)278-7222 (T)

ESTEPHAN TALENT AGENCY, 6018 Greenmeadow Road, Lakewood (90713) (310)421-8048 (FS-A)

FPA, TALENT AGENCY, 12701 Moorpark, Suite 205, Studio City (91604) (818)508-6691 (T-A)

FARRELL EILEEN/ COULTER CATHY TALENT AGE, 7313 Kraft Avenue, NH (91605) (818)765-0400 (FS)

FAVORED ARTISTS AGENCY, 122 South Robertson Blvd, Suite 202 (90048) (310)247-1040 (T-A)

FELBER & ASSOCIATES, WILLIAM, 2126 Cahuenga Boulevard (90068) 466-7629 (FS)

FERRAR-MAZIROFF ASSOCIATES, 8430 Santa Monica Blvd, Suite 220 (90069) 654-2601 (C-A)

FIELDS TALENT AGENCY, LIANA, 3325 Wilshire Blvd, Suite 749 (90010) 487-3656 (FS)

FILM ARTISTS ASSOCIATES, 7080 Hollywood Blvd, Suite 1118 (90028) 463-1010 (FS)

FIRST ARTISTS AGENCY, 10000 Riverside Drive, Suite 10, Toluca Lake (91602) (818)509-9292

FLICK EAST & WEST TALENTS, INC., 9057 Nemo Street, Suite #A, West Hollywood (90069) (310)271-9111 (FS-A)

FONTAINE AGENCY, JUDITH, 9255 Sunset Blvd (90069) (310)285-0545 (C)

FREED, BARRY COMPANY, 2029 Century Park East, Suite 600 (90067) (310)277-1260 (T-A)

FRIES, ALICE AGENCY, 6381 Hollywood Blvd, Suite 600 (90028) 464-6491 (T)

FUTURE AGENCY, 8929 S. Sepulveda Blvd., Suite 314 (90045) (310)338-9602 (FS)

GAGE GROUP INC, 9255 Sunset Boulevard, Suite #515 (90069) (310)859-8777 (T-A)

GARRETT TALENT AGENCY, HELEN, 6525 Sunset Blvd, 5th Floor (90028) 871-8707 (FS)

GARRICK INTERNATIONAL, DALE, 8831 Sunset Boulevard, Suite #402 (90069) (310)657-2661

GEDDES AGENCY, THE, 1201 Green Acre Avenue, West Hollywood (90046) 878-1155 (T-A)

GELFF ASSOCIATES, LAYA, 16133 Ventura Boulevard, Suite #700, Encino (91436) (818)713-2610 (T-A)

GERARD TALENT AGENCY, PAUL, 11712 Moorpark Street, Suite 112, Studio City (91604) (714)644-7950 (T-A)

GERLER, DON AGENCY, 3349 Cahuenga Blvd., West, Suite #1, Los Angeles, (90068) 850-7386 (FS)

GERSH AGENCY, THE, 232 N Canon Drive, BH (90210) (310)274-6611 (FS-A)

GERSHENSON, DAVID S TALENT AGENCY, 11757 San Vicente Blvd, Suite 2 (90049) (310)207-1345

GILLY, GEORGIA TALENT AGENCY, 8721 Sunset Blvd, Suite #104 (90069) (310)657-5660 (T-A)

GOLD/MARSHAK & ASSOCIATES, 3500 West Olive Avenue, Suite 1400, Burbank (91505) (818)972-4300 (FS)

GOLDEY COMPANY, INC, 116 N. Robertson Blvd., Suite 700 (90048) (310)657-3277 (T)

GORDON, MICHELLE & ASSOCIATES, 260 S. Beverly Drive, Suite 308, BH (90212) (310)246-9930 (FS-A)

HWA TALENT REPRESENTATIVES, INC, 1964 Westwood Blvd, Suite 400 (90025) (310)446-1313 (FS-A)

HAEGGSTROM OFFICE, TALENT AGENCY, 8721 Sunset Blvd., Suite 103 (90069) 658-9111 (T-A)

HALLIDAY, BUZZ & ASSOCIATES, 8899 Beverly Blvd, Suite 620 (90048) (310)275-6028 (FS-A)

HALPERN & ASSOCIATES, 12304 Santa Monica Blvd., Suite 104 (90025) (310)571-4488 (FS-A)

HAMILBURG AGENCY, MITCHELL J., 292 S La Cienega #312, BH (90211) (310)657-1501

HART & ASSOCIATES, VAUGHN D., 8899 Beverly Blvd., Suite #815 (90048) (310)273-7887 (T-A)

HEADLINE ARTISTS AGENCY, 16400 Ventura Blvd., Suite 324, Encino (91436) (818)986-1730

HECHT AGENCY, BEVERLY, 8949 Sunset Boulevard, Suite #203 (90069) (310)278-3544 (FS)

HENDERSON/HOGAN AGENCY, 247 S Beverly Dr, BH (90212) (310)274-7815 (T-A)

HERVEY/GRIMES TALENT AGENCY, 12444 Ventura Boulevard, Suite #103, Studio City (91404) (818)981-0891 (FS)

HOLLYWOOD CNTV TALENT AGENCY, 1680 N. Vine, Suite 1105 (90028) 463-5677 (FS)

HOUSE OF REPRESENTATIVES TALENT AGENCY, 9911 Pico Boulevard, Suite 1060 (90035) (310)772-0772 (T-A)

HOWARD TALENT WEST, 12178 Ventura Blvd, Suite 201, Studio City (91604) (818)766-5300 (FS-A)

HURWITZ ASSOC, MARTIN, 427 N Canon Drive, Suite #215, BH (90210) (310)274-0240 (T-A)

IFA TALENT AGENCY, 2049 Century Park East, Suite 2500 (90067) (310)659-5522 (T-A)

IMAGE TALENT AGENCY, 259 South Robertson Blvd., BH (90212) (310)277-9134 (FS)

INNOVATIVE ARTISTS, 1999 Ave Of The Stars, Suite 2850 (90067) (310)553-5200 (T-A)

INTERNATIONAL CREATIVE MANAGEMENT, 8942 Wilshire Blvd., BH (90211) (310)550-4000 (FS-A)

IT MODEL MANAGEMENT, 526 N Larchmont Blvd. (90004) 962-9564 (FS)

JACKMAN & TAUSSIG, 1815 Butler Ave., Suite #120 (90025) (310)478-6641 (FS)

JAY AGENCY, GEORGE, 6269 Selma Avenue #15 (90028) 466-6665 (FS)

JENNINGS & ASSOCIATES, THOMAS, 28035 Dorothy Drive, Suite #210A, Agoura (91301) (818)879-1260 (FS)

KAPLAN-STAHLER AGENCY, THE, 8383 Wilshire Blvd #923, BH (90211) 653-4483 (T-A)

KARG/WEISSENBACH & ASSOCIATES, 329 N Wetherly Drive #101, BH (90210) (310)205-0435 (T-A)

KAZARIAN/SPENCER & ASSOCIATES, 11365 Ventura Blvd, Suite 100, Studio City (91604) (818)769-9111 (FS-A)

KELMAN/ARLETTA, 7813 Sunset Boulevard (90046)
851-8822 (FS)

KEMP, SHARON TALENT AGENCY, 9812 Vidor
Drive (90035) (310)552-0011

KERWIN WILLIAM AGENCY, 1605 N. Cahuenga
Boulevard, Suite #202 (90028) 469-5155 (FS-A)

KJAR AGENCY, TYLER, 10653 Riverside Drive,
Toluca Lake (91602) (818)760-0321 (FS)

KLASS, ERIC AGENCY, 144 S Beverly Drive, Suite
405, BH (90212) (310)274-9169 (T-A)

KOHNER, PAUL INC, 9300 Wilshire Blvd., Suite 555,
BH (90212) (310)550-1060 (FS-A)

KRUGLOV & ASSOCIATES, VICTOR, 7060
Hollywood Boulevard, Suite #1220 (90028) 957-9000
(FS)

L A TALENT, 8335 Sunset Blvd, 2nd Floor (90069)
656-3722 (FS)

L A ARTISTS, 2566 Overland Avenue, Suite 550 (90064)
(310)202-0254 (T-A)

LW 1, INC., 8383 Wilshire Blvd, Suite 649, BH (90211)
653-5700 (C-A)

LAINE, LAUREN TALENT AGENCY, 1370 N. Brea
Blvd., Suite 200 D, Fullerton (92633) (714)441-1140
(FS)

LANE TALENT AGENCY, STACEY, 13455 Ventura
Blvd, Suite 240, Sherman Oaks (91423) (818)501-2668
(FS)

LAWRENCE AGENCY, THE, 3575 Cahuenga Blvd,
West, Suite #125-3 (90068) 851-7711 (T)

LEE & ASSOCIATES, GUY, 4150 Riverside Drive,
Suite 212, Burbank (91505) (818)848-7475 (FS)

LENHOFF/ROBINSON TALENT AND LIT.
AGENCY, 1728 S. La Cienega Boulevard (90035)
(310)558-4700 (T-A)

LEVIN AGENCY, THE, 8484 Wilshire Blvd., Suite 745,
BH (90211) 653-7073 (FS-A)

LEVY, ROBIN & ASSOCIATES, INC., 9701 Wilshire
Blvd, Suite 1200, BH (90212) (310)278-8748 (FS-A)

LICHTMAN CO, TERRY, 4439 Wortser Avenue,
Studio City (91604) (818)783-3003 (T-A)

LIGHT AGENCY, ROBERT, 6404 Wilshire Blvd, Suite
900 (90048) 651-1777 (FS-A)

LINDNER & ASSOCIATES, KEN, 2049 Century Park
East, Suite 2750 (90067) (310)277-9223 (T-A)

LOFT AGENCY, THE, 369 S Doheny Drive, Suite
#203, BH (90211) (310)576-9012 (FS-A)

LOS ANGELES PREMIERE ARTISTS AGENCY,
8899 Beverly Blvd., Suite 510 (90048) (310)271-1414
(FS)

LOVELL & ASSOCIATES, 1350 N. Highland Avenue
(90028) 462-1672

LYNNE & REILLY AGENCY, Toluca Plaza Building,
6735 Forest Lawn Drive, Suite 313 (90068) 850-1984
(FS)

MGA/MARY GRADY AGENCY, 4444 Lankershim
Blvd, Suite 207, NH (91602) (818)766-4414 (FS)

MADEMOISELLE TALENT AGENCY, 8693 Wilshire
Blvd., Suite 200, BH (90211) (310)289-8005 (FS)

MAJOR CLIENTS AGENCY, 345 Maple Drive, Suite
395, BH (90210) (310)205-5000 (T-A)

MARSHALL MODEL & COMML AGNCY, ALESE,
23900 Hawthorne Blvd, Suite 100, Torrance (90505)
(310)378-1223 (C)

MARTEL AGENCY, THE, 1680 N Vine Street, Suite
203 (90028) 461-5943 (FS-A)

MAXINE'S TALENT AGENCY, 4830 Encino Avenue,
Encino (91316) (818)986-2946 (FS-A)

MEDIA ARTISTS GROUP, 8383 Wilshire Boulevard,
Suite 954, BH (90211) 658-5050 (FS)

METROPOLITAN TALENT AGENCY, 4526 Wilshire
Boulevard (90010) 857-4500 (FS-A)

MIRAMAR TALENT AGENCY, 9157 Sunset
Boulevard, Suite 300 (90069) (310)858-1900 (FS-A)

MITCHELL AGENCY, PATTY, 4605 Lankershim
Blvd., Suite 201, NH (91602) (818)508-6181 (FS-Y)

MOORE ARTISTS, TALENT AGENCY, 1551 S.
Robertson Blvd. (90035) (310)286-3150 (A

MORRIS AGENCY, WILLIAM, 151 El Camino Dr,
BH (90212) (310)274-7451 (FS)

MOSS & ASSOC, H DAVID, 733 North Seward Street,
Penthouse (90038) 465-1234 (T-A)

MURPHY AGENCY, MARY, 6014 Greenbush Avenue,
Van Nuys (91401) (818)989-6076 (FS-A)

NATHE & ASSOCIATES, SUSAN/C P C, 8281
Melrose Avenue, Suite 200 (90046) 653-7573 (FS-A)

OMNIPOP INC, 10700 Ventura Blvd, Second Floor,
Studio City (91604) (818)980-9267 (FS-A)

ORANGE GROVE GROUP, INC., 12178 Ventura
Blvd., Suite 205, Studio City (91604) (818)762-7498
(T)

OSBRINK TALENT AGENCY, CINDY, 4605
Lankershim Blvd., Suite 401, NH (91602)
(818)760-2488 (FS-Y)

OTIS, DOROTHY DAY & ASSOCIATES, 13223
Ventura Blvd., Suite F, Studio City (91604)
(818)905-9510 (FS)

PAKULA KING & ASSOCIATES, 9229 Sunset Blvd.,
Suite 315 (90069) (310)281-4868 (T-A)

PARADIGM TALENT AGENCY, 10100 Santa Monica
Boulevard, Suite 2500 (90067) (310)277-4400 (T-A)

PARAGON TALENT AGENCY, INC., 8439 Sunset
Blvd., Suite 301 (90069) 654-4554 (FS-A)

PARTOS COMPANY, THE, 3630 Barham Blvd #Z108
(90068) 876-5500 (T)

PERSEUS MODELING & TALENT, 3807 Wilshire
Boulevard, Suite 1102 (90010) 383-2322 (FS)

PLAYERS TALENT AGENCY, 8770 Shoreham Drive,
Suite 2, West Hollywood (90069) (310)289-8777 (FS)

PRIMA EASTWEST MODEL MGMT INC, 933 N La
Brea Avenue, Suite 200 (90038) 882-6900 (FS)

PRIVILEGE TALENT AGENCY, 8170 Beverly Blvd,
Suite 204 (90048) 658-8781 (FS-A)

PRO-SPORT & ENTERTAINMENT CO, 1990 S Bundy
Drive, Suite 700 (90025) (310)207-0228 (FS-A)

PROGRESSIVE ARTISTS, 400 S Beverly Drive, Suite
#216, BH (90212) (310)553-8561 (T-A)

RAEL COMPANY, GORDON, 9255 Sunset Blvd., Suite
425 (90069) (310)285-9552 (C-A)

RENAISSANCE TALENT & LITERARY AGENCY,
8523 Sunset Blvd. (90069) (310)289-3636 (T-A)

ROGERS & ASSOC, STEPHANIE, 3575 West
Cahuenga Blvd., Suite 249 (90068) 851-5155 (T-A)

ROMANO MODELING & TALENT AGENCY,
CINDY, 414 Village Square West, Palm Springs
(92262) (619)323-3333 (FS)

ROOS WEST LTD , GILLA, 9744 Wilshire Blvd, Suite
#203, BH (90212) (310)274-9356 (FS-A)

ROSENBERG OFFICE, THE MARION, 8428 Melrose
Place, Suite #B (90069) 653-7383 (T-A)

S D B PARTNERS, INC., 1801 Avenue of the Stars,
Suite 902 (90067) (310)785-0060 (T-A)

SANDERS AGENCY, THE, 8831 Sunset Blvd #304
(90069) (310)652-1119 (FS)

SARNOFF COMPANY, INC, 3900 W. Alameda
Avenue, Burbank (91505) (818)972-1779 (T-A)

SAVAGE AGENCY, THE, 6212 Banner Ave (90038)
461-8316 (FS)

SCAGNETTI TALENT AGENCY,JACK, 5118
Vineland Avenue, Suite 102, NH (91601)
(818)762-3871 (FS-A)

SCHECHTER COMPANY, THE IRV, 9300 Wilshire
Blvd #410, BH (90212) (310)278-8070 (FS)

SCHIOWITZ/CLAY/ROSE, INC., 1680 N. Vine Street,
Suite 614 (90028) 463-7300 (T-A)

SCHNARR TALENT, SANDIE, 8281 Melrose Ave #200
(90046) 653-9479 (C-A)

SCHOEN & ASSOCIATES, JUDY, 606 N Larchmont
Blvd, Suite 309 (90004) 962-1950 (T-A)

SCHWARTZ ASSOCIATES, DON, 8749 Sunset
Boulevard (90069) (310)657-8910 (FS)

SCREEN ARTISTS AGENCY, 12435 Oxnard Street,
NH (91606) (818)755-0026 (FS)

SCREEN CHILDREN'S TALENT AGENCY, 4000
Riverside Drive, Suite A, Burbank (91505)
(818)846-4300 (FS-Y)

SELECTED ARTISTS AGENCY, 3575 Cahuenga Blvd
West, Second Floor (90068) 368-1271 (FS-A)

SHAPIRA & ASSOC, 15301 Ventura Blvd, Suite 345,
Sherman Oaks (91403) (818)906-0322 (FS-A)

SHAPIRO-LICHTMAN, INC., 8827 Beverly Blvd
(90048) (310)859-8877 (T-A)

SHOWBIZ ENTERTAINMENT, 6922 Hollywood
Boulevard, Suite #207 (90028) 469-9931 (FS)

SHREVE AGENCY, DOROTHY, 2665 N Palm Canyon
Drive, Palm Springs (92262) (619)327-5855

SHUMAKER TALENT AGENCY, THE, 6533
Hollywood Blvd, Suite #301 (90028) 464-0745 (FS)

SIEGEL ASSOCIATES, JEROME, 7551 Sunset Blvd,
Suite 203 (90046) 850-1275 (T)

SIERRA TALENT AGENCY, 14542 Ventura Blvd.,
Suite 207, Sherman Oaks (91403) (818)907-9645
(FS-A)

SILVER MASSETTI & ASSOCIATES/WEST LTD.,
8730 Sunset Boulevard, Suite #480 (90069)
(310)289-0909 (FS-A)

ORANGE GROVE GROUP, INC., 12178 Ventura Blvd., Suite 205, Studio City (91604) (818)762-7498 (T)

OSBRINK TALENT AGENCY, CINDY, 4605 Lankershim Blvd., Suite 401, NH (91602) (818)760-2488(FS-Y)

OTIS, DOROTHY DAY & ASSOCIATES, 13223 Ventura Blvd., Suite F, Studio City (91604) (818)905-9510(FS)

PAKULA KING & ASSOCIATES, 9229 Sunset Blvd., Suite 315 (90069) (310)281-4868(T-A)

PARADIGM TALENT AGENCY, 10100 Santa Monica Boulevard, Suite 2500 (90067) (310)277-4400(T-A)

PARAGON TALENT AGENCY, INC., 8439 Sunset Blvd., Suite 301 (90069) 654-4554 (FS-A)

PARTOS COMPANY, THE, 3630 Barham Blvd #Z108 (90068) 876-5500 (T)

PERSEUS MODELING & TALENT, 3807 Wilshire Boulevard, Suite 1102 (90010) 383-2322 (FS)

PLAYERS TALENT AGENCY, 8770 Shoreham Drive, Suite 2, West Hollywood (90069) (310)289-8777(FS)

PRIMA EASTWEST MODEL MGMT INC, 933 N La Brea Avenue, Suite 200 (90038) 882-6900 (FS)

PRIVILEGE TALENT AGENCY, 8170 Beverly Blvd, Suite 204 (90048) 658-8781 (FS-A)

PRO-SPORT & ENTERTAINMENT CO, 1990 S Bundy Drive, Suite 700 (90025) (310)207-0228 (FS-A)

PROGRESSIVE ARTISTS, 400 S Beverly Drive, Suite #216, BH (90212) (310)553-8561 (T-A)

RAEL COMPANY, GORDON, 9255 Sunset Blvd., Suite 425 (90069) (310)285-9552(C-A)

RENAISSANCE TALENT & LITERARY AGENCY, 8523 Sunset Blvd. (90069) (310)289-3636 (T-A)

ROGERS & ASSOC, STEPHANIE, 3575 West Cahuenga Blvd., Suite 249 (90068) 851-5155 (T-A)

ROMANO MODELING & TALENT AGENCY, CINDY, 414 Village Square West, Palm Springs (92262) (619)323-3333(FS)

ROOS WEST LTD , GILLA, 9744 Wilshire Blvd, Suite #203, BH (90212) (310)274-9356(FS-A)

ROSENBERG OFFICE, THE MARION, 8428 Melrose Place, Suite #B (90069) 653-7383 (T-A)

S D B PARTNERS, INC., 1801 Avenue of the Stars, Suite 902 (90067) (310)785-0060(T-A)

SANDERS AGENCY, THE, 8831 Sunset Blvd #304 (90069) (310)652-1119(FS)

SARNOFF COMPANY, INC, 3900 W. Alameda Avenue, Burbank (91505) (818)972-1779(T-A)

SAVAGE AGENCY, THE, 6212 Banner Ave (90038) 461-8316 (FS)

SCAGNETTI TALENT AGENCY,JACK, 5118 Vineland Avenue, Suite 102, NH (91601) (818)762-3871 (FS-A)

SCHECHTER COMPANY, THE IRV, 9300 Wilshire Blvd #410, BH (90212) (310)278-8070(FS)

SCHIOWITZ/CLAY/ROSE, INC, 1680 N. Vine Street, Suite 614 (90028) 463-7300 (T-A)

SCHNARR TALENT, SANDIE, 8281 Melrose Ave #200 (90046) 653-9479 (C-A)

SCHOEN & ASSOCIATES, JUDY, 606 N Larchmont Blvd, Suite 309 (90004) 962-1950 (T-A)

SCHWARTZ ASSOCIATES, DON, 8749 Sunset Boulevard (90069) (310)657-8910(FS)

SCREEN ARTISTS AGENCY, 12435 Oxnard Street, NH (91606) (818)755-0026(FS)

SCREEN CHILDREN'S TALENT AGENCY, 4000 Riverside Drive, Suite A, Burbank (91505) (818)846-4300(FS-Y)

SELECTED ARTISTS AGENCY, 3575 Cahuenga Blvd West, Second Floor (90068) 368-1271 (FS-A)

SHAPIRA & ASSOC, 15301 Ventura Blvd, Suite 345, Sherman Oaks (91403) (818)906-0322(FS-A)

SHAPIRO-LICHTMAN, INC., 8827 Beverly Blvd (90048) (310)859-8877(T-A)

SHOWBIZ ENTERTAINMENT, 6922 Hollywood Boulevard, Suite #207 (90028) 469-9931 (FS)

SHREVE AGENCY, DOROTHY, 2665 N Palm Canyon Drive, Palm Springs (92262) (619)327-5855

SHUMAKER TALENT AGENCY, THE, 6533 Hollywood Blvd, Suite #301 (90028) 464-0745 (FS)

SIEGEL ASSOCIATES, JEROME, 7551 Sunset Blvd, Suite 203 (90046) 850-1275 (T)

SIERRA TALENT AGENCY, 14542 Ventura Blvd., Suite 207, Sherman Oaks (91403) (818)907-9645 (FS-A)

SILVER MASSETTI & ASSOCIATES/WEST LTD., 8730 Sunset Boulevard, Suite #480 (90069) (310)289-0909 (FS-A)

SINDELL, RICHARD & ASSOCIATES, 8271 Melrose Avenue, Suite #202 (90046) 653-5051 (T-A)

SIRENS MODEL MANAGEMENT, 6404 Wilshire Blvd., Suite 720 (90048) 782-0310 (C-A)

SLESSINGER ASSOC, MICHAEL, 8730 Sunset Boulevard, Suite 220 (90069) (310)657-7113(T-A)

SMITH & ASSOCIATES, SUSAN, 121 N San Vicente Blvd, BH (90211) 852-4777 (T)

SORICE TALENT AGENCY, CAMILLE, 16661 Ventura Boulevard, Suite 400-E, Encino (91436) (818)995-1775(FS)

SPECIAL ARTISTS AGENCY, 335 North Maple Drive, Suite 360, BH (90210) (310)859-9688(C)

STAR TALENT AGENCY, 4555 1/2 Mariota Avenue, Toluca Lake (91602) (818)509-1931(FS)

STARWILL TALENT AGENCY, 6253 Hollywood Blvd #730 (90028) 874-1239 (FS)

STERN AGENCY, CHARLES H., 11766 Wilshire Blvd, Suite 760 (90025) (310)479-1788

STEVENS, STEVEN R TALENT AGENCY, 3518 West Cahuenga Blvd., Suite 301 (90068) 850-5761 (FS)

STONE MANNERS AGENCY, 8091 Selma Avenue (90046) 654-7575 (FS-A)

SUTTON, BARTH & VENNARI INC., 145 S Fairfax Avenue, Suite 310 (90036) 938-6000 (C)

TALENT GROUP INC, 9250 Wilshire Blvd, Suite 208, BH (90212) 852-9559 (FS)

TALON THEATRICAL AGENCY, 567 South Lake, Pasadena (91101) (818)577-1998(FS)

TANNEN & ASSOC, 1800 N Vine Street, Suite #120 (90028) 466-6191 (FS)

THOMAS TALENT AGENCY, 124 S. Lasky Drive, Beverly Hills, (90212) (310)247-2727(FS)

THORNTON & ASSOCIATES, ARLENE, 5657 Wilshire Blvd, Suite 290 (90036)(818)760-6688(FS-A)

TISHERMAN AGENCY, INC., 6767 Forest Lawn Drive, Suite 101 (90068) 850-6767 (C-A)

TOTAL ACTING EXPERIENCE, A, 20501 Ventura Blvd., Suite 112, Woodland Hills (91364) (818)340-9249(FS)

TURTLE AGENCY, THE, 12456 Ventura Boulevard, Suite #1, Studio City (91604) (818)506-6898(T-A)

TWENTIETH CENTURY ARTISTS, 15315 Magnolia Boulevard, Suite 429, Sherman Oaks (91403) (818)788-5516(T)

UMOJA TALENT AGENCY, 2069 W. Slauson Avenue (90047) 290-6612 (FS)

UNITED TALENT AGENCY, INC, 9560 Wilshire Blvd., 5th Floor, BH (90212) (310)273-6700(FS-A)

WAIN AGENCY, ERIKA, 1418 N Highland Ave #102 (90028) 460-4224 (T-A)

WALLIS AGENCY, 1126 Hollywood Way, Suite 203-A, Burbank (91505) (818)953-4848(FS)

WATT & ASSOCIATES, SANDRA, 7551 Melrose Avenue, Suite 5 (90046) 851-1021 (FS-A)

WAUGH TALENT AGENCY, ANN, 4731 Laurel Canyon Boulevard, Suite #5, NH (91607) (818)980-0141(FS)

WEBB ENTERPRISES, RUTH, 7500 Devista Drive (90046) 874-1700 (FS)

WHITAKER AGENCY, THE, 4924 Vineland Avenue, NH (91601) (818)766-4441 (FS-A)

WILSON & ASSOCIATES, SHIRLEY, 5410 Wilshire Boulevard, Suite #227 (90036) 857-6977 (FS)

WORLD CLASS SPORTS, 9171 Wilshire Blvd #404, BH (90210) (310)278-2010(FS-A)

WORLD WIDE ACTS, TALENT AGENCY, 5830 Las Virgenes Road, Suite 492, Calabasas (91302) (818)340-8151(FS-A)

WRIGHT ENTERPRISES, CARTER, 6513 Hollywood Blvd, Suite 210 (90028) 469-0944 (FS)

WRITERS AND ARTISTS AGENCY, 924 Westwood Blvd., Suite 900, Los Angeles, (90024) (310)824-6300 (FS-A)

ZADEH & ASSOCIATES, STELLA, 11759 Iowa Avenue (90025) (310)207-4114(T-A)

ZEALOUS ARTISTS P., INC., 139 S. Beverly Drive, Suite 222, BH (90212) (310)281-3533(FS)

NEW YORK

ABRAMS ARTISTS & ASSOCIATES, 420 Madison Avenue, 14th Floor, New York (10017)(212)935-8980 (FS-Y-A)

(310)289-0909(FS-A)

DUVA-FLACK ASSOCIATES, INC., 200 West 57th Street, Suite 1407, New York (10019) (212)957-9600 (FS-A)

EASTWOOD TALENT GROUP, LTD., 214 East 9th Street, New York (10003) (212)982-9700(FS)
EISEN ASSOCIATES, DULCINA, 154 East 61st Street, New York (10021) (212)355-6617(FS)
EPSTEIN/WYCKOFF & ASSOCIATES, 311 West 43rd Street, Suite 401, New York (10036) (212)586-9110 (FS-Y)

FLICK E & W TALENTS, INC., 881 Seventh Avenue, Suite 1110, New York (10019) (212)307-1850(FS)
FRONTIER BOOKING INTERNATIONAL, 1560 Broadway, Suite 1110, New York (10036) (212)221-0220(FS-Y)

GRANT, A THEATRICAL AND LITERARY AGENCY, 1120 Avenue of the Americas, 4th Floor, New York (10036) (212)626-6730(T-A)
GAGE GROUP INC., THE, 315 West 57th Street, Suite 4H, New York (10019) (212)541-5250(FS)
GERSH AGENCY NEW YORK, INC., 130 West 42nd Street, Suite 2400, New York (10036) (212)997-1818 (FS)
GILCHRIST TALENT GROUP, 310 Madison Avenue, Suite 1025, New York (10017) (212)692-9166(FS-Y)

H W A TALENT REPRESENTATIVES, 36 East 22nd Street, 3rd Floor, New York (10010) (212)529-4555 (FS)
HADLEY ENTERPRISES, LTD., PEGGY, 250 West 57th Street, New York (10019) (212)246-2166(FS)
HARTIG AGENCY LTD., MICHAEL, 156 Fifth Avenue, Suite 820, New York (10010) (212)929-1772 (FS)
HENDERSON/HOGAN AGENCY INC., 850 Seventh Avenue, Suite 1003, New York (10019) (212)765-5190 (FS-Y)
HODGES TALENT AGENCY, INC., 156 Fifth Avenue, Suite 515, New York (10010) (212)691-2756(FS)
BARBARA HOGENSON AGENCY, 19 West 44th Street, Suite 1000, New York (10036) (212)730-7306 (FS-A)

INGBER & ASSOCIATES, 274 Madison Avenue, Suite 1104, New York (10016) (212)889-9450(C)
INNOVATIVE ARTISTS, Talent & Literary Agency, 1776 Broadway, Suite 1810, New York (10019) (212)315-4455(T-A)
INTEGRITY TALENT, INC., 165 West 46th Street, Suite 1210, New York (10036) (212)575-5756(FS)
INTERNATIONAL CREATIVE MANAGEMENT, 40 West 57th Street, New York (10019) (212)556-5600 (FS)
IT MODELS/OMARS MEN, 251 Fifth Avenue, 7th Floor, Penthouse, New York (10016) (212)481-7220 (FS)

JAM THEATRICAL AGENCY, INC, 352 Seventh Avenue, Suite 1500, New York (10001) (212)376-6330 (FS-A)
JAN J. AGENCY, 365 West 34th Street, New York (10001) (212)967-5265(FS-Y)
JORDAN, GILL & DORNBAUM TALENT AGENCY, 156 Fifth Avenue, Suite 711, New York (10010) (212)463-8455(FS-Y)

KERIN, INC., CHARLES, 155 East 55th Street, New York (10022) (212)838-7373(FS)
KING, ARCHER, 10 Columbus Circle, Suite 1492, New York (10019) (212)765-3103(FS)
KMA ASSOCIATES, 11 Broadway Rm #1101, New York (10004) (212)581-4610(FS)
KRASNY OFFICE INC., THE, 1501 Broadway, Suite 1510, New York (10036) (212)730-8160(FS)

LALLY TALENT AGENCY, 630 Ninth Avenue, New York (10036) (212)974-8718(FS)
LANTZ OFFICE, 888 Seventh Avenue, New York (10106) (212)586-0200(FS)
LARNER, LIONEL LTD., 130 West 57th Street, New York (10019) (212)246-3105(FS)
BRUCE LEVY AGENCY, 335 West 38th Street, Suite 802, New York (10018) (212)563-7079(FS)
LURE INTERNATIONAL TALENT GROUP, INC., 915 Broadway, Suite 1210, New York (10010) (212)260-9300(FS)

MADISON TALENT GROUP, INC., 310 Madison Avenue, Suite 1508, New York (10017)(212)922-9600 (FS-Y)
MCDONALD/RICHARDS MODEL MANAGEMENT, INC., 156 Fifth Avenue, Suite 222, New York (10010) (212)627-3100(FS)
MEREDITH MODEL MANAGEMENT, 10 Furler Street, Totowa (07512) (201)812-0122(FS)
MORRIS AGENCY, INC. WILLIAM, 1325 Avenue Of the Americas, New York (10019) (212)586-5100 (FS-A)

NOUVELLE TALENT MANAGEMENT, INC., 20 Bethune Street, Suite 3B, New York (10014) (212)645-0940(FS)

OMNIPOP, INC., 55 West Old Country Road, Hicksville (11801) (516)937-6011(FS-A)
OPPENHEIM/CHRISTIE ASSOCIATES, LTD., 13 East 37th Street, New York (10016) (212)213-4330 (FS)
OSCARD AGENCY, INC., FIFI, 24 West 40th Street, Suite #17, New York (10018)(212)764-1100(FS-Y-A)

PACKWOOD TALENT LTD., HARRY, 250 West 57th Street, Suite 2012, New York (10107) (212)586-8900 (FS)
PALMER TALENT AGENCY, DOROTHY, 235 West 56th Street, #24K, New York (10019) (212)765-4280
PARADIGM, A TALENT & LITERARY AGENCY, 200 West 57th Street, Suite 900, New York (10019) (212)246-1030(FS-A)
PAULINE'S TALENT CORPORATION, 379 West Broadway, Suite 502, New York (10012) (212)941-6000(FS)
PREMIER TALENT ASSOCIATES, 3 East 54th Street, New York (10022) (212)758-4900(FS)
PROFESSIONAL ARTISTS UNLTD., 513 West 54th Street, New York (10019) (212)247-8770(FS)
PYRAMID ENTERTAINMENT GROUP, 89 Fifth Avenue, New York (10003) (212)242-7274(FS-A)

RADIOACTIVE TALENT INC., 240-03 Linden Boulevard, Elmont (11003) (212)315-1919(FS)
REICH AGENCY, NORMAN, 1650 Broadway, Suite 303, New York (10019) (212)399-2881(FS)
ROOS, LTD. GILLA, 16 West 22nd Street, 7th Floor, New York (10010) (212)727-7820(FS-Y)

SAMES & ROLLNICK ASSOCIATES, 250 West 57th Street, Suite 703, New York (10107) (212)315-4434 (FS)
SANDERS AGENCY LTD., THE, 1204 Broadway, Suite 306, New York (10001) (212)779-3737(FS)
SCHIFFMAN, EKMAN, MORRISON, AND MARX, 22 West 19th Street, 8th Floor, New York (10011) (212)627-5500(FS-Y)
SCHILL AGENCY INC., WILLIAM, 250 West 57th Street, Suite 1429, New York (10107) (212)315-5919 (FS)
SCHULLER TALENT, INC. AKA NEW YORK KIDS, 276 Fifth Avenue, 10th Floor, New York (10001) (212)532-6005(FS)
SHEPLIN ARTISTS & ASSOCIATES, 160 Fifth Avenue, Suite 909, New York (10010) (212)647-1311 (FS)
SILVER, MASSETTI & ASSOCIATES/EAST,LTD., 145 West 45th Street, #1204, New York (10036) (212)391-4545(FS)
SPECIAL ARTISTS AGENCY, INC., 111 East 22nd Street, Suite 4C, New York (10010) (212)420-0200(C)
PETER STRAIN & ASSOCIATES, INC., 1501 Broadway, Suite 2900, New York (10036) (212)391-0380(FS)

TALENT REPRESENTATIVES,INC., 20 East 53rd Street, New York (10022) (212)752-1835(FS)
TANTLEFF OFFICE, THE, 375 Greenwich Street, Suite 700, New York (10013) (212)941-3939(FS)
MICHAEL THOMAS AGENCY, INC., 305 Madison Avenue, Suite 4419, New York (10165) (212)867-0303 (FS)
TRANUM, ROBERTSON, & HUGHES, INC., 2 Dag Hammarskjold Plaza, New York (10017) (212)371-7500(FS)

VAN DER VEER PEOPLE, INC., 401 East 57th Street, New York (10022) (212)688-2880(FS)

WATERS & NICOLOSI, 1501 Broadway, Suite 1305, New York (10036) (212)302-8787(FS)

RUTH WEBB ENTERPRISES, INC., 445 West 45th Street, New York (10036) (212)757-6300(FS)

HANNS WOLTERS THEATRICAL AGENCY, 10 West 37th Street, New York (10018) (212)714-0100 (FS)

ANN WRIGHT REPRESENTATIVES,INC., 165 West 46th Street, New York (10036) (212)764-6770(FS)

WRITERS & ARTISTS AGENCY, 19 West 44th Street, Suite 1000, New York (10036) (212)391-1112(FS)

ZOLI MANAGEMENT, INC. 3 West 18th Street, 5th Floor, New York (10011) (212)242-7490(FS)

ARIZONA

ACT, 6264 East Grant Road, Tucson (85712) (520)885-3246(FS)

BLACK AGENCY, ROBERT, 7525 E. Camelback Road, Suite 200, Scottdale (85251) (602)966-2537

BLUE OX TALENT AGENCY, 2323 E. Cactus Road, Phoenix (85022) (602)788-5258(FS-A)

DANIS AGENCY, One East Camelback Road, Suite 550, Phoenix (85012) (602)263-1918

FOSI'S TALENT AGENCY, 2777 N Campbell Avenue, #209, Tucson (85719) (520)795-3534

LEIGHTON AGENCY, INC., 3333 N 44th Street #2, Phoenix (85018) (602)224-9255

SAVAGE TALENT AGENCY, ELIZABETH, 4949 East Lincoln Drive, Paradise Valley (82523) (602)840-3530

SIGNATURE MODELS & TALENT, 2600 N. 44th St., Suite #209, Phoenix (85008) (602)966-1102

BOSTON

MAGGIE, INC., 35 Newbury Street, Boston (02116) (617)536-2639

MODELS GROUP, THE, 374 Congress Street, Suite #305, Boston (02210) (617)426-4711

CHICAGO

AMBASSADOR TALENT AGENTS, 333 N. MICHIGAN AVE, Suite 314, Chicago (60601) (312)641-3491

ARIA MODEL & TALENT MGMT., 1017 W Washington Street, #2A, Chicago (60607) (312)243-9400

CUNNINGHAM, ESCOTT, & DIPENE, One East Superior Street, Suite 505, Chicago (60611) (312)944-5600(C)

DAVID & LEE, 70 W Hubbard Street, Suite 200, Chicago (60610) (312)670-4444

DAVIDSON & ASSOC , HARRISE, 65 E Wacker Place, Suite 2401, Chicago (60601) (312)782-4480

E T A INC, 7558 S Chicago Ave, Chicago (60619) (312)752-3955

GEDDES AGENCY, 1633 N. Halsted Street, Suite 400, Chicago (60614) (312)348-3333

HAMILTON, SHIRLEY, 333 E Ontario, Suite B, Chicago (60611) (312)787-4700

JACK TALENT, LINDA, 230 East Ohio Street, Suite #200, Chicago (60611) (312)587-1155

JEFFERSON & ASSOCIATES, 1050 N State Street, Chicago (60610) (312)337-1930

LILY'S TALENT AGENCY, 5962 North Elston, Chicago (60646) (312)792-3456

LORENCE, EMILIA, 619 N Wabash, Chicago (60611) (312)787-2033

MERCURY, INC, C J, 1330 Lake Avenue, Whiting (46394) (219)659-2701

NORTH SHORE TALENT, INC, 450 Peterson Road, Libertyville (60040) (708)816-1811

NOUVELLE TALENT MANAGEMENT, 15 W. Hubbard Street, 3rd Floor, Chicago (60610) (312)944-1133(FS)

SA-RAH, 1935 S Halsted, Suite 301, Chicago (60608) (312)733-2822

SALAZAR & NAVAS, INC, 367 W Chicago Ave. Chicago (60610) (312)751-3419

SCHUCART, NORMAN ENT, 1417 Green Bay Rd, Highland Park (60035) (708)433-1113

STEWART TALENT MANAGEMENT, 212 W Superior St #406, Chicago (60610) (312)943-3131

SUSANNE'S A-PLUS TALENT, 108 W Oak Street, Chicago (60610) (312)943-8315

VOICES UNLIMITED, INC, 680 N Lake Shore Dr. Suite 1330, Chicago, (60611) (312)642-3262

WILSON TALENT, ARLENE, INC, 430 W Erie Street. Suite #210, Chicago (60610) (312)573-0200

COLORADO

BALDWIN TALENT, DONNA, 50 South Steele Street, Suite #260, Denver (80209) (303)320-0067

BARBIZON AGENCY, 7535 E Hampden #108, Denver (80231) (303)337-6952

MATTAS THEATRICAL AGENCY, 1026 W Colorado Avenue, Colorado Springs (80904) (303)577-4704

MAXIMUM TALENT, INC., 3900 East Mexico Avenue, Suite 105, Denver (80210)(303)691-2344(FS)

VOICE CHOICE, 1805 S. Bellaire Street, Suite 130, Denver (80222) (303)756-9055(FS-A)

DALLAS

CAMPBELL AGENCY, THE, 3906 Lemmon Avenue, Suite 200, Dallas (75219) (214)522-8991

COLLINS, MARY AGENT C TALENT, 5956 Sherry Lane, Suite #917, Dallas, (75225) (214)360-0900

DANIEL-HORNE AGENCY, INC, 1576 Northwest Hwy., Garland (75041) (214)613-7827(FS)

DAWSON AGENCY, KIM, 700, Tower North, 2710 N. Stemmons Freeway, Dallas (75207) (214)630-5161

MARQUEE TALENT, INC., 5911 Maple Avenue, Dallas (75235) (214)357-0355(FS-A)

STONE AGENCY, IVETT, 6309 N O'Connor Road, Suite 100, Irving (75039) (214)506-9962 .

TAYLOR TALENT, PEGGY, 1825 Market Center Blvd, Suite 320A/LB37, Dallas (75207) (214)651-7884

DETROIT

AFFILIATED MODELS INC, 1680 Crooks Road, Suite #200, Troy (48084) (810)244-8770

JEFFREY MODEL & TALENT, MICHAEL, 118 S. Main Street, Suite 133, Ann Arbor (48104) (313)663-6398

PASTICHE MODEL AND TALENT, 1514 Wealthy Street, S.E., Suite 280, Grand Rapids (49506) (616)451-8417

PRODUCTIONS PLUS, 30600 Telegraph Road, Suite #2156, Bloomfeild (48301) (810)644-5566

TALENT SHOP, THE, 30100 Telegraph Road, Suite #116, Birmingham (48025) (810)644-4877

FLORIDA

A-1 PEG'S TALENT AGENCY, 133 E Lauren Court, Fern Park (32730) (407)834-0406

ACT ONE TALENT AGENCY, 1205 Washington Avenue, Miami Beach (33139) (305)672-0200

ALEXA MODEL & TALENT, 4100 W Kennedy Blvd., Suite 228, Tampa (33609) (813)289-8020

AZUREE MODELING AND TALENT, 140 N Orlando Ave #120, Winter Park (32789) (407)629-5025

BAILEY TALENT GROUP, INC., 513 W. Colonial Drive, Suite #5, Orlando (32804) (407)843-3215

BERG TALENT & MODEL AGENCY, 12614 Twisted Oak Dr., Tampa (33624) (813)877-5533

BOCA TALENT AND MODEL AGENCY, 829 SE 9th Street, Deerfield Beach (33441) (305)428-4677(FS)

BREVARD TALENT GROUP, INC, 405 Palm Springs Boulevard, Indian Harbour Beach (32937) (407)773-1355

BURNS MODEL & TALENT, DOTT, 478 Severn Ave., Davis Island, Tampa (33606) (813)251-5882

CHRISTENSEN GROUP, THE, 120 International Parkway, Suite 262, Heathrow (32746) (407)333-2506

COCONUT GROVE TALENT AGENCY, 3525 Vista Court, Coconut Grove (33133) (305)858-3002

COLOURES MODEL & TALENT AGENCY, 1655 Drexel Avenue, Suite 206, Miami Beach (33139) (305)531-2700

DIMENSIONS 3 MODELING, 5205 S Orange Avenue, Suite 209, Orlando (32809) (407)851-2575

FAMOUS FACES ENT CO, 2013 Harding St, Hollywood (33020) (305)922-0700

FLICK EAST-WEST TALENTS, INC., 161 Ocean Dr. #8, Miami Beach (33139) (305)674-9900

GORDON, ADA TALENT AGENCY, 1995 Ne 150th Street, Suite C, No Miami, (33181) (305)940-1311

GREEN AND GREEN, 1688 Meridian Avenue, 8th Floor, Miami Beach (33139) (305)532-9880

HALEY TALENT, SUSANNE, 618 Wymore Rd #2, Winter Park (32789) (407)644-0600

HAMILTON-HALL TALENT AGENCY, 13700 58th Street North, Suite 201, Clearwater, (34620) (813)538-3838

HURT-GARVER TALENT, 400 N New York Avenue, Suite #207, Winter Park (32789) (407)740-5700

INTERNATIONAL ARTISTS GROUP, INC., 420 Lincoln Road, Suite #382, Miami Beach (33139) (305)538-6100

KARR, PHILIP TALENT AGENCY, 5979 Vineland Road, Suite 319, Orlando (32819) (407)363-7773

LOUISE'S PEOPLE MODEL & TALENT AGENCY, 863 13th Avenue North, St. Petersburg (33701) (813)823-7828(FS)

MARIE, IRENE AGENCY, 728 Ocean Drive, Miami Beach (33139) (305)672-2929

MCMILLAN TALENT AGENCY, ROXANNE, 12100 NE 16th Avenue, Suite #106, North Miami (33161) (305)899-9150

PARKES MODELS, PAGE, 660 Ocean Drive, Miami Beach, (33139) (305)672-4869

POLAN TALENT AGENCY, MARIAN, 10 Ne 11th Avenue, Ft Lauderdale (33301) (305)525-8351

POMMIER, MICHELE MODELS INC, 81 Washington Avenue, Miami Beach (33139) (305)672-9344

STELLAR TALENT AGENCY, 407 Lincoln Road, Suite 2K, Miami Beach (33139) (305)672-2217

STEWART'S MODELING, EVELYN, 911 Samy Drive, Tampa, (33613) (813)968-1441

TAKE 1 EMPLOYMENT GUILD, INC., 3800 S. Tamiami Trail, Suite 18, Sarasota (34239) (941)364-9285

WORLD OF KIDS INC., 1460 Ocean Drive, Suite 205, Miami Beach (33139) (305)672-5437

GEORGIA

ATLANTA MODELS & TALENT, INC., 2970 Peachtree Road, NW, Suite #660, Atlanta (30305) (404)261-9627(FS)

AW/ATLANTA, 887 West Marietta Street, Suite #N-101, Atlanta (30318) (404)876-8555(FS-A)

BORDEN & ASSOCIATES, TED, 2434 Adina Drive, NE,, Suite B, Atlanta (30324) (404)266-0664

BURNS AGENCY, THE, 602 Hammett Drive, Decatur (30032) (404)299-8114(FS-A)

ELITE MODEL MANAGEMENT CORP/ATLANTA, 181 14th Street, Suite #325, Atlanta (30309) (404)872-7444(FS-A)

GENESIS MODELS AND TALENT, INC., 1465 Northside Drive, Suite #120, Atlanta (30318) (404)350-9212(FS)

KENNEDY MODELS & TALENT, GLYN, 659 Peachtree Street NE, Atlanta (30308) (404)892-5500 (FS)

PEOPLE STORE, THE, 2004 Rockledge Road NE, Suite 60, Atlanta (30324) (404)874-6448

SUMMERS' TALENT, DONNA, 8950 Laurel Way, Suite #200, Alpharetta (30202) (404)518-9855

HAWAII

ADR MODEL & TALENT AGENCY, 431 Kuwili Street, Honolulu (96817) (808)524-0477(FS)

KOTOMORI AGENT SERVICES, AMOS, 1018 Hoawa Lane, Honolulu (96826) (808)955-6511(FS)

MULLER TALENT AGENCY, KATHY, 619 Kapahulu Ave, Penthouse, Honolulu (96815) (808)737-7917(FS)

HOUSTON

ACTORS, ETC, 2620 Fountainview, Suite #210, Houston (77057) (713)785-4495

INTERMEDIA TALENT AGENCY, 5353 W Alabama, Suite #222, Houston (77056) (713)622-8282

PASTORINI BOSBY TALENT AG, 3013 Fountain View Drive, Suite 240, Houston(77057)(713)266-4488

QUAID TALENT AGENCY, 5959 Richmond, Suite 310, Houston (77057) (713)975-9600(FS)

YOUNG AGENCY, SHERRY, 2620 Fountain View, Suite #212, Houston (77057) (713)266-5800

NASHVILLE

ACTOR AND OTHERS TALENT AGENCY, 6676 Memphis-Arlington Road, Bartlett (38134) (901)385-7885(FS)

BOX OFFICE, INC TALENT AGENCY, 1010 16th Avenue South, Nashville (37212) (615)256-5400(FS)

CREATIVE ARTISTS AGENCY, INC., 3310 West End Avenue, 5 Floor, Nashville (37203) (615)383-8787 (FS)

LEE ATTRACTIONS, BUDDY, 38 Music Square East, SUITE 300, Nashville (37203) (615)244-4336

MORRIS AGENCY, WILLIAM, 2100 W End Avenue, Suite 1000, Nashville (37203) (615)385-0310(FS)

TALENT & MODEL LAND, 4516 Granny White Pike, Nashville (37204) (615)321-5596

TALENT TREK AGENCY, 406 11th Street, Knoxville (37916) (615)977-8735

NEVADA

BASKOW, J & ASSOCIATES, 6075 South Eastern Avenue, Las Vegas (89119) (702)733-7818(FS)

BASS CREATIVE BOOKING AGENCY, 6188 S. Sandhill Rd., Las Vegas (89120) (702)388-2898(FS)

SUPREME AGENCY, 4180 South Sandhill Road,, Suite B8, Las Vegas (89121) (702)433-3393

NEW MEXICO

AESTHETICS, INC, 489 1/2 Don Miguel, Santa Fe (87501) (505)982-5883(FS)

APPLAUSE TALENT AGENCY, 225 San Pedro NE, Albuquerque (87108) (505)262-9733

CHARACTERS, Rt 9, Box 73HH, Santa Fe (87505) (505)982-9729(FS)

CIMARRON TALENT AGENCY, 10605 Casador Del Oso NE, Albuquerque (87111) (505)292-2314

EATON AGENCY, INC, 3636 High Street N E, Albuquerque (87107) (505)344-3149

FLAIR MODELING & TALENT, 7001 Menaul Blvd. NE, Albuquerque (87110) (505)881-4688(FS)

MANNEQUIN AGENCY, THE, 2021 San Mateo Blvd Ne, Albuquerque (87110) (505)266-6829

PHOENIX AGENCY, THE, 6400 Uptown Blvd , Ne, Suite #481-W, Albuquerque (87110) (505)881-1209

SOUTH OF SANTA FE TALENT GUILD, INC., 6921-B Montgomery NE, Albuquerque (87109) (505)880-8550(FS)

PHILADELPHIA

ASKINS, DENNISE, New Market, Suite 200, Head House Square, Philadelphia (19147) (215)925-7795

CLARO MODELING AGENCY, THE, 1513 West Passyunk Ave, Philadelphia (19145) (215)465-7788

EXPRESSIONS MODELING & TALENT, 110 Church Street, Philadelphia (19106) (215)923-4420

LANGE GREER & ASSOCIATES, 18 Great Valley Parkway, Suite 180, Malvern (19355) (215)647-5515

MCCULLOUGH ASSOCIATES, 8 South Hanover Avenue, Margate (08402) (609)822-2222(FS)

PLAZA 7, 160 N Gulph Road, King Of Prussia (19406) (610)337-2693

REINHARD AGENCY, 2021 Arch Street, Suite 400, Philadelphia (19103) (215)567-2008

SAN DIEGO

AGENCY 2 MODEL & TALENT AGENCY, 2425 San Diego Avenue, Suite #209, San Diego (92110) (619)291-9556

ANDERSON,ANDY AGENCY, 7801 Mission Center Court, San Diego (92108) (619)294-4629(C)

ARTIST MANAGEMENT, TALENT AGENCY, 835 Fifth Avenue, Suite #411, San Diego (92101) (619)233-6655(FS)

ELEGANCE TALENT AGENCY, 2975 Madison Avenue, Carlsbad (92008) (619)434-3397(FS)

LILY, BEATRICE TALENT AGENCY, 1250 Prospect Street, Suite 100, San Diego (92037) (619)454-3579

NOUVEAU MODEL MANAGEMENT,TALENT AGENCY, 9823 Pacific Heights Blvd., Suite M, San Diego (92121) (619)453-2727(FS)

PATTERSON, JANICE TALENT AGENCY, 2254 Moore Street, Suite 104, San Diego (92110) (619)295-9477

SAN DIEGO MODEL MANAGEMENT, 824 Camino Del Rio North, Suite 552, San Diego (92108) (619)296-1018(FS)

SHAMON FREITAS & COMPANY, 2400 Kettner Boulevard, Suite #212, San Diego (92101) (619)234-3043(FS)

SAN FRANCISCO

BOOM MODELS & TALENT, 2565 Third Street, #206, San Francisco (94107) (415)626-6591 (FS)

COVERS MODEL & TALENT AGENCY, 4716 Foulger Drive, Santa Rosa (95405) (707)539-9252

DELL TALENT, MARLA, 2124 Union Street, San Francisco (94123) (415)563-9213

FILM THEATRE ACTORS XCHNGE, 582 Market St, Suite 302, San Francisco (94104) (415)433-3920

FRAZER AGENCY, THE, 4300 Stevens Creek Blvd, Suite #126, San Jose (95129) (408)554-1055

LOOK MODEL & TALENT AGENCY, 166 Geary Blvd, Suite 1406, San Francisco (94108)(415)781-2841

LOS LATINOS TALENT AGENCY/TALENT PLUS, 2801 Moorpark Ave #11, Dyer Building, San Jose (95128) (408)296-2213

MITCHELL TALENT MANAGEMENT, 323 Geary Street, Suite 303, San Francisco (94102)(415)395-9291

PALMERS MODEL TALENT AGENCY, 699 Eighth Street, Suite 3260-A, San Francisco (94103) (415)553-4100(FS)

PANDA AGENCY, 3721 Hoen Avenue, Santa Rosa (95405) (707)576-0711

QUINN ASSOCIATES, CLAUDIA, 533 Airport Boulevard, Suite #400, Burlingame (94010) (415)615-9950

QUINN-TONRY, INC, 601 Brannan Street, San Francisco (94107) (415)543-3797

SAN FRANCISCO TOP MODELS AND TALENT, 870 Market Street, Suite 1076, San Francisco (94102) (415)391-1800(FS)

STARS, THE AGENCY, 777 Davis Street, San Francisco (94111) (415)421-6272

WASHINGTON, DC

CENTRAL AGENCY, 623 Pennsylavania Ave., S.E., Washington (20003) (202)547-6300

CHARACTERS AGENCY INC, THE, P.O. Box #73643, Washington (20056) (202)232-2230

ERICKSON AGENCY, THE, 1481 Chain Bridge Road, Suite 200, McLean (22101) (703)356-0040(FS)

FOX ENTERPRISES, INC., 7700 Leesberg Pike, Center Towers, Suite 100, Fall Church (22043) (703)506-0335 (FS)

KIDS INTERNATIONAL TALENT AGENCY, 938 East Swan Creek Rd., Suite 152, Ft. Washington (20744) (301)292-6093(FS)

TAYLOR ROYALL AGENCY, 2308 South Road, Baltimore (21209) (410)466-5959

THE BERGMAN TALENT AGENCY, INC., 12208 Turley Drive, North Potomac (20878) (301)869-8500 (FS)

KANSAS

JACKSON ARTISTS, 7251 Lowell Dr #200, Overland Park (66204) (913)384-6688

MISSOURI

TALENT PLUS, INC, 55 Maryland Plaza, St Louis (63108) (314)367-5588

TALENT UNLIMITED,LLC, 4049 Pennsylvania, Suite 300, Kansas City (64111) (816)561-9040(FS)

SEATTLE

ACTORS GROUP, 114 Alaskan Way South, Suite 104, Seattle (98104) (206)624-9465

E. THOMAS & ASSOCIATES, INC. BLISS, 219 1st Avenue S., #420, Seattle (98104) (206)340-1875(FS)

HALLOWELL AGENCY, LOLA, 1700 Westlake Ave North, Suite 702, Seattle (98109) (206)281-4646

JAMES AGENCY, CAROL, 117 S Main St, Seattle (98104) (206)447-9191

SEALS INTERNATIONAL, EILEEN, 600 Stewart Street, Seattle (98101) (206)448-2040

STUDIOS
Television Studios

Sunset-GowerStudios
ABC - NBC.- *Hollywood*

Warner Bros.Studio
Burbank

Walt Disney Studio
Burbank

CBS MTM Radford Studio
Burbank

NBC TV Studio
Burbank

ABC
Sunset-GowerStudios
1438 N. Gower St.
Hollywood, CA 90028
(213) 467-1001
THOMAS GUIDE PG: 563 CO-ORD:G-5.

ABC
4151 Prospect Avenue
Hollywood, CA 90027
(213) 557-7777
THOMAS GUIDE PG: 564 CO-ORD: B-3

CBS-TV CITY
7800 Beverly Blvd.
Los Angeles, CA 90036
(213) 852-2345
THOMAS GUIDE PG: 633 CO-ORD: B-1

THE COMPLEX
2323 Corinth
West Los Angeles, CA 90064
(310) 477-1938
THOMAS GUIDE PG: 632 CO-ORD: B-6

FOX TELEVISION CENTER
5746 Sunset Blvd
Hollywood, CA 90028
(213) 462-7111
THOMAS GUIDE PG: 593 CO-ORD: G-5

OAKRIDGE STUDIOS
1239 S. Glendale Ave.
Glendale, CA 91205
(818) 502-5300
THOMAS GUIDE PG: 564 CO-ORD: E-7

HOLLYWOOD CENTER STUDIOS
6753 Hollywood Blvd., 7th Floor
Hollywood, CA 90028
(213) 469-5000
THOMAS GUIDE PG: 593 CO-ORD: E-4

KCAL TV
5515 Melrose Blvd.
Los Angeles, CA 90038
(213) 467-5459
THOMAS GUIDE PG: 593 CO-ORD: G-6

KCBS - LOCAL CBS
6121 Sunset Blvd.
Hollywood, CA 90028
(213) 460-3000
THOMAS GUIDE PG: 593 CO-ORD: F-4

KCOP
915 N. La Brea
Los Angeles, CA 90038
(310) 851-1000
THOMAS GUIDE PG: 593 CO-ORD: D-6

KCOP
Hollywood

KTTV TV Studio
Hollywood

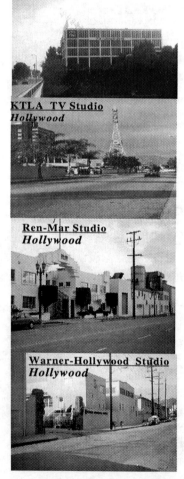

KTLA TV Studio
Hollywood

Ren-Mar Studio
Hollywood

Warner-Hollywood Studio
Hollywood

KTLA - CHANNEL 5
Hollywood Center Studios
5842 Sunset Blvd., Bldg. #1
Hollywood, CA 90028
(213) 460-5500
THOMAS GUIDE PG: 593 CO-ORD: G-4

NBC - BURBANK
3000 W. Alameda Ave.
Burbank, CA 91523
(818) 840-4444
THOMAS GUIDE PG: 563 CO-ORD: E-4

POST GROUP STUDIOS
6335 Homewood Ave.
Hollywood, CA 90028
(213) 462-2300
THOMAS GUIDE PG: 593 CO-ORD: E-5

PRODUCTION GROUP
1330 N. Vine St.
Hollywood, CA 90028
(213) 469-8111
THOMAS GUIDE PG: 593 CO-ORD: F-5

SUNSET THEATRE
6230 Sunset Blvd.
Los Angeles, CA 90028
(213) 962-1991
THOMAS GUIDE PG: 593 CO-ORD: F-4

T.A.V. STUDIOS Trans American
Video
1541 Vine St.
Hollywood, CA 90028
(213) 466-2141
THOMAS GUIDE PG: 593 CO-ORD: F-4

WARNER HOLLYWOOD

STUDIOS
1041 N. Formosa
Hollywood, CA 90046
(213) 850-2500
THOMAS GUIDE PG: 593 CO-ORD: D-6

NBC - HOLLYWOOD
Sunset-Gower Studios
1420 N Beachwood Ave.
Hollywood, CA 90028
(213) 467-1001
THOMAS GUIDE PG: 593 CO-ORD: G-5

HOLLYWOOD CENTER
STUDIOS
1041 N. Las Palmas
Hollywood, CA 90038
(213) 469-5000

THOMAS GUIDE PG: 593 CO-ORD: E-6

FEATURE STUDIOS

Universal Studio- Lankershim
Universal City

Universal Studios-Barham gate
Burbank

Raleigh Studio
Hollywood

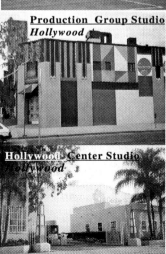

Production Group Studio
Hollywood

Hollywood Center Studio
Hollywood

WARNER BROS.
4000 Warner Blvd.
Burbank, CA 91522
(818) 954-6000
OLIVE & HOLLYWOOD WAY
THOMAS GUIDE PG: 563 CO-ORD: D-5

CULVER STUDIOS
9336 W. Washington Blvd.
Culver City, CA 90230
(213) 836-5537
ROBERTSON & WASHINGTON
THOMAS GUIDE PG:672 CO-ORD: G-1

DON CARLOS STAGE
1360 E. 6TH STREET
Los Angeles, CA
ALAMEDA & MATEO

THOMAS GUIDE PG: 634 CO-ORD:H-6

LINSEY STUDIOS
25241 Avenue Stanford.
Valencia, CA 91355
THOMAS GUIDE PG:4550 CO-ORD: C-1

PARAMOUNT STUDIOS
5555 Melrose Ave.
Hollywood, CA 90038
(213) 956-5000
GOWER & MELROSE
THOMAS GUIDE PG: 593 CO-ORD: G-6

REN-MAR STUDIOS
846 N. Cahuenga Blvd.
Hollywood, CA 90038
(213) 463-0808
MELROSE & VINE
THOMAS GUIDE PG: 593 CO-ORD: F-6

SANTA CLARITA STUDIOS
25135 Anza Drive
Valencia, CA 91355
THOMAS GUIDE PG: 4550 CO-ORD: D-1

TWENTIETH CENTURY-FOX
10200 Pico Blvd..
Century City, CA 90067
(213)
PICO & MOTOR AVE.
THOMAS GUIDE PG: 632 CO-ORD: E-4

WALT DISNEY STUDIOS
500 S. Buena Vista St.
Burbank, CA 91506
(818) 840-1000

Paramount Studios
Hollywood

CBS TV-CITY Studio
Los Angeles

SONY Studio
Culver City

Culver Studio
Culver City

Warner-Hollywood Studio
Hollywood

ALAMEDA & BUENA VISTA
THOMAS GUIDE PG: 563 CO-ORD: F-4

CBS/MTM STUDIOS
4024 Radford Ave.
Studio City, CA 91604
(818) 760-5000
LAUREL CANYON & VENTURA
THOMAS GUIDE PG: 562 CO-ORD: G-5

**SONY PICTURES ENTERTAIN-
MENT**
10202 W. Washington Blvd.
Culver City, CA 90232
(310) 280-8000
OVERLAND & WASHINGTON
THOMAS GUIDE PG: 672 CO-ORD: F-2

RALEIGH STUDIOS
5300 Melrose Ave.
Hollywood, CA 90004
(213) 466-3111
VAN NESS & MELROSE
THOMAS GUIDE PG: 593 CO-ORD: G-6

UNIVERSAL STUDIOS
100 Universal City Plaza
Universal City, CA 91608
(818) 777-1000
FOREST LAWN & BARHAM
(EXTRAS ENTER HERE)
THOMAS GUIDE PG: 563 CO-ORD: D-5

**VALLEY PRODUCTION
CENTER**
6633 Van Nuys Blvd.
Van Nuys, CA 91401
(818) 988-6601
THOMAS GUIDE PG: 532 CO-ORD: A-6

V.P.S. STUDIOS
800 No. Seward St.
Hollywood, CA 90038
(213) 469-7244
(213) 462-2473
THOMAS GUIDE PG: 593 CO-ORD: E-6

EXTRA NOTE

THEATRICAL BOOK STORES

TRADE PUBLICATIONS

LARRY EDMUNDS BOOKSTORE
6644 HOLLYWOOD BLVD.
HOLLYWOOD, CA 90028
213 463-3273
STORE HOURS: MON-SAT 10A-6P
THOMAS BROTHER GUIDE
PAGE: 593 CO-ORD: E-4

SAMUEL FRENCH THEATRE & FILM BOOKSTORE-HOLLYWOOD
7623 SUNSET BLVD.
HOLLYWOOD, CA 90046
213 876-0570
STORE HOURS: MON-FRI 10A-6P,
SAT 11A-5P
THOMAS BROTHER GUIDE
PAGE 593 CO-ORD C-5

SAMUEL FRENCH THEATRE & FILM BOOKSTORE-STUDIO CITY
11963 VENTURA BLVD.
STUDIO CITY, CA 91604
818 762-0535
STORE HOURS: MON-FRI 10A-6P, SAT 11A-5P, SUN 12P-5P
THOMAS BROTHER GUIDE
PAGE: 562 CO-ORD: H-6

PERFORMING ARTS BOOKS
7215 OWENSMOUTH AVE.
CANOGA PARK, CA 91303
818 703-7311
STORE HOURS: MON-SAT 11A-5P
THOMAS BROTHER GUIDE
PAGE: 530 CO-ORD: A-5

DRAMA BOOKSHOP
DRAMA BOOK SHOP
723 7th Ave.
NEW YORK CITY, NY 10019
212 944-0595

BACKSTAGE WEST
5055 WILSHIRE BLVD.
6TH FLOOR
LOS ANGELES, CA 90036
(213) 525-2356
PUBLISHED: WEEKLY
COST PER ISSUE: $1.85

BLACK TALENT NEWS
P.O. Box 7374
CULVER CITY, CA 90036
(213) 525-2356
PUBLISHED: MONTHLY
COST PER ISSUE: $3.00

DRAMALOGUE
146 GORDON AVE
HOLLYWOOD
(213) 464-5079
PUBLISHED: WEEKLY
COST PER ISSUE: $1.85

HOLLYWOOD REPORTER
5055 WILSHIRE BLVD.
6TH FLOOR
LOS ANGELES, CA 90036
(213) 525-2000
PUBLISHED: DAILY
COST PER ISSUE: $1.00

VARIETY
5700 WILSHIRE BLVD.
LOS ANGELES, CA 90036
(213) 857-6600
PUBLISHED: DAILY
COST PER ISSUE: $1.25

PUBLISHERS BOOKSHELF

Most of these reference books maybe found in your local library. All are in my personal library. There are many good books on acting, writing, producing and directing as well as those about crew and other aspects of the Film & TV industry. The best are listed here. All are available from **Back To One Publishing**. Call the friendly toll-free order desk. For those not available here send $2.00 U.S., for the 120 ppg, **1996 MEGA-CATALOG** of 1,000's of movie & T.V. scripts, industry directories, guides and books along with audio/video seminars & software and much more including Hundreds of Gift Items from your favorite Movies, TV Shows & Studios.

Never give up, especially never give up learning. You have taken steps to your acting or background acting career, now you have an obligation to have fun and excel. Review what has worked and do more of it. Review what has not work and cut your losses.

THE L.A. AGENTS BOOK

Get The Agent You Need & The Career You Want
K. Callan - 302 pgs.

This is the only book written to include background on the agents, their histories and information regarding size and quality of their client lists. Personal interviews with over 130 L.A. agents and 20 years in the business have helped the author produce this indispensable book.

~$15.95

THE NEW YORK AGENT BOOK

Get The Agent You Need & The Career You Want
K. Callan - 282 pgs. 4th edition.

This is the only book written to include background on the agents, their histories and information regarding size and quality of their client lists. Personal interviews with over New York agents and 20 years in the business have helped the author produce this indispensable book.

~$17.95

THE ADDRESS BOOK

Michael Levine- 269 pgs. How to reach anyone who is anyone. Direct access to nearly 4,00 Celebrities, Corporate Execs, and other VIP's. This remarkable book contains the addresses of thousands of the world's most powerful, popular and influential people especially those in the entertainment industry. It is a must!

~$11.00

DEALMAKING IN THE FILM & TELEVISION INDUSTRY

FROM NEGOTIATIONS TO CONTRACTS
Mark Litwak - 350 pgs.

Dealmaking is the first "self-defense" book for everyone working in the film and television industry. Armed with this book, filmmakers can save themselves thousands of dollars in legal fees as they navigate the shark-infested waters of the entertainment business. Whether you are a producer, writer, director, or actor Mark Litwak will help you steer clear of the many contractual traps that may await you.

-$26.95

THE MOVIE BUSINESS BOOK

Jason Squire - editor - 480 pgs

Behind the glitter of Hollywood lies a high-powered, multi-billion dollar business whose workings are known only to industry insiders. In this book, forty of Hollywood's most celebrated producers, directors, screenwriter, agents lawyers marketers, distributors, exhibitors and deal makers reveal the secrets of their trade in personal accounts that are both highly informative and wonderfully entertaining.

-$14.00

WHAT A PRODUCER DOES

Buck Houghton - 200 pps

What exactly does a TV producer do, anyway? This book really is the inside story, going behind the scene from veterans who know, the producer of the first one hundred plus episode of Twilight Zone Outlining the key functions such as the tools, techniques and resources required to deal with script development, budgeting, casting, crew development and management, and much, much more. Reading this book should be one of the first steps that any prospective producer takes

-$14.95

GAFFERS, GRIPS & BEST BOYS

Eric Taub - 276 pgs.

From producer to director to gaffer and computer special - effects creator, A behind-the-scene look at who does what in the making of a motion picture. It examines the essentials of personnel in a style that is simple and light in its approach.

-$24.95

COMMERCIALS JUST MY SPEED

Verne'e Watson Johnson -192 pgs.

Revealed are 25 years of various approaches to successful commercial acting by a CLIO award winning actress. Covering all the basics on preparing for and developing a lasting career in TV commercials.

-$15.95

AN ACTOR SUCCEEDS

Career Management for the Actor - 397 pgs.

Chapters include Getting the Jobs; Choosing the Jobs; Making the Deals; and Turns in the Road. Of particular note are discussions concerning what various casting directors look for in a "cold reading" and a "call back," as well as advice on photos, resumé and tapes.

-$15.95

FROM AGENT TO ACTOR

Edgar Small - 200 pgs.

A very realistic point of view of acting as a profession. Topics include No Actor Is Irreplaceable; Not About Acting But About Money; The People For Whom You Audition; Lies, Bluffs And Threats; Personal Managers; New York vs. Los Angeles; and many others. Written by a man who started as an actor in the 40's and has also devoted thirty years to being an agent so you will see both perspectives.

-$14.95

HOW TO BE A WORKING ACTOR

Mari Lu Henner & Lynne Rogers - 320 pgs.

Launching your acting career involves dedication, training, and learning the most crucial skill of all: how to land a role. This book shows you how to manage an acting career as a business, how to have a successful audition, how to network, and how to make your dreams come true.

-$18.95

YOUR FILM ACTING CAREER

M. K. Lewis & Rosemary R. Lewis - 302 pgs.

Here is a working guide for today's actors. It provides answers to hundreds of questions asked about the Hollywood scene: Finding work in TV, movies commercials etc., Living in Los Angeles ... choosing classes ..resumés.. contracts and much, much more. The classic work on the business of acting!

-$15.95

ACTING IN TELEVISION COMMERCIALS

Squire Fridell - 216 pgs.

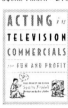

Acting in television commercials is fun, challenging, and often very lucrative. Squire Fridell, a veteran of over 1,700 television commercials, including 15 years as the Toyota spokesman and six years as TV's Ronald McDonalds, offers tips and advice that will give you the edge necessary to break in and keep on working.

-$15.00

ACTING IS EVERYTHING

Judy Kerr - 392 pgs.

The ultimate reference guide for planning, promoting and expanding your acting career. Where to go, Who to call, What to spend, What not to do, Right to the point. Actress, Acting Coach and Director - shares a lifetime of techniques and tricks of the trade. These special resources provide everything that you need to develop your talent, your career, your life.

-$14.95

Micro- Budget HOLLYWOOD

Philip Gaines & David J. Rhodes - 220 pgs.

The first book to offer to offer micro-budget filmmakers a fully explained - line-by-line, account-by-account - sample budget specifically geared to their economic bracket. This straight forward, commonsense approach to shoe-string budgeting is an invaluable aid to understanding how to keep a film on track and within budget. Includes interviews with eleven who did and does Micro-Budgeting.

$17.95

The NEW TAX GUIDE FOR PERFORMERS WRITERS, DIRECTORS DESIGNERS & OTHER SHOW BIZ FOLK

R. Brendan Hanlon - 130 pgs.

From how to get organized to what to do if you are audited, including a monthly travel expense diary. A must read for those in for the long haul .

-$10.95

THE CELEBRITY ALMANAC

Ed Lucaire - 278 pgs.

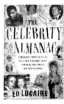

A treasure trove of facts, fun, list, and lore about the rich, the famous and the infamous. Here's the latest Insider's Scoop on the celebrities and newsmakers. A fabulous feast of tantalizing tidbits, and juicy morsels, this is a bonanza for people-watchers, moviegoers, sports fans and of course trivia buffs.

-$10.00

THE SCRIPT IS FINISHED, NOW WHAT DO I DO?

K. Callan - 296 pgs

Deals with query letters, meetings writer/agent relationships and how to nurture them; what the writer has a right to expect and what is too much to expect; the relative value of no agent, a star agent and discerning which is the agent with whom you would have the most fruitful relationship.

-$15.95

SCREEN WRITING TRICKS OF THE TRADE

William Froug - 158 pgs.

Distills William Froug's many years as a Hollywood professional and a highly respected screenwriting teacher into a fresh and timeless primer that takes the novice screenwriter on an insightful journey from the first urge to write through the completion and sale of a well wrought script.

-$10.95

MAKING A GOOD SCRIPT GREAT

Linda Seger - 244 pgs.

Making a good script great is not just a matter of having a good idea. Nor is it a matter of just putting that good idea down on paper. In script-writing, it's not just the writing but also the rewriting that counts. Making a Good Script Great focuses on the rewriting process and offers specific methods to help you craft tighter, stronger, and more workable scripts. Especially if you are writing your first script.

-$12.95

THE SCREENWRITER'S BIBLE

David Trottier - 196 pgs 8 x 11

A wealth of practical information and straightforward explanations of screenwriting fundamentals. A concise presentation of screen-writing basics. Formatting for both screenplays and teleplays. Work-book that walks the writer through the writing process, from nascent ideas through revisions. Sales and marketing guide that presents proven marketing plans and sales strategies.

-$18.95

HOW TO WRITE A MOVIE IN 21 DAYS

Viki King - 192 pgs

The ultimate survival guide. It takes the aspiring screenwriter the short-est distance from blank page to completed script. A step-by-step process designed to get the story in the write's heart onto the page. King's friendly style is like having a first-rate writing partner every step of the way.

-$12.00

HOW TO SELL YOURSELF AS AN ACTOR

K. Callan - 250 pgs. 3rd. ED.

A necessity for the beginning actor as well as the trained veteran, this popular book addresses the age-old question of how to merchandise your craft after you have learned it. Whether you are in Dallas, des Moine, Los Angeles, or New York. Step-by-step instructions for pack-aging your talents, finding and choosing agents being your own agent, networking, appraising the market and more.

-$17.95

AFRICAN-AMERICAN SCREENWRITERS NOW

Conversations with Hollywood's Black Pack
Eric Leon Harris - 300 pgs

Hollywood is currently seeing a great influx of young African-American filmmakers who collec-tively are altering the face of American filmmaking. Bringing to-gether both up-and-coming and established screenwriters these writers discuss their influences, their goals, the birth of stories, the writing process, getting work, and getting films made alongside their comments on racial barriers and the portrayal of blacks in film.

-$16.95

REBEL WITHOUT A CREW

Robert Rodriguez - 259 pgs

The remarkable story of how a 23 year old filmmaker with $7,000 became a Holywood Player. From the director of El Marachi and Desparado. How you too can do it with a crash course in his Ten- Minute film school

$22.95

THE HOLLYWOOD REPORTER STUDIO BLU-BOOK DIRECTORY

Ed. by Toni Smithson - 550 pgs, 9x12

For over 60 years, the BLU-BOOK has been an invalu-able resource to the entertainment industry. THOU-SANDS of listings cover everything from film/video post production services to foreign press representatives worldwide.

$59.95

THE WORKING ACTOR'S GUIDE L.A.

Ed. by Karin Mani - 580 pgs

Complete sourcebook for L.A. actors with over 85 categories including Agents, Business and personal Man-agers, Casting Directors, Photographers, Production Companies, Theaters, Acting Schools, etc. Also included are helpful articles. Terrific guide for those living inside or outside of LA.

$35.95

EXTRA RELATED SERVICES

Hollywood Background Artist Association

H.B.A.A., one of the most effective, informative, comprehensive, exciting and rewarding entertainment industry organizations. They deserve your talents, skills, abilities, ideas, information and support!

Your voice in the entertainment industry!

Visit us on the WWW

http://hollywoodnetwork.com/hn/acting/

http://www.hollywoodnetwork.com/Chambers

The **H.B.A.A.** is one the **BEST** opportunity to learn about casting that is going on in the industry on a daily basis. The purpose of this organization is to network on a daily basis what casting is going on, what auditions are taking place, where to send or submit photos and resumés, which casting companies have projects, and which casting companies will really give you work. This information is valuable in helping every member achieve their career goals.

The information is geared to Union and Non-Union Principal Actors and Union and Non-Union Non-Principal Performers & Background Actors.

The benefits gained from belonging to the H.B.A.A. is the opportunity to learn about everything that is going on in the industry every day and to be able to use this information to your best advantage. As an member, you are able to get discounts on many of the "TOOLS OF THE TRADE" needed to present yourself professionally in a very competitive industry.

Come hear great enetertainment and casting persons guest speakers share their career opportunities information at the monthly meetings, special coaches and instructors will also be available. Thus increasing your knowledge of industry information.

Membership meeting the last Saturday of every month from 12:00 p.m.-3:00 p.m.. 11:30 p.m.- 12:00 p.m. is a prospective members orientation, 12:00 p.m. 2:00 p.m. is the general meeting for members. **Guest may audit one orientation meeting before membership is required.** Handouts are given out at meetings with the latest casting information for principal and background work. We will place your photo & info before every virtual casting and talent agent via our webpage on World Wide Web.

H.B.A.A. work very closely with many of the casting agencies and many casting agents network job directly with us as to their casting needs. All casting information is networked through a **"FOR MEMBERS ONLY"** coded broadcast line.

The membership fees is very small. The only requirement other than fees is that you are professional on the set and are willing to work and network with others. I have discovered that if everyone does a little, everyone accomplishes a lot!

You are invited to become be a part of the

fastest growing information network in the

entertainment industry.

Send your name, address including country and telephone number on a post card or E-mail us for more information about this exciting new opportunity to:

H.B.A.A.
c/o Back To One
P.O . Box 753
Hollywood, CA 90078-0753
E-mail:backtoone@earthlink.net

HOLLYWOOD BACKGROUND ARTIST ASSOCIATION

H.B.A.A. offers its members many opportunities and discounts on various tools and material necessary for the aspiring actor including but not limited to an industry newsletter, discounts on photos, photo duplication, resumés, envelopes, garments bags, tote bags, chairs, vitamins, makeup and wardrobe to list a few.

The **H.B.A.A.** membership cost only $100.00 per year and a trial subscription to the very informative newsletter is included, a great bargain!

The **H.B.A.A.** can also arrange for friends and relatives or as your groups fund-raiser to have a *WALK-ON PART* on the set of their favorite TV show or to work alongside their favorite actor or actress during or as part of a vacation in HOLLYWOOD. Full services, complete with airline reservations, hotel accommodation, limousine and ground trans-portation, and our new exclusive *"V.I.P.- Behind The Scene"* sight-seeing tours and much more. Travel and services fees range from $250.00 - $2500.00

For more information write/call <u>or</u> to become a member send Visa, MasterCard, check or money order payable to Back To One at:

H.B.A.A.
c/o BACK TO ONE PUBLICATIONS
P.O. BOX 753-H
HOLLYWOOD, CA 90078-0753
213 969-4897 or 818 907-0908

E-mail: backtoone@earthlink.net

 Visa - MasterCard Accepted

JUDY KERR'S ACTING WORKSHOP

Each workshop begins with sensory exercises, learning to develop your own personal methods for evoking emotion, anger, tears and sensuality.

The second half of each class is usually on camera, doing cold readings, scenes and monologues. Every actor has the opportunity to work in both sections of each class. This is a safe place to prepare for auditions and showcases and to discover and expand your acting instrument.

JUDY KERR
ACTRESS-DIRECTOR-COACH

Judy Kerr teaches THE TECHNIQUE.

Developing a basic craft is your insurance that you'll be able to 'deliver the goods' on demand. Actors succeed by developing basic acting tools in a loving supportive atmosphere, and then viewing their work on video. In addition, we explore actor's secrets and the "tricks of the trade." There is a lot of individual attention, career counseling and work on your audition and interview skills.

She has been working with beginning professionals as well as experienced actors who want to develop technique or work on specific acting problems.

Actor may bring a videotape to class to keep a record of their work. Copies of this work as well as scenes from her cable television show have been successful in generating interest from agents, managers and casting directors

JUDY KERR......... acting coach, actress, author and director, has been working with actors to develop careers for over fifteen years. She just finished the second season of coaching on *THE NEW LASSIE* series. Her television show on Continental and Century cable in Los Angeles, **Judy Kerr's Acting Workshop**, is in it's eighth season.

Actors and celebrities she has coached have appeared in such features as *SOAP DISH, TEEN WITCH, TANGO & CASH* and *DO THE RIGHT THING*. Others are currently series regulars on *SEINFELD*, SISTERS, *BOLD & BEAUTIFUL, SANTA BARBARA* and *NORTHERN EXPOSURE*.
THE PROGRAM: WEEKLY EVENING CLASSES.
LOCATION: HOLLYWOOD HILLS.
ADMISSION BY INTERVIEW. 4 CLASSES PER MONTH $125.00 CLASS SIZE LIMITED. ALL NEW STUDENTS MUST TAKE A PRIVATE PREPARATION CLASS FEE $30.00. AUDITING PERMITTED BY APPOINTMENT. PRIVATE COACHING AVAILABLE.

CALL (818) 505-9373 TODAY!

ACTING IS EVERYTHING
by JUDY KERR

AN ACTOR'S GUIDEBOOK FOR A SUCCESSFUL CAREER IN LOS ANGELES

START YOUR FILM CAREER

AND BEGIN WORKING IN TELEVISION, MOVIES AND COMMERCIALS IN THE NEXT 24 HOURS.

In this 3-hour fact filled fun seminar Cullen Chambers actor, Best-Selling, Award-Winning author of 'BACK TO ONE' How To Make Good Money As A Hollywood Extra, will teach you the fastest way to break into movies, television and commercials.

You can be on the set of your favorite show and make good money at the same time! Sounds too good to be true? Well, it isn't. Background actors do it every day. Whether your interest lie in the movies, television or commercials, there is a great demand for people to fill the needs of production companies. Working as a background actor is perfect for housewives, students, retirees, anyone in-between jobs, or anyone with a flexible schedule who is interested in working alongside your favorite actor or on the set of their favorite TV show. If you're waiting on your big break into show business, it's the perfect day job-- studying the pros! The best thing is that anyone can be a background actor, people of all shapes, sizes and colors are needed-- no special talent or experience is required.

In this exciting fun fact-filled seminar you will learn insider tips and tricks on how to get started, where to find the jobs, how to work with the casting agencies, how to market yourself for success and much more.

THIS SPECIAL SEMINAR IS ONLY $39.00 PER PERSON
REGISTER NOW!

ENROLLMENT IN THIS SPECIAL SEMINAR IS LIMITED IN THE HEART OF HOLLYWOOD

TO RESERVE YOUR SEAT(S) TODAY
CALL (818) 907-0908

EXTRA NOTES

ALLIANCE of BLACK
ENTERTAINMENT TECHNICIANS

The Alliance of Black Entertainment Technicians (ABET) was formed in June 1988 by Shirley Moore. The purpose of A.B.E.T. has been to provide, promote, enhance and assist Black technicians in the motion picture entertainment industry by increasing awareness, visibility and opportunities through education, networking and promotional activities. A.B.E.T. have been extremely successful just a few of their numerous accomplishments to date include:

✪ABET Annual Entertainment Industry Networking Brunch.

✪ABET Call-sheet Newsletter promotes, recognize and informs.

✪UCLA EXTENTION SCHOLARSHIP PROGRAM.

✪ABET Resources Directory - Jobs and Technicians Listings.

✪Filled over 250 industry job positions through networking in the first 2 years.

✪ABET Reception honoring two Black Academy Award Winners.

✪Two time recipient Russell Williams for sound "GLORY" & "DANCES WITH WOLVES" 1990 & 1991. Willie Burton for sound "BIRD" 1989.

✪TV Talkshow interviews for members including Behind The Scene interviews of crew members on "BoyZ N the Hood" & "White Men Can't Jump".

In addition, through a series of public awareness program ABET conducts Career Day presentations at secondary school and colleges, seminar & workshops, award ceremonies and other activities that involve the industry and the community.

For further information regarding membership please send $10.00 to Shirley Moore at:

ABET, c/o Back To One Publications,
P.O. Box 753-T, Hollywood, CA 90078-0753
**A great organization for those pursuing careers
behind the camera!**

THE ASSOCIATION OF
ASIAN PACIFIC AMERICAN ARTISTS

The Association of Asian Pacific American Artists is going into its third decade as a non-profit organization concerned with the positive images and balanced portrayal of Asian Pacific Americans. The purpose of A.A.P.A.A. has been to provide, promote, enhance and assist Asian Pacific talent and technicians in the motion picture entertainment industry by increasing awareness, visibility and opportunities through education, networking and promotional activities. A.A.P.A.A. has been extremely successful. Just a few of their numerous accomplishments to date include:

✪A.A.P.A.A. Annual Entertainment Industry "JIMMIE" Awards for excellence.
✪A.A.P.A.A. INSIDE MOVIES Newsletter.
✪A.A.P.A.A. Resources Directory- Casting Notices, Crew Jobs and Technicians Listings.

In addition, through a series of public awareness programs, A.A.P.A.A. conducts activities that involve the industry and the Asian Pacific community. They feel "We are near, yet so far, far away. The 1990's can become an enormous opportunity for Asian Americans in film and on television."

They deserve your support!!

For further information regarding membership please contact Beulah Ku by mail or telephone at:

A.A.P.A.A.
3518-B. Cahuenga Blvd West, Suite 302
Los Angeles, CA 90068

EXTRA PROMOTIONAL SERVICES

In no other business does the old saying ... "It pays to advertise" ring truer.

Promotion and publicity is the name of the game. You should be sending at least 25 pieces of promotional material to industry people each week. It is <u>your</u> business!

The people in the casting section of the industry must know you exist before they can hire you. They see hundreds of people a week. You must plan a promotional and marketing campaign like big companies. You must keep yourself in the casting agents mind. The more they know of you the more familiar you are, the more they can trust you, the more familiar, the more trust and confidence they have in you , the more acting assignments you will land.

The following promotional and marketing tools are just what you need to pump up your act and make it easier to promote and publicize your look, your experiences, your talent, your professionalism, your business and your career.

Use of them liberally will bring amazing results! Be creative! It is your dynamic career you are promoting.

SEE YOU <u>IN</u> THE MOVIES!!!

EXTRA NOTES

𝕭ecause First Impressions are Lasting Impressions...

DocChristopher Chambers
P.O. Box 753
Hollywood, CA 90078

(213) 969-4897
(818) 972-9474

Dennis Tracey
(213) 969-4897
SAG   AFTRA

Lisa Marie Stagno

actress - model -
voice-over
SAG - AFTRA - AE
(213) 969-4897

Cheryl Felton
213 969-4897
MODEL   ACTRESS

...and one picture is worth a thousand words!

"BACK TO ONE" Graphics Services
Presents...

Photo Business & Postcards

First Quality, Fast Professional Service
at very, very affordable prices

Marc Urgello

P.O. Box 753
Hollywood, CA 90078

(213) 969-4897
(818) 972-9474

SAG/AFTRA

Horizontal

Photo may be on either left or right side. Text limited to 8 lines, including blank lines, maximum 24 characters per line, including spaces

R.C. BATES
(213) 969-4897
SAG   AFTRA

Vertical

Text is limited to 4 lines. Maximum 24 characters per line, including spaces

BUSINESS CARDS AVAILABLE ON WHITE
GLOSSY AND STANDARD CARD STOCK

**Claude 'Pete'
Bryant**
SAG AFTRA
(213) 969-4897

500 Portrait Photo
Business Cards

**Evangeline
Fasig**

SAG AFTRA AE

Actress

213 969-4897

500 Landscape Photo Business Cards

500
Portrait
Photo
Post
Cards
4¼"x5½"

Maritess Villutuya
(213) 969-4897

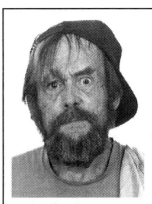

CLOWN

Rent-A-Gang

(213) 969-4897

500
Landscape
Photo
Post
Cards
4¼"x5½"

Post Card shown actual size (4 -1/4" x 5 -1/2")

Vertical

Text is limited to 4 lines. Maximum 24 characters per line, including spaces.

100 - Typeset Photo Résumés (8½"x11")

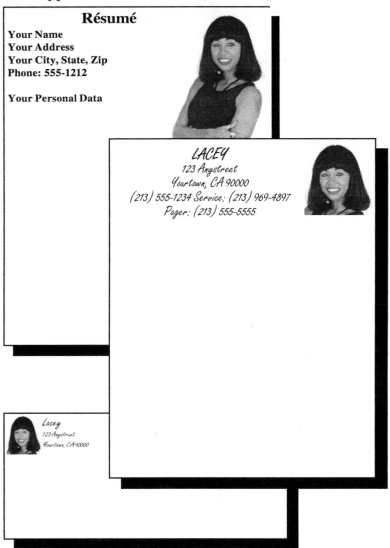

Résumé

Your Name
Your Address
Your City, State, Zip
Phone: 555-1212

Your Personal Data

LACEY
123 Anystreet
Yourtown, CA 90000
(213) 555-1234 Service: (213) 969-4897
Pager: (213) 555-5555

Lacey
123 Anystreet
Yourtown, CA 90000

100 No. 10 Photo Envelopes

From the desk of
Lacey

250 -
4¼"x11"
THINGS
TO DO

200 - 5½"x 8½" Notes

THINGS TO DO TODAY

1. _____
2. _____
3. _____
4. _____
5. _____
6. _____
7. _____
8. _____
9. _____
10. _____
11. _____
12. _____

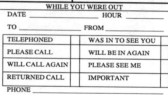

WHILE YOU WERE OUT		
DATE _____	HOUR _____	
TO _____	FROM _____	
TELEPHONED	WAS IN TO SEE YOU	
PLEASE CALL	WILL BE IN AGAIN	
WILL CALL AGAIN	PLEASE SEE ME	
RETURNED CALL	IMPORTANT	

PHONE _____
MESSAGE _____
_____

SIGNED

CALLING SERVICE
PHONE NUMBER
TALENT AGENT
PHONE NUMBER
BEEPER
PHONE NUMBER

YOUR NAME

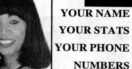

YOUR NAME
YOUR STATS
YOUR PHONE
NUMBERS

6O 4¼"x5½"
PHONE MESSAGE
PADS

EXTRA NOTES

ORDERING IS AS EASY AS 1..2..3..

1. FILL IN NAME
2. CARD TYPE
3. QUANITY
4. STYLE
5. CARD STOCK
6. CARD COLOR
7. BORDER
8. TYPEFACE
9. TEXT ON CARD
10. SEND ORDER

8. Borders

① ━━━━━ ⑤ ═══ ⑨ ▬ ▬ ▬
② ━━━━━ ⑥ ■ ■ ■ ■ ⑩ ━ ━ ━
③ ━━━━━ ⑦ ═══ ⑪ ▬ ▬ ▬
④ ▬▬▬▬ ⑧ ● ● ● ● ⑫ ━━━━

9. Type-Main Line is set in 12 & 24 pt. type , all body copy will be set in 8 pt. type.

⓪. TIMES NEW ROMAN ①. **Times New Roman Bold**
②*Times New Roman Italic* ③***Times New Roman Bold Italic***
④Arial ⑤**Arial bold** ⑥*Arial Italic* ⑦***Arial Bold Italic***
⑧**Bodnoff** ⑨Homeward ⑩*FREEPORT* ⑪QUANTUM
⑫**Renfrew** ⑬ Lincoln

Base Price For Standard Black & White Photo Business Cards And Photo Post Cards

500 Photo Business Cards
only $55.00
500 Photo Post Cards
only $65.00

Custom Variation Charges

1. Printing on back of card (for 1st 500 or 1000)	30.00	_____
2. Border from list	N/C	_____
3. Logo or Art (each)	4.00	_____
4. Extra lines over 8 on horizontal (per line) *4 lines max. on vertical*	2.00	_____
5. Proof (black & white)	10.00	_____
6. Reproduction of customer supplied art	10.00	_____
7. Reproduction of 2nd photo needed**	10.00	_____
8. Bleed printing which runs off card (per. side)	10.00	_____

TOTAL FROM BASE PRICE & CUSTOM VARIATIONS LIST $ _____

PROFESSIONAL Studio Photo Session with famous Hollywood photographer RICH HOGAN. Special Photo cards package includes 8 poses/2 wardrobe changes/processing/ prints/negatives only $35.00. Call (213) 467-2628

BACK TO ONE
GRAPHICS SERVICES
DEPT. ____
P.O. BOX 753
HOLLYWOOD, CA 90078-0753
(213) 969-4897

FOR OFFICE USE ONLY
☐SR ____
☐CK MO CA ____
☐DATE REC'D ____
☐PROOF ____
☐PRINT ____
☐INVOICE ____
☐REFERENCE ____
☐REPRO NEEDED ____
☐SHIP ____

PLEASE PRINY CLEARLY

1:NAME: _____

ADDRESS: _____

CITY: _____ STATE: ____ ZIP _____

TELEPHONE:[   ] _____

PLEASE CIRCLE DESIRED CHOICES

2. CARD TYPE: BUSINESS   POST
3. QUANITY: 500   1000   *PHOTO POSITION*
4. STYLE: VERTICAL   HORIZONTAL   ☐RIGHT   ☐LEFT
5: CARD STOCK: STANDARD   GLOSSY   LINEN
6: CARD COLOR: WHITE   OFFWHITE
7: BORDER DESIGN: NONE 1   2 3 4   5   6   7   8   9   10   11   12
8:TYPEFACE: 0 1   2   3   4   5   6   7   8   9   10   11   12   13

9:TEXT ON CARD: Please print text desired on the lines below. Text will be copied exactly, line for line, so identify upper and lower case letters clearly.

Mark an "X" in box for Main Line

Line 1 _____ ☐
Line 2 _____ ☐
Line 3 _____ ☐
Line 4 _____ ☐
Lines below are for horizontal cards <u>only</u>!
Line 5 _____ ☐
Line 6 _____ ☐
Line 7 _____ ☐
Line 8 _____ ☐

Please add $3.50 for S&H each card ordered.Free shipping for order over $100.00

GUARANTEED FAST SERVICE! Orders shipped within 7 days!

CA. resident add 8.25% sales tax to order

10. A check or money order for $ _____ , made payable to: BACK TO ONE and (two) identical B/W or Color photos is enclosed.

VISA   Visa - MasterCard Accepted

EXTRA NOTES

BACK TO ONE
GRAPHICS SERVICES
DEPT. ____
P.O. BOX 753
HOLLYWOOD, CA 90078-0753
(213) 969-4897

FOR OFFICE USE ONLY
☐SR _____
☐CK MO CA _____
☐DATE REC'D _____
☐PROOF _____
☐PRINT _____
☐INVOICE _____
☐REFERENCE _____
☐REPRO NEEDED _____
☐SHIP _____

PLEASE PRINY CLEARLY

1:NAME: _____

ADDRESS: _____

CITY: _____ STATE: ____ ZIP _____

TELEPHONE:[   ] _____

PLEASE CIRCLE DESIRED CHOICES

2. CARD TYPE:	BUSINESS	POST	
3. QUANITY:	500	1000	*PHOTO POSITION*
4. STYLE:	VERTICAL	HORIZONTAL	☐RIGHT ☐LEFT
5: CARD STOCK:	STANDARD	GLOSSY	LINEN
6: CARD COLOR:	WHITE	OFFWHITE	

7: BORDER DESIGN: NONE 1   2 3 4   5   6   7   8   9   10   11   12

8:TYPEFACE: 0 1   2   3   4   5   6 7   8   9   10   11   12   13

9:TEXT ON CARD: Please print text desired on the lines below. Text will be copied exactly, line for line, so identify upper and lower case letters clearly.

Mark an "X" in box for Main Line

Line 1 _____ ☐

Line 2 _____ ☐

Line 3 _____ ☐

Line 4 _____ ☐

Lines below are for horizontal cards only!

Line 5 _____ ☐

Line 6 _____ ☐

Line 7 _____ ☐

Line 8 _____ ☐

Please add $3.50 for S&H each card ordered.Free shipping for order over $100.00

GUARANTEED FAST SERVICE! Orders shipped within 7 days!

CA. resident add 8.25% sales tax to order

10. A check or money order for $ _____ , made payable to: BACK TO ONE and (two) identical B/W or Color photos is enclosed.

VISA   Visa - MasterCard Accepted

EXTRA NOTES

EXTRA NOTES

EXTRA PERSONAL DATA

Complete the the following data information form. Highlight those sports, hobbies, skills, and training that apply to you. Use as a guide when you fill out the Extra Casting Agency applications.

NAME_____ HOME# _____

ADDRESS _____ MESS# _____

CITY _____ STATE _____ ZIP _____

EMERGENCY PHONE _____

SOCIAL SECURITY NO. _____

DRIVERS LICENSE NO._____

UNION MEMBERSHIP NO.# - S.A.G. _____

A.F.T.R.A. _____ S.E.G. _____

	MEN	WOMEN
AGE RANGE _____	SHIRT/NECK _____	BUST _____
WEIGHT _____	SUIT _____	WAIST _____
HAIR_____	PANTS _____	HIP _____
EYES _____	CHEST _____	BLOUSE_____
HEIGHT _____	WAIST _____	DRESS _____
SHOE _____	INSEAM _____	SLACK _____
HAT _____	COAT _____	INSEAM _____

FOREIGN LANGUAGES _____

ACCENTS _____

Aerobics, Archery, Airplane Pilot, Announcer, Badminton, Ballooning, Baseball, Basketball, Baton Twirling, Bicycling-(BMX- Racing- Veldrome- Wheelies), Boating-(Canoeing Kayaking- Sailing Sculling), Bowling, Boxing, Cabaret Singer, Car Racing, Cartoon Voices, Celebrity Look-alike, Comedian, Character Voices, Choreographer, Club Performer, Computer, Crochet, Dance-(Disco - Modern - Jazz- Tap- Exotic- Swing- Waltz- Square- Ballroom- etc.), Disc- Jockey, Diving, Fencing, Field Hockey, Fishing, Football, Frisbees, Golf, Gunmanship, Gymnastics-(Floor-Parallel Bars- Rings- Side Horse- Vaulting) Hackey-Sack, Handball, Hang Gliding, Ice Hockey, Ice Skating, Impression, Impersonations, Hiking, Horsemanship-(Western- Bareback- Jumps-English-Show), Jet Skiing, Jogging, Judo, Juggling, Jump Rope-Double-Dutch- Hot Peas), Karate, Kung-Fu, Magician, Mime, Motorcycling-(Racing- Wheelies - MotoCross- Hill Climbing- Trail- Dirt- ATV), Mountaineer, Musical Instruments-(Be Specific), Parachuting, Paddleball, Ping-Pong, Pinball, Pool-(Billiards- Nineball- Snooker- Bumper-Eightball), Racquetball, Reporter, Riflery, Rope Tricks, Sailing, SCUBA, Skateboarding, Skating, Sky-Diving, Snowskiing, Snorkeling, Soccer, Softball, Spokesperson, Squash, Stage Combat, Stand-up Comedy, Surfing, Swimming, Tennis, Track & Field, Trampoline, Ventriloquist, Volley Ball, Water Polo, Water-skiing, Weapons, Windsurfing, Wrestling, Yachting, etc.

EXTRA CALL SHEET

Use this handy Call Sheet to keep accurate record of your daily activity on the set. Very helpful come tax time.

DATE: _____ DAY: _____

PRODUCTION TITLE: _____

CASTING AGENCY: _____

LOCATION: _____

THOMAS BROS. PAGE: _____ CO-ORD: _____

DIRECTIONS: _____

PARKING: _____

CALL TIME: _____ (A.M. P.M.) ASK FOR: _____

CHARACTER: _____

WARDROBE: _____

BASE PAY: $ _____ HRS. ____ TTL HRS WORKED: ____

BUMP $: _____ WARDROBE $: _____ AUTO $: _____

MILEAGE: $ _____ EXPECTED GROSS: $ _____

DATE P'D: _____ CK ___ CASH ___ NET PAID: $_____

NOTES: _____

_____

_____

_____

EXTRA THINGS TO DO

Date: ---------------------Day: -------------------------

Item		Wrapped
1.		
2.		
3.		
4.		
5.		
6.		
7.		
8.		
9.		
10.		
11.		
12.		
13.		
14.		
15.		
16.		
17.		

EXTRA NOTE

EXTRA NOTES

Extra Quick & E-Z REFERENCE
Phone Directory

EXTRA CASTING AGENCIES-Hollywood CA

ACADEMY KIDS MANAGEMENT	(818) 769-8091
ACTOR'S REPETORIE BANK	(818) 996-0505
ALLISON & ASSOC. CASTING	(818) 782-3676
AMC -ANNA MILLER Casting	(213) 957-4696
ANNISA WILLIAMS CASTING	(213) 668-0454
ARTIST CONNECTION CASTING	(213) 782-9315
AXIUM CASTING	(818) 557-2997
B.J. CASTING	(213) 851-7881
BACK TO ONE/HOLLYWOOD CASTING	(213) 969-4897
BILL DANCE CASTING	(213) 878-1131
CASTING WORKS LA	(818) 784-6218
CENEX CASTING	(818) 562-2800
CENTRAL CASTING	(818) 562-2700
CHRISTOPHER GRAY CASTING	(213) 850-7114
CREATIVE IMAGE	(213) 655-9505
DAVID ANTHONY'S BACKGROUND PLAYERS	(213) 243-1974
FIRST ACTION CASTING	(818) 754-0906
FRANZ PIERRE CASTING	(310) 366-3833
DENNIS HANSEN CASTING	(310) 558-4870
HAGERMAN & ASSOCIATES CASTING	(310) 285-7765
IDELL JAMES CASTING	(310) 394-3919
LANE MODEL AND TALENT AGENCY	(714) 731-1420
LATIN CONNECTION	(213) 257-9748
M & J MANAGEMENT	(818) 286-4008
MAGIC CASTING	(805) 688-3702
MESSENGER & ASSOCIATES CASTING	(818) 995-3575
M.R. COOPER CASTING	(213) 526-2951
NAT JOHNSON CASTING	(310) 418-2019
NATIVE AMERICAN CASTING	(213) 255-6880
JEAN PAGE MANAGEMENT	(818) 703-7328
PRIME CASTING	(213) 962-0377
PRODUCERS CASTING	(310) 454-5233
RAINBOW CASTING	(818) 752-CAST
RON SMITH'S CELEBRITY LOOK-ALIKES	(213) 467-3030
SCREEN CHILDREN AGENCY	(818) 846-4300
SUNSET CASTING	(310) 478-2664
T.B.S. CASTING	(310) 854-1955
terrence/atmosphere casting	MAIL ONLY
WEBSTER - KOLICH	(818) 567-0524
WILD BUNCH, The	(818) 342-8282

Extra Quick & E-Z REFERENCE
Phone Directory

BOOKSTORES - THEATRICAL
DRAMA BOOKS -NEW YORK CITY, NY .... (212) 944-0595
LARRY EDMUNDS -HOLLYWOOD .... (213) 463-3273
PERFORMING ARTS BOOKS -CANOGA PARK, CA .... (818) 703-7311
SAMUEL FRENCH THEATRE & FILM-HOLLYWOOD (818) 876-0570
SAMUEL FRENCH THEATRE & FILM- STUDIO CITY (818) 782-0535

EXTRA CALLING IN SERVICES-Hollywood CA
DIRECT LINE CALLING IN & BOOKING SERVICE(818) 753-8064
EXTRA EFFORT.. (818) 981-1144
EXTRA PHONE .... (818) 972-9474
RAPID CASTING Calling-In Service .... (818) 558-6270
STARTING POINT CALLING SERVICE .... (213) 730-8509
T.C.A. .... (818) 769-3350
VALENTINA Casting Management .... (213) 467-4469

EXTRA RELATED SERVICES-Hollywood CA
BACK TO ONE GRAFX .... (213) 969-4897
CA STATE LABOR COMMISSION .... (818)901-5484
HOLLYWOOD BACKGROUND ARTIST ASSOC. .. (213) 969-4897
JUDY KERR'S ACTING WORKSHOP .... (213) 874-7330
METRO TRANPORTATION SYSTEM .... (800) 371-5465
"STARTING YOUR FILM CAREER" SEMINARS ... (213) 467-2628

PHOTOGRAPHERS-Hollywood CA
CARRIE CAVALIER... (818) 840-9148
CHARLES FRETZIN PHOTOGRAPHY .... (818) 876-1783
RICH HOGAN PHOTOGRAPHY .... (213) 467-2628

PHOTO LAB & DUPLICATING HOUSE
BIG SHOTS, 8x 10 PHOTO DUPS & LITHOS ...... (818) 763-2202
CHOICE PHOTO LAB .... (213) 463-5381
DUPLICATE PHOTOS .... (213) 466-7544
GRAPHICS REPRODUCTIONS .... (213) 874-4335
HOUR IMAGE .... (213) 653-0130
PAPER CHASE .... (213) 874-2300
PRINTS CHARMING - W. HOLLYWOOD .... (310) 288-1786
PRINTS CHARMING - STUDIO CITY .... (818) 753-9055
PRINTS CHARMING - W. LOS ANGELES .... (310) 312-0904

PRODUCTION COMPANIES-Hollywood CA
BOB BOOKER PROD. .... (310) 477-3757
BRILLSTEIN-GREY ENTERTAINMENT .... (310) 275-6135
DICK CLARK PROD. .... (818) 841-3003
RALPH EDWARDS/STU BILLETT .... (213) 462-2212
GTG SERVICES, INC. .... (310) 836-5537
HOPE ENTERPRISES .... (818) 841-2020
FOX TELEVISION CTR. .... (213) 462-7111
NBC PRODUCTIONS .... (818) 840-7500
NEW WORLD TELEVISION .... (310) 444-8100
PIERRE COSSETTE PROD. .... (213) 278-3366
GEORGE SCHLATTER PROD ....(310) 655-1400
SMITH HEMION...(213) 871-1200
TPI-IDC ....(818) 569-5100

PRODUCTION COMPANIES

20TH CENTURY FOX ....(310) 277-2211
W-F PRODUCTIONS ....(213) 850-3800

UNIONS-Hollywood CA

ACTOR'S EQUITY ....(213) 462-2334
AFTRA MAIN OFFICE ....(213) 461-8111
   TDD ....(213) 463-9264
   CASTING/ INFORMATION HOTLINE ....(213) 461-1377
   HEALTH & RETIREMENT FUND ....(213) 462-3244
   AFTRA /SAG CREDIT UNION..(213) 461-3041
   ACTORS' WORK PROGRAM ....(213) 461-6133
   AIPADA ABUSE HOTLINE .... (800) 756-HOPE
   CASTING SHOWCASES & SEMINARS ....(213) 467-8702
   SEXUAL HARRASSMENT HOTLINE.................. (213) 461-8111 X243
SAG MAIN OFFICE ....(213) 954-1600
   AFFIRMATIVE ACTION ....(213) 549-6444
   COMMUNICATIONS ....(213) 549-6745
   CONSERVATORY ....(213) 549-6654
   CONTRACTS
   COMMERCIALS/MUSIC VIDEOS ....(213) 549-6858
   INDUSTRIAL/INTERACTIVE ....(213) 549-6847
   PRODUCTION SERVICES .... (213) 549 -6811
   SINGERS' REPRESENTATIVE ....(213) 549-6864
   TELEVISION...(213) 549-6835
   THEATRICAL FILMS ....(213) 549-6828
   DUES INDORMATION ....(213) 549-6755
   EMERCENCY FUND ....(213) 549-6773
   FILM SOCIETY HOTLINE ....(213) 549-6657
   InFo CAST ....(213) 937-3441
   LEGAL AFFAIRS ....(213) 549-6657
   MEMBERSHIP SERVICES ....(213) 549-6778
   PRESIDENT'S OFFICE ....(213) 549-6828
   RECEPTIONIST .... (213) 549-66404
   RESIDUAL ....(213) 549-6505
   SIGNATORY RECORDS...(213) 549-6869
   SAG FOUNDATION ....(213) 549-6709

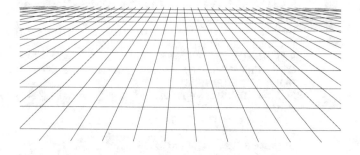

EXTRA IMPORTANT NUMBERS

NAME   **PHONE**

EXTRA IMPORTANT NUMBERS

NAME   **PHONE**

EXTRA IMPORTANT NUMBERS

NAME   **PHONE**

EXTRA NOTE

EXTRA NOTE

EXTRA NOTE

Index

Symbols

3/4" TAPE 123
3x5 color w/ white background 37
4-As 114

A

A.D 100
AARON SPELLING 21
ABET 265
accessories 175
ACTION 107
AD LIB 107
ADELE SIMMONS 10, 17
ADR 107
AEA 108
Affordable Studio Teachers'
    Association 94
AFI 108
AFL-CIO 108
AFM 108
age range 40
AGMA 108
AGVA 108
AISHA JOHNSON 38
Aisha Johnson 10
Aixa Maldonado 153
Alan Bates 157, 160
ALAN LADD 20
ALICIA SASSANO 37
ALL-AMERICAN LOOK 108
ALLIANCE of BLACK
    ENTERTAINMENT
    TECHNICIANS 265
Alphonso Jones 164
amateur photographs 31
AMPTP 108
ANGELICA HUSTON 20
Anjanette Sierra 143
ANNE WHITE PHOTOGRAPHY
    39
Antoinette Mosley 11
APPLICATION FOR
    CHILDRENS WORK
    PERMIT 98
ART DIRECTOR 108
Art Director 105
Assistant Art Director 105
Assistant Auditor 106
Assistant Costume Designer 105
Assistant Electrician 105
Assistant Hair Stylist 105
Assistant Location Manager 106
Assistant Make-Up Person 105
Assistant Production Office
    Coordinator 106
Assistant Property Person 105
ASSOCIATION OF ASIAN
    PACIFIC AMERICAN
    ARTISTS 266
ATA 108
AUDITION 108
AVAIL 108

B

Baby Wranglers 94
BACK TO ONE" Graphics Services
    269
BACK-UP 108
BACKGROUND ACTOR 108
Background Artist 45
Barbara Schiffman 97
BEAUTY SHOT 108
Bernard Weisman 9
BEST BOY 109
Betty Mccormick Aggas 11
BILL COSBY 20
BILLING 109
BIO 109
Bishop Charles E. Blake 10
Blanket permits 95
BLOCKING 109
BOB HOPE 20
Body Make-Up Person 105
BOOKING 109
BOOM 109
Boom 104
BoyZ N the Hood 265
Brad Bradbury 133, 139
BREAKDOWN 109
BUMP 109
Bump 57
BUMPS 179
BURT REYNOLDS 20
BURY 109
business 128
BUYOUT 109

C

Cable Person 104
California Labor Department 64
CALL SHEET 109
CALL TIME 109
CALLBACK 109
Calling-In Service 53
CAMERA DEPARTMENT 104
CAMERA LEFT 109
Camera Operator 104
CAMERA RIGHT 109
Camera Truck 106
Carol Florence 9
Cast Trailers 106
CASTING DIRECTOR 109
Casting Director 46
Catch 22 situation 18
CATERER 106
Caterer Assistants 106
CATTLE CALL 110
Cellular phones 30
CHANGES 110
CHARACTER 46
CHARACTER SHOT 36
CHARLES ALESSI 219
Cheryl Felton 10, 12
Child Labor Laws 95
CHILDREN IN ACTION 93
Children Labor Laws 93
Chuck Loch 145
Cinematographer 104
City Police 105
CLAPBOARD 111
CLARK GABLE 20
CLASSIC CAR SUPPLIES 57

Claude Oatts 141, 144
CLINT EASTWOOD 20
CLOSE-UP 110
CLOSED SHOP 68
clothing bag. 175
Clown 271
CLOYDE HOWARD 37
COLD READING 110, 111
Colleagues 42
COMMERCIAL HALF-BODY 38
COMMERCIAL HEADSHOT 35
COMMISSION 110
COMPOSITE 110
composite head and body shots 32
composite head shots 32
CONFLICT 110
Construction Truck 106
CONTINUITY 111
contract. 45
COPY 110
Costume Designer 105
CRAFT SERVICES 110
Craft Services 104
Crane Operator 104
CRANE SHOT 110
CRAWL 110
CREDITS 110
Crew Cabs 106
CROSS 111
crosses 177
CU 110
CUE 110, 111
Cullen Chambers 12, 18, 19
CUT 111
CUT & HOLD 111
CUTAWAY 110
Cynthia Noritake 143, 150, 157

D

D.L.S.E. 93
D.L.S.E. complaint form 66
D.P. 112
Dallas 128
Dave Sales 166
David Calhoun 1
DAVID NIVEN 21
Dawn Emerick 152
DAYTIME DRAMA 111
DEALER COMMERCIAL 111
Debbie Rock 155
DEMO TAPE 111
Dependable Transportation 57
Derrell P. Woods 271
DGA 112
DIALECT 112
DIALOGUE 112
DIRECTOR 112
Director 103
Director Of Photography 104
Director's Assistant 106
DIRECTORY LISTINGS 183
DOC 33, 34
Doc Christopher Gary Chambers
    270
DOLLY 112
Dolly Grip 104
DON STROUD 20
DONALD PLEASENCE 20
DONALD SUTHERLAND 21
Donna Marcou 134

EXTRA NOTE

EXTRA ORDER FORM

1. **"Back To One" The MOVIE EXTRA Guidebook** $19.95
2. **"Back To One" Pocket-Size (4 1/2 x 5 1/2)** $19.95
3. **Labels For Extra Casting Agents** $10.00
4. **Labels For S.A.G. Franchised Agents** $15.00
5. **"Screen Parents Bookshelf" directory** $5.95
6. **BTO Hollywood Extra Casting Agent directory** $6.95
7. **The Hollywood Callsheet & Recordkeeper** $4.00
8. **1996 Thomas Brothers Guide Mapbook** $25.95

PROMOTIONAL TOOLS

9. **Photo Extra Things To Do Pad** 10 pads of 100-4 ½ x 11 .... $10.00
10. **Photo Extra Phone Message Pads** 20 pads of 100-4 ½ x 5 ½ $15.00
11. **Photo From The Desk Of...** 20 pads of 100-5 ½ x 8 ½ $10.00
12. **Simple Resumé w/wo Photo** 100-8 x 10 .... $45.00/35.00
    Writing and Special Requirements Negotiated
13. **Photo Letterhead** 250-8 ½ x 11 .... $35.00
14. **Photo Envelopes** 250 #10 Business Size $50.00
15. **Photo Business Cards** 500 - Horizontal $55.00
16. **Photo Business Cards** 500 - Vertical $55.00
17. **Photo Post Cards** 300-Horizontal 4 X 5 .... $65.00
18. **Photo Post Cards** 300-Vertical 4 X 5 .... $65.00

SUB-TOTAL: $ _____
(Please include $3.50 for first item

and $1.75 for each additional item.   SHIPPING: $ _____

Sales Tax: Add 8 ¼ % to orders shipped to California addresses. $ _____

Here is my ☐Check ☐M.O. -TOTAL ENCLOSED: $ _____

Charge my ☐VISA ☐MasterCard   Here is my ☐Check ☐M.O.
NAME _____ PHONE _____
ADDRESS _____
CITY _____ STATE _____ ZIP _____
CARD # _____ Exp Date _____
SIGNATURE _____

**Checks payable to: Back To One Publications, P.O. Box 753-T,
Hollywood, CA 90078-753 U.S.A. (213) 969-4897**

 Visa - MasterCard Accepted

EXTRA NOTE

EXTRA ORDER FORM

1. **"Back To One" The MOVIE EXTRA Guidebook** $19.95
2. **"Back To One" Pocket-Size (4 1/2 x 5 1/2)** $19.95
3. **Labels For Extra Casting Agents** $10.00
4. **Labels For S.A.G. Franchised Agents** $15.00
5. **"Screen Parents Bookshelf" directory** $5.95
6. **BTO Hollywood Extra Casting Agent directory** $6.95
7. **The Hollywood Callsheet & Recordkeeper** $4.00
8. **1996 Thomas Brothers Guide Mapbook** $25.95

PROMOTIONAL TOOLS

9. **Photo Extra Things To Do Pad** 10 pads of 100-4 ½ x 11 .... $10.00
10. **Photo Extra Phone Message Pads** 20 pads of 100-4 ½ x 5 ½ $15.00
11. **Photo From The Desk Of...** 20 pads of 100-5 ½ x 8 ½ $10.00
12. **Simple Resumé w/wo Photo** 100-8 x 10 .... $45.00/35.00
Writing and Special Requirements Negotiated
13. **Photo Letterhead** 250-8 ½ x 11 .... $35.00
14. **Photo Envelopes** 250 #10 Business Size $50.00
15. **Photo Business Cards** 500 - Horizontal $55.00
16. **Photo Business Cards** 500 - Vertical $55.00
17. **Photo Post Cards** 300-Horizontal 4 X 5 .... $65.00
18. **Photo Post Cards** 300-Vertical 4 X 5 .... $65.00

SUB-TOTAL: $ _____
(Please include $3.50 for first item

and $1.75 for each additional item.   SHIPPING: $ _____

Sales Tax: Add 8 ¼ % to orders shipped to California addresses. $ _____

Here is my ☐Check ☐M.O. -TOTAL ENCLOSED: $ _____

Charge my ☐VISA ☐MasterCard   Here is my ☐Check ☐M.O.
NAME _____ PHONE _____
ADDRESS _____
CITY_____ STATE _____ ZIP _____
CARD # _____ Exp Date _____
SIGNATURE _____

**Checks payable to: Back To One Publications, P.O. Box 753-T,
Hollywood, CA 90078-753 U.S.A. (213) 969-4897**

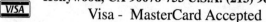 Visa - MasterCard Accepted